THE
ANGRY
SKIES

THE
ANGRY
SKIES

A PHYSICIAN'S JOURNEY INTO
CAMBODIA'S HEART OF DARKNESS

BLAKE KERR, MD

EAST END PRESS
BRIDGEHAMPTON • NEW YORK

Copyright © 2025 by Blake Kerr

All rights reserved. No portion of this book may be reproduced, distributed, or transmitted in any form or by any means, electronic or mechanical, including photocopying, recording, or information storage or retrieval system, without the prior written permission of the publisher.

Published by EAST END PRESS Bridgehampton, NY

ISBN: 979-8-9873266-9-5
Ebook ISBN: 979-8-9926869-0-6

First Edition

Book Design by Pauline Neuwirth, Neuwirth & Associates, Inc.
Cover Design by Johnathan Sinclair, 6 x 9 Design

Manufactured in the United States of America
10 9 8 7 6 5 4 3 2 1

ACKNOWLEDGMENTS

I would like to thank Zack, Kaley, and Kate for tolerating my trips to the Land of Smiles. I am grateful for edits and encouragement from John Eastman, Peter Emerson, Gloria Jones, Ben Kiernan, Joanie McDonell, Camille Petrillo, Margaret Kerr Richenburg, and Ann-Lise and Philip Spitzer, and for William Henderson's advice to throw out half of the manuscript and start over, twice. I am also grateful to Cindy Durand for copy editing, Pauline Neuwirth for East End Press, and Bruce McMaster for goading me to get my head out of the guidebook and ride motorcycles into Kampot Province where we met the child soldier who killed the last Western backpackers who came to Phnom Vor in 1994: David Wilson from Australia, Mark Slater from Britain, Jean-Michel Braquet from France.

Although the Phnom Vor Gang tried to kill me, I would not have met the architects of the Khmer Rouge Revolution without them. I remain proud of Dr. Noun for regaining his practice for rural Cambodians afflicted with tuberculosis, typhoid, malaria, malnutrition, and AIDS.

Most of all, I applaud the Cambodian people's struggle to overcome centuries of foreign domination.

There is a saying in Asia that if you
show up at your mortal enemies' home,
they will invite you in for tea.

CONTENTS

Map xii
Foreword *by Leakhena Nou, PhD* xiii
Introduction xv

PART I: SOFT TRAVEL TO HARD PLACES

Soft Travel to Hard Places 3
Kissinger, Nixon, and the American Bombing of Cambodia 8
Siem Reap 13
The Angkor Wats 17
Mr. Land Mine 21
Fast Boat 24
Phnom Penh 27
Phnom Penh's Nightly Death 30
Tuol Sleng 33
Choeung Ek 36
Don't Break 39
Phnom Vor 44
Child Soldier 47
Mercenary 52
Kep Killing Fields 56
Hermaphrodite Beach 59
Lariam Dreams 63
How Can You Be Mad at a Spirit? 68
Beggar in the Land of Smiles 71
Jean-Michel Braquet, Mark Slater, and David Wilson 73

PART II: MY ENEMIES, MY FRIENDS

The Elephant Bar	77
Off the Road to Kampot	82
Not Meeting Chhouk Rin	84
What Do You Call a Doctor With One Leg?	88
Warlord	95
Kampot Karaoke	101
My Land	104
AIDS in the Jungle	107
Doctor Kroh and American Bombing	113
Khat Mann Stories	116
My Enemies, My Friends	120

PART III: SEARCHING FOR THE TRUTH

Searching for the Truth	127
Pol Pot	129
Youk Chhang and the Documentation Center of Cambodia	132
Tuol Sleng Survivors	136
Victory Coconuts	141
The Good Dr. Noun	146
The Phnom Vor Gang	149
Travels to Pailin	158
The Ghost Party	165
Khieu Samphan	167
Second Wife	173
Nuon Chea	175
The Liver Eaters	183
Barbarians at the FCC	188
Repercussions	190
Genocide Tribunal	194

PART IV: THE ANGRY SKIES

Thai Riot	203
Breaking Down	211
Malcolm Caldwell's Murder	219
Pol Pot's UN Secretary	226
Pol Pot's Death	230
Brother Number Two Again	233
Mr. Muhn	237
The Angry Skies	245
Justice Is for the Gods	247
Defense Intelligence	249
Farewell to Harm	252
Slouching Toward a Tribunal	255
Epilogue	260

Alphabetical Listing of Cambodians Mentioned in *The Angry Skies*	263
Bibliography	265
Notes	267

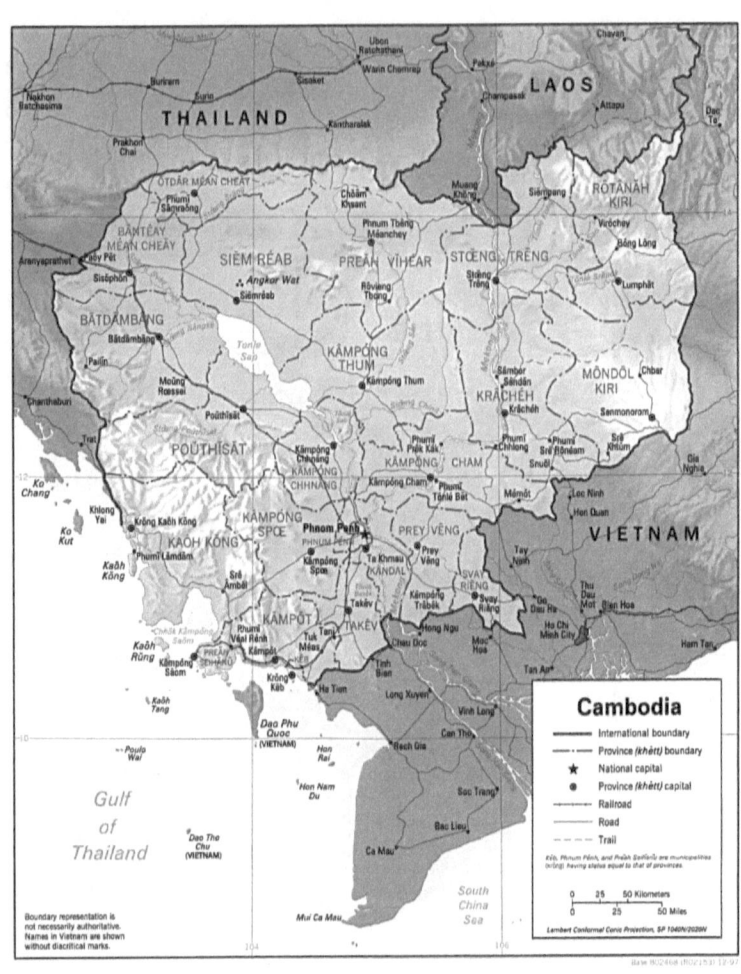

FOREWORD

Five decades after the Khmer Rouge genocide where one-quarter of Cambodia's population perished between 1975 and 1979, both survivors and perpetrators have continued to experience chronic and pervasive traumatic stress and violence in the subsequent decades. The Extraordinary Chambers in the Courts of Cambodia (ECCC), also known as the Khmer Rouge International War Crimes Tribunal, has fundamentally failed to deliver accountability and reparative justice for victims.[1] As a university professor and one of the world's only American-trained medical sociologists of Cambodian descent, my commitment is professional and personal.

In 2003, as Dean of the College of Social Sciences at the University of Cambodia, I created the first curriculum on the sociology of Cambodia in the post-Khmer Rouge era. Understandably, the rigorous empirical study of corruption and the systematic brutality of the Khmer Rouge was unwelcome, even decades after the genocide's end. At the time, Dr. Kerr was risking his life to interview senior Khmer Rouge officers and their associates, individuals responsible for the genocide as well as the killings of Western backpackers Jean-Michel Braquet, Mark Slater, and David Wilson, and journalist Malcolm Caldwell.

---

1 Nou, L. 2024. "Violence and Traumatic Stress among Cambodian Survivors and Perpetrators for the Khmer Rouge Genocide." Social Science Medicine-Mental Health, 6, 100341. https://doi.org/10.1016/j.ssmmh.2024.100341

The Angry Skies leads readers on a wild ride as we follow Dr. Kerr, an activist and medical doctor, into Cambodia's most remote corners (and its darkest hour) to uncover the inner workings of the Khmer Rouge and its structural fundamentalism. Strategic U.S. foreign policy in Southeast Asia and the geopolitics of the Vietnam War also inflicted multi-generational harm on Cambodians. The book is difficult to put down and offers a rare, intimate, existential stare into Khmer Rouge social psychology and the group's paranoia in fighting the "foreign devils."

The Angry Skies is significant and timely as political violence erupting globally coincides with the fiftieth anniversary of the Khmer Rouge seizing power on April 17, 1975, and the ECCC wrapping up its decades-delayed judicial proceedings. The Khmer Rouge's radical violence and atrocities against innocent civilians caused the deaths of two million victims, forever changing Cambodian social psychology. Kerr's unconventional, bottom-up investigation represents an emblematic departure from the top-down approach common in international justice systems, demands judicial reform in international and humanitarian law, and serves as a model for urgent lessons learned when unchecked abuse of geopolitical power causes nation-states to collapse.

Riveting and illuminating, *The Angry Skies* offers insights into the past that remain devastatingly relevant today not only for Cambodians, but also for vulnerable indigenous people and societies facing political violence and devastation in Afghanistan, Armenia, Bosnia-Herzegovina, China, Democratic Republic of Congo, Ethiopia, Haiti, Iraq, Israel, Lebanon, Myanmar, Palestine, Rwanda, Somalia, Sudan, Syria, Tibet, Ukraine, United States, Yemen, and beyond.

Leakhena Nou, PhD
Professor of Sociology
California State University, Long Beach (CSULB)

INTRODUCTION

Investigating crimes against humanity did not come easily. After graduating from SUNY Buffalo School of Medicine in 1987, I traveled to Tibet with John Ackerly, Esq., to get as high as we could on the Tibetan side of Mount Everest. We had spent seasons rock climbing in Yosemite as Dartmouth College undergrads, and a winter mountaineering in Peru. Traveling overland with nomads and pilgrims, getting food and clothing on the way like explorers from previous centuries, seemed like a good idea at the time.

Long before we got to the Tibetan capital of Lhasa, it became apparent that Chinese immigrants outnumbered Tibetans in cities and towns, most jobs were reserved for Chinese immigrants, Tibetan was not taught in schools, and monks could not study Tibetan Buddhism in monasteries. One monk said he was a "tour guide in a museum." Tibetans were second-class citizens in their own country.

China's security forces introduced us to state-sponsored terrorism on October 1, 1987, Chinese National Day. John did not know he would photograph the largest independence demonstration in Lhasa since the Dalai Lama fled into exile in 1959. The morning started with a handful of monks circumambulating Tibet's most holy temple, the Jokhang, chanting, "China out of Tibet," and "Free Tibet now." When Chinese police arrived, beat the monks with rifles and dragged them inside the police station, a handful of Tibetans stormed the building to free the monks. I documented twelve deaths while Chinese police fired AK-47s and automatic pistols from the rooftops and the street at unarmed Tibetan men, women, children, and monks. One sixteen-year-old boy was beaten to death inside the police station with a shovel.

I will never forget the ten-year-old boy who was shot through the heart and died with my hands pressed against entrance and exit wounds. His father's stare carrying his son's lifeless body through the maddening crowd. Sixty Chinese police in riot gear yelling their death cries and charging the Jokhang Temple, the heart of Tibetan Buddhism. Running toward the police with rocks in my hands alongside a dozen Khampas who had removed the red tassels wrapped around their heads. Focusing on eyes, throats, and groins. Prepared to kill or be killed. And to our amazement, the police turned and fled at the last moment.

That evening John organized a travelers' underground to gather confirmed, firsthand accounts of the demonstration, and donations of any medical supplies. I snuck out to treat wounded Tibetans in the Barkhor, the two-story Tibetan homes with flat rooftops around the Jokhang. One room sheltered sixteen monks who had been beaten by the police. I did not have any medicines, but I documented that the long, purple bruises on backs, legs, and arms were consistent with the monks' accounts of repeated strikes by police truncheons. Irregular, macerated blotches came from rocks. Rifle butts left triangular divots on scalps and torsos.

In addition to the victims of torture, I encountered something worse. While cleaning an abscess on a twenty-six-year-old man who had been shot in the calf, I asked his nineteen-year-old wife if she had any children. Anger replaced shame as Kunyang described having been six months pregnant with her first child.

When Kunyang's work unit leader noticed that she was showing, he ordered her to go to the People's Hospital where a Chinese doctor insisted that she needed an operation to save her life. Kunyang argued that she was healthy before the nurse injected her abdomen with something that made her deliver the baby the next day. Kunyang heard her baby cry twice: once when his head appeared in the birth canal, and when the nurse gave a lethal injection into the soft spot on his forehead. The next day Kunyang was forced to have an operation that, she was told, prevented her from having another child.

With Chinese soldiers searching every home in the Barkhor and dragging anyone suspected of participating in the demonstration or possessing pictures of the Dalai Lama to prison, John and I snuck onto the last flight to Nepal. Reporters from international news organizations were waiting for the "two American Mountaineers'" who had witnessed a massacre in Lhasa.[1] John's graphic photos of the riot that a traveler took to Hong Kong had landed on the international news, and the Dalai Lama invited us to visit him in Dharamsala, Northern India, a British hill station that became home to the Tibetan government in exile.

Tenzin Gyatso, the fourteenth Dalai Lama, put us at ease by saying that he was a simple Buddhist monk, and he joked that he was not a very good monk because he did not have enough time for his own studies and meditation. His Holiness was eager to know if any Khampas, nomads from his home in eastern Tibet who were known for their bravado and banditry, had participated in the demonstration. Since he fled to India in 1959, His Holiness knew of over fifty independence demonstrations throughout Tibet, but it took months or years for the Tibetans who escaped across the Himalayas to get to Dharamsala before he heard any details. John and I were the first Westerners who had seen independence demonstrations inside Tibet since China suppressed the Lhasa Rebellion in 1959.

When the Dalai Lama asked if monks had thrown rocks at the police, John replied that many Tibetans had thrown rocks at the police station, where Chinese police had taken the leaders of the demonstration. Tears welled in my eyes as I described the ten-year-old boy who died in my hands, and the sixteen-year-old boy beaten to death with a shovel inside the police station. His Holiness expressed grave concern for the loss of life. He also understood how a monk or layperson throwing rocks at a Chinese policeman could be a natural reaction to an extreme situation.

I was so moved by the Dalai Lama saying that he held no anger at the Chinese people, or the Chinese government, that I confessed to throwing rocks at Chinese police who were shooting unarmed Tibetans and children. John kicked me under the table, as he had done many times when I argued with the police in Lhasa during our arrest and interrogation.

The Dalai Lama's mischievous laughter released a wellspring of guilt from my strict Catholic upbringing. As a child, if I did not have any sins to confess, and the priest wanted numbers, I lied about how many times I had hit my brother or teased my sister. His Holiness did not seem to mind my impertinence and said there were many paths to enlightenment. At that moment John and I both knew that our paths would return to Tibet, as lawyer and physician, to document the underside of China's military occupation.

Continued independence demonstrations in Lhasa prompted China to impose martial law in March 1989 and deny visas to parliamentarians and human rights groups that wanted to visit. China's insistence that Tibet was an "internal affair," and that Tibetans were "thriving," prompted John and me to interview Tibetans at refugee camps in India and Nepal. After Physicians for Social Responsibility published our report on torture and imprisonment in Tibet that was in no danger of wide circulation,[2] we testified before the Senate Foreign Relations Committee. Criticisms included, "How can you trust refugees? How can you be sure where they are from? Why did they leave China in the first place?" Exiting the great hall, I could hear my deceased father saying, "Don't get mad. Get even."

Working as a general practitioner in Eastern Long Island, I continued to write reports on China's prison system and Family Planning Policy in Tibet[3,4,5] and *Sky Burial: An Eyewitness Account of China's Brutal Crackdown in Tibet.*[6] Writing helped me cope with post-traumatic stress disorder from seeing Tibetans slaughtered like baby seals. So did John's and my returning to Tibet separately seven times in the next decade. Although I never got used to the many individual accounts of institutionalized cruelty, the Tibetans' indomitable spirits tempered my introduction to the first tenet of Buddhism: All life is suffering.

In 2011, I testified at the Spanish National Court against China's past president and prime minister who were accused of committing crimes against humanity in Tibet. After focusing on what I had seen, Judge Ismael Moreno accepted twenty kilos of John's and my photographs of Chinese prisons and prisoners in Tibet, torture of Tibetan political prisoners, and my written, audio, and hidden camera documentation of Tibetan women subjected to coerced abortion, sterilization, and infanticide at People's Hospitals in Lhasa and remote regions throughout Tibet. Judge Moreno also authorized money for their translation.

In 2014, Judge Moreno convicted Jiang Zemin, Li Peng, and five other Chinese officials for committing genocide in Tibet and issued warrants for their arrest to Interpol. Five months later, when China pressured Spain to reverse its National Court's findings, I made a documentary film, *Eye of the Lammergeier*, for the Court of World Opinion. *Eye of the Lammergeier* won the Science and Educational Award, and was nominated for Best Short Documentary and Best Director of a Short Documentary at the Berlin International Filmmaker Festival of World Cinema in 2017. The same year the film was nominated for the Science and Educational Award at the Madrid International Film Festival.

But awards are rare and fleeting and do nothing for the Tibetans living under Chinese military occupation since 1959. Trying to raise awareness of human rights abuses in any country is like swimming upstream. After becoming persona non grata in China in 1999, I thought of traveling to Cambodia to see how people were faring two decades after the Khmer Rouge genocide. Cambodia was another intersection of the long arms of US and China foreign policies.

As the Khmer Rouge routed the US-backed Lon Nol government and army in 1975, China sponsored Pol Pot's Khmer Rouge Revolution where 2 million Cambodians died from starvation, disease, and executions.[7] When Vietnamese troops routed the Khmer Rouge from Cambodia in 1979, US and British Special Forces were waiting on the Thai border to help the Khmer Rouge regroup.[8,9] US President Carter befriended the Khmer Rouge, as long as they continued fighting the Vietnamese Communists who had just dealt a humiliating defeat to the US in Vietnam.

On my first trip to Cambodia in the winter of 2000, I met a Khmer Rouge soldier who boasted about killing the last three Western backpackers who traveled to Phnom Vor in 1994: David Wilson from Australia, Mark Slater from England, and Jean-Michel Braquet from France.[10] As a child soldier for the local Khmer Rouge commander in 1975, Khat Mann had killed thousands of people. He also presented a remarkable opportunity to find out more about the Western backpackers' treatment during three months of captivity before their execution. Working with Tibetan victims of torture and sterilization had taught me the importance of interviewing the perpetrators of their crimes, whenever possible.

The following year I started a clinic with a Khmer Rouge surgeon in Phnom Vor, a Khmer Rouge stronghold in southern Cambodia controlled by the Phnom Vor Gang. Dr. Noun's uncle turned out to be Ta Mok, the most powerful and feared general in the Khmer Rouge Army, who killed Pol Pot in 1998. This gave Dr. Noun a "Pure Biography." I had a "Bad Biography." Working with Dr. Noun helped protect me from the warlord in Phnom Vor who kidnapped the backpackers and threatened to kill me until we found common dialogue about the rise of the Khmer Rouge before they "Liberated Cambodia" from "Foreign Devils." A litany of horrors from US bombing ensued.

I was nervous every day traveling with the Phnom Vor Gang to meet Khmer Rouge leaders, including Khieu Samphan, the prime minister of Democratic Kampuchea; Nuon Chea, Brother Number

Two; Teph Kunnal, Pol Pot's secretary to the United Nations Transitional Authority in Cambodia (UNTAC); Mr. Muhn, Pol Pot's telegraph operator who translated and conveyed Pol Pot's orders to his regional commanders; and Pol Pot's wife and daughter.

There have been many books about the Cambodian genocide, including Haing Ngor's *A Cambodian Odyssey*, with Roger Warner;[11] Elizabeth Becker's *When the War Was Over: Cambodia's Revolution and the Voices of Its People*;[12] Ben Kiernan's *The Pol Pot Regime: Race, Power, and Genocide in Cambodia under the Khmer Rouge, 1975-1979*;[13] David Chandler's *The Tragedy of Cambodian History*;[14] and Laurence Picq's *Beyond the Horizon, Five Years with The Khmer Rouge: A Western Woman's Firsthand Account of the Drama, Passion, and Horror of Pol Pot's Cambodia*.[15] But none of these would be published for a decade or include the perspectives of Khmer Rouge soldiers and their leaders on how they used the hatred from American bombing to rise to power and overthrow the "American Foreign Devils."

The Angry Skies follows my documentary film, *The Angry Skies: A Cambodian Journey*, that helped pressure the Cambodian government to arrest Nuon Chea and Khieu Samphan in 2007, and to accept Cambodian judges working with the United Nations (UN) in an international tribunal that tried five architects of the Khmer Rouge Revolution. The tribunal has been criticized for spending $300 million to convict Nuon Chea and Khieu Samphan of crimes against humanity in 2018, but the historical record needed straightening. Unfortunately, time has passed for Henry Kissinger to answer charges that the American bombing of Cambodia was state-sponsored terrorism.

PART I

SOFT TRAVEL TO HARD PLACES

SOFT TRAVEL TO HARD PLACES

Knocking on the door startled me. As a general practitioner in East Hampton, New York, playground for the rich and famous, I treated migrant workers and movie stars and many people in between, especially in the summer when our seaside population quadrupled. I did not expect the tanned, forty-nine-year-old Navy pilot with tinted Ray-Bans who introduced himself by his call sign. Swan appeared to be in excellent physical condition but woke up fitfully every night. His speech was pressured as he recounted clandestine missions in 1970 when President Nixon authorized bombing North Vietnamese bases in Cambodia that were launching attacks against the American-backed South Vietnamese government.

"In the beginning we dropped pods manufactured by Ross Perot to track troop movements in Cambodia," Swan said. "Ross Perot made a lot of money during the Vietnam War. I bet you didn't know that! Once the pods landed they transmitted any motion back to our base and we bombed them into the Stone Age. But the Cambodians were smart. They learned to send one or two people to walk in circles around the pod. Then only one or two people died."

More knocking.

What should have been a ten-minute visit for insomnia was rolling on. I got nervous not because of the pilot's catharsis. I was the only physician on duty. Besides people with Lyme disease from tick bites, infections, diabetes, heartburn, hypertension, high cholesterol, and other vagaries of overconsumption, there could be victims of domestic violence, lacerations, or anaphylactic shock who did not share my interest in history. I was also not very good at terminating a visit if someone needed time.

"What happened over Cambodia?"

"We flew at night, without uniforms or ID. Our targets were classified but we knew we were over Cambodia. You wouldn't believe the satellite photos after each mission. We could read the top of a cigarette pack in a shirt pocket. We could tell how much someone was carrying from the depth of their footprint in the dirt." Swan paused to stare at the wall. After each sortie he also saw pictures of dismembered men, women, children, and water buffaloes.

"When I was twenty years old, I didn't spend much time thinking that I had killed entire villages. Now I can't stop thinking about what I have done."

I did not think about Cambodia again until the fall when a disheveled gardener complained of unusual headaches, tiredness, and different joint pains every day. Gardeners and people who spend a lot of time outdoors are at high risk of getting Lyme disease, a tick-borne illness that is easy to treat with antibiotics if it is caught early. When I started practicing medicine there was a widespread perception that Lyme disease could never be cured. This came from people who were infected for years going from one doctor and specialist to another before being labeled as crazy by friends, relatives, and physicians who grew tired of their ever-changing litany of complaints.

Beneath the gardener's veneer of tranquility, I sensed a cauldron of guilt. As the product of a strict Catholic upbringing, I marveled at how people coped with guilt that had been instilled in me at an early age. One of the many Catholic horrors: original sin. Catholics were guilty before they were even born. Not believing that Jesus was born to a virgin mother, that Jesus was the only son of an all-knowing male god who made the world in seven days, or that Jesus was resurrected and ascended into heaven after his crucifixion, I suspected that I was a heathen when I was ten years old.

I explained to the gardener that his symptoms were caused by *Borrelia burgdorferi*, a corkscrew-shaped spirochete that burrowed into muscles, joints, nerves, heart conduction fibers, and the brain. Lyme disease is remarkably similar to syphilis and, fortunately for him, easy to cure.

"I thought I was getting old. When the fevers started, I got flashbacks to Nam. You know how I got interested in gardening?" The clinic was less chaotic in the fall. I had more time to listen to his tales of search and destroy missions in Cambodia in 1974. Like the Navy pilot, he never wore a uniform. Sometimes he went in with several men and was the only one who returned. Once he went in with thirty men and three came out. He could do anything he wanted, kill anyone in his path. By his own account he was almost killed dozens of times.

"We were bad motherfuckers. You know what saved me? I got malaria."

The mercenary turned gardener explained that the army had flown him to a hospital in Japan where it took two months of treatment before the fevers stopped. After being discharged without any money or strength, a Japanese family invited him into their home. He spent two months listening to fountains, watching fish in the lily pool, reflecting on all the crazy shit that he had done.

"I couldn't do special ops after that. I stayed in Japan for a year studying Japanese gardens. Now I make gardens for a living."

Meeting the second US soldier who had served in Cambodia got me reading how the Cambodians, like the Tibetans, had fallen victim to Chinese Communism. After two decades investigating the underside of China's military occupation of Tibet, I wondered how the Cambodians were faring after the Khmer Rouge genocide. Many of the Tibetans I interviewed in India and Tibet who were victims of torture, coerced abortion, or sterilization felt that the Chinese were trying to eliminate their race. Although this was catastrophically depressing, the spirits of Tibetan Buddhists who could forgive their captors inspired me.

I was too young to register as 50,000 US soldiers were killed in Indochina from 1964 to 1975. My father was a lieutenant colonel in the US Air Force that dropped 8 million tons of bombs—the equivalent of 640 Hiroshimas—on Laos, Vietnam, and Cambodia.[16] By comparison, the US dropped 2 million tons of bombs during World War II, which does not include chemicals, defoliants, and land mines.[17] Unlike World War II, when the US dropped 70 percent of the bombs on military targets, and 30 percent on civilian areas, in Indochina 80 percent of the bombing targeted or struck civilians.[18]

In the fall of 1999, reading that a Cambodian soldier drove a tank up to the first cash machine in Phnom Penh and dragged it on a chain down the boulevard in broad daylight, I figured cash would be safer than traveler's checks. Kate surprised me by agreeing that it would be good for me to get away. I had been working without a break for one year since the Chinese police in Lhasa accused me of entering Tibet illegally and made me persona non grata.

Kate also understood that my going to Cambodia to see how Cambodians were faring two decades after two million people died unnatural deaths was not normal, but understandable. Although we were having difficulty with our marriage and had been separated for six months, Kate had both sets of grandparents to help with our children. Kaley was a healthy, beautiful, three-year-old already looking after her older brother, Zachary, who had Down syndrome. Zachary was much better now that he was seven. For the first few years of early intervention, I thought Zack would never talk. Now he was in first grade and wouldn't stop talking.

Kate gave me a big goodbye "be careful" hug. And so began another leap to the other side, freed from the responsibilities of everyone else's infirmities. Never free from Zack and Kaley whom I already missed. Worrying that it was irresponsible for me to leave my children, I tried telling myself that going to Cambodia would make me a better father.

In January 2000, I was a khaki eclipse in a sea of dark suits and polished black leather shoes flying first class on frequent-flier miles from New York to Thailand. Korean Air lived up to its reputation for Asian hospitality with seats that fully reclined and hostesses serving five-star meals from New York to Seoul and continuing to Bangkok. Before takeoff, changing into the same navy blue chamois pajamas as the other passengers in our luxurious cabin, I entertained the illusion of camaraderie with US businessmen hoping to sell Sikorsky helicopters and a Korean movie star with gel-spiked hair.

KISSINGER, NIXON, AND THE AMERICAN BOMBING OF CAMBODIA

The modern history of Cambodia is not complicated. In 1968 US President Johnson tried to end the Vietnam War that was intended to prevent Vietnam from becoming another communist "domino." Early in the year the US troop commitment had peaked at 550,000. The Tet Offensive shocked the US military and people at home when the Vietcong simultaneously attacked all major US bases on Vietnamese New Year, killing 4,000 Americans, 4,954 South Vietnamese soldiers, 58,373 Vietcong and North Vietnamese soldiers and 14,300 civilians.[19] Support for the war was further eroded by repeated news coverage of the US use of napalm, and Lieutenant Calley and his men burning every hut in Mai Lai, raping women and girls, and disemboweling pregnant women while they machine-gunned and bayoneted 500 civilians to death.[20]

Henry Kissinger sabotaged the Paris peace talks by convincing the South Vietnamese government that a US Republican administration would back them.[21,22] With the election of Richard Nixon to the White House, Henry Kissinger became the national security advisor. Besides escalating the US involvement and bombing of Vietnam, he orchestrated the elaborate falsification of American pilots' flight records to conceal the large-scale illicit bombing of Cambodia. Behind the backs of the Secretary of the Air Force, Dr. Robert Seamans, most of the intelligence community, and the US Congress, the US bombed encampments of North Vietnamese and Viet Cong soldiers along Cambodia's eastern border with Vietnam where they had established sanctuaries from the US bombing in Vietnam.

British journalist William Shawcross's *Sideshow: Kissinger, Nixon and the Destruction of Cambodia* painstakingly exposes the covert US bombing of Cambodia.[23] The first bombing mission of the Vietnamese sanctuaries in Cambodia was inaugurated on March 18, 1969, code-named "Operation Breakfast." Subsequent courses in Operation Menu included "Operations Lunch," "Snack," "Dinner," "Supper," and "Dessert." As the Vietnamese soldiers fled the US bombing and moved farther into Cambodia, US bombs followed.

Cambodia avoided being dragged into the Vietnam War until March 18, 1970, exactly one year after Operation Breakfast, when Cambodia's Prince Norodom Sihanouk was overthrown in a coup d'état. There are many conspiracy theories about the events that transpired when Sihanouk left his palace in Phnom Penh for a spa in Southern France. Whether or not Sihanouk had asked General Lon Nol to stage a series of demonstrations to whip up anti-communist fervor in his absence, Lon Nol assumed power with the CIA's blessings.[24] Lon Nol and the CIA had long believed that Sihanouk was too lenient with the Vietnamese Communists. For ten years the CIA had supported the Khmer Serei, armed anti-communist rebels in Southern Vietnam dedicated to overthrowing Prince Sihanouk.

After Lon Nol seized power, the CIA backed the new, extraordinarily inept Cambodian government and army. In 1972, Lon Nol announced that it was time to end "the sterile game of outmoded liberal democracy," and declared himself president, prime minister, and secretary of defense. At the same time it was widely known that the Cambodian Army was better prepared for parades than warfare. As a foreign correspondent for the *New York Times*, Henry Kamm described his first encounter with the "First Battalion of Commandos of the Teaching Profession." The "commandos" consisted of 474 schoolteachers who were each given eight rounds of ammunition for the rifles that they had never fired before being thrust to the front lines battling the Khmer Rouge.[25]

Like many other corrupt Southeast Asian leaders propped up by the CIA, Lon Nol was superstitious. Secluded and out of touch in his Phnom Pehn villa, Lon Nol relied on the advice of a mystical monk, Mam Prum Moni, or "Great Intellectual of Pure Glory." Lon Nol was well known for having planes sprinkle blessed sand around the capital, Phnom Penh, to protect him from his communist foes. Although the Cambodian Army outnumbered the Khmer Rouge, soldiers that did not defect were preoccupied with enriching themselves and became dependent on US aid dollars.

Sihanouk went to Peking and established a government in exile when the Russians shunned the arrogant Cambodian prince after a coup. In a remarkable about-face, Sihanouk appealed to the Khmer Rouge Communists, whom he had long opposed, to help overthrow the American imperialists. Meanwhile Kissinger's cabal of rogue US military who argued that surgical strikes would cripple the Communists the previous year, now pushed for more sustained bombing and a US ground invasion.

Nixon ordered 31,000 US and 43,000 South Vietnamese soldiers to invade Cambodia and wipe out the North Vietnamese strongholds in April 1970. In his "Address to the Nation on Military Action in Cambodia," Nixon said, "If, when the chips are down, the world's most powerful nation—the United States of America—acts like a pitiful, helpless giant, the forces of totalitarianism and anarchy will threaten free nations and free institutions throughout the world."[26]

Before the US Congress halted the US bombing of Cambodia in August 1973, American B-52s had dropped half a million tons of bombs from 30,000 feet that were neither accurate nor discriminate. Half of the tonnage culminated in a six-month carpet bombing of the entire country from February to August 1973.[27] Besides the economic devastation from US bombing, the CIA estimates there were 600,000 to 700,000 "war-related deaths" during the 1970–1975 civil war between the Khmer Rouge and the Lon Nol government.[28] Ultimately the US would spend $1.85 billion to prop up the Lon Nol regime.[29]

Irate that a *New York Times* article had disclosed his illegal war in Cambodia, Nixon ordered the CIA and FBI to conduct wiretaps that would become known as Watergate and lead to his impeachment.[30] Although Kissinger thought the leak might have been from his assistant, Mort Halpern, a political scientist who had worked in the Pentagon during the Johnson administration, the FBI's wiretaps broadened to include seventeen people, including White House aides, National Security Council staffers, and journalists.

In the summer of 1973 with angry street demonstrations against the Nixon administration's massive carpet bombing of Cambodia and the Watergate scandal, the US Congress came close to including war crimes in Cambodia in Nixon's articles of impeachment. Nixon resigned on August 8, 1974. In January 1975, US Attorney General John Mitchell was convicted of conspiracy to cover up the Watergate burglaries with the CIA's help. John Mitchell was the first attorney general to go to jail. He was also Nixon's campaign manager.

As the Nixon administration imploded, the Khmer Rouge walked into Phnom Penh on April 17, 1975. After five years of US bombing and covert war in Cambodia, the Khmer Rouge Communists defeated the American-backed Lon Nol government. Pol Pot was proud that his forces had freed Cambodia from US hegemony two weeks before the Vietnamese Communists defeated the American-backed South Vietnamese government.

Luong Ung's *First They Killed My Father* describes Khmer Rouge soldiers "liberating" Phnom Penh.[31] Wearing sandals made from tires and black pajama pants, red-and-white *kramas*[32] around their waists, the soldiers shouted, "Take as little as you can! You will not need your city belongings! You will be able to return in three days! No one can stay here! The city must be clean and empty! The U.S. will bomb the city! Leave and stay in the country for a few days! Leave now!"

While evacuating Phnom Penh's 2 million inhabitants to the countryside, 1.2 million of whom had fled US bombing there, Khmer Rouge soldiers executed anyone with any ties to the American-backed Lon Nol government or the Cambodian Army. The men and women in black pants and *kramas* also targeted any people identified as wealthy, skilled, or influential. Eleven thousand people died on the initial forced march to the countryside.[33]

Women giving birth bled to death by the side of the road. In order to turn Cambodia into a Maoist-inspired agrarian society, parents and children were separated and forced into slave labor gangs. The Khmer Rouge abolished currency, clocks, cars, newspapers, radios, foreign contacts, and all government and public references to civilization. For the next three years, eight months and twenty days the world knew very little about conditions in Cambodia during Pol Pot's Khmer Rouge Revolution. Anyone who resisted resetting the Cambodian calendar to Year Zero was killed.[34]

SIEM REAP

A "Happy New Year 2000" banner greeted passengers on the two-hour flight from Bangkok to Siem Reap. Every cell in my body cried for sleep that was out of the question. My biological clock was still twelve hours behind on New York time. I tried to imagine the Angkor temples built to honor Khmer "God Kings" when Cambodia dominated Southeast Asia from the ninth to thirteenth centuries.[35]

King Jayavarman II founded the Khmer Empire in 802 with Angkor as its capital, north of Cambodia's great inland lake, the Tonle Sap.[36] Jayavarman II ruled until 850, anointing himself a God King with supernatural powers inspired by Shiva. He also built a temple mountain at Phnom Kulen that symbolized the mythical Mount Meru, the holy mountain at the center of the Hindu universe. Massive irrigation canals flanked the temple, just as lakes surrounded Mount Meru. For the next five hundred years each Khmer God King built temple mountains to commemorate their reign while the Khmer civilization extended its domain into what are now Siam (Thailand), Myanmar (Burma), Vietnam, Laos, and Malaysia.

Jet lag evaporated as the plane descended over the Cambodian jungle. I strained for glimpses of flat-topped limestone towers rising above the canopy. Except for Angkor Wat, which had been restored in the sixteenth century as a Buddhist shrine, most of the temple complexes in forty square miles were overgrown by the jungle and had succumbed to the vagaries of time, erosion, and Western robbers.

For $20 and a visa application with a photo, a very efficient line of customs agents took turns fleecing an additional $5 while they perused foreigners' passports. Despite my pathetic phonic rendition of "Su Serei?" ("Hello" in Khmer) that I gleaned from the Lonely Planet guidebook, the last soldier in a brown uniform with gold epaulettes returned my passport without requesting a gratuity.

Siem Reap was a frantic frontier town with hotels sprouting next to unpaved boulevards. Legions of tourists and dust devils patrolled the red dirt streets. During Cambodia's decade of Vietnamese occupation in the 1980s, the Vietnamese Army clear-cut so much jungle around Siem Reap that the average daily temperature went up ten degrees. Stepping into hundred-degree heat on the shimmering tarmac, hot wind blasting our faces, confirmed that Vietnam's spoils of war were not worth their ill-gotten gains.

Crossing a line of soldiers with AK-47s and dark glasses, I entered the throng of taxi drivers shouting from the parking lot. A scrawny twenty-six-year-old, who drove an ancient Toyota while his wife stayed home with their four children, chose me. Hak seemed to have an appropriate name for someone born during the Khmer Rouge time. I offered to pay $20 to take me to a clean hotel and then the Sunset Wat before sunset. This was twice the going rate and ignited a best friend smile with two missing upper incisors. Offering $20 a day for the next two days to drive me around cemented Hak's enthusiasm for a few days' work.

The trickle-down theory espoused by Ronald Reagan stated that giving tax breaks to the wealthy would benefit the working classes in the creation of more and better paying jobs. Travelers in Asia had a chance to institute the trickle-up theory. Although many Westerners followed the local custom of not tipping, a generous tip could positively impact an extended family. It also gave Hak incentive to watch my back.

"On one condition," I said and Hak looked at me quizzically. "With four kids you need to save your money. I pay for your gas and meals."

After taking me to a modest hostel where rooms were $10, and Hak got a $2 commission, Hak set a land speed record driving twenty kilometers on a dirt road past palm trees and sweeping views of terraced rice fields to reach the Sunset Wat before sunset. Starting from the parking lot where empty air-conditioned buses coughed thick, black smoke into the air, we walked as quickly as we could up the steep hill, passing tourists on elephants, weaving around ancient, discombobulated stone steps and people struggling against the heat.

Hundreds of travelers from dozens of countries packed the flat-topped tower of the temple mountain that rose above a tiered base. The fading light bathing the temple in magenta and vermilion lifted my spirits, but the throng of tourists taking thousands of pictures diminished the view of the sun setting into jungle greens. As a cacophony of camera clicks drowned out the chorus of insects and the jungle swallowed the last rays of light, I realized I needed a Wat strategy.

Over dinner at the Bayon restaurant, Hak agreed to pick me up at 4:30 a.m. and go to Angkor Wat before it was inundated with tourists. In honor of French colonial influence and Siem Reap's extensive wetlands, I ordered frog legs sautéed in garlic butter. When Hak said he wasn't hungry I had to insist three times before he ordered a large bowl of rice noodles and shrimp in coconut milk and vegetables. It was hard not to notice how stunning our waitress looked in her red sarong, her ivory white teeth and beautiful brown skin. I was embarrassed when Hak caught me staring while she squeezed lime juice into dishes of black pepper for a dipping sauce. When Leakhena went for another plate of frog legs, Hak reported that Leakhena had been in Siem Reap for one month. Her family lived near the Vietnamese border. He could ask her to come to my hotel.

After I told Hak that my wife had just left me, he admonished to not tell any Cambodian woman that I was divorced or my wife was dead. "Then they will feel sorry for you and assume you have bad karma."

When the check came to $19, Hak put $5 on the table and grabbed a toothpick to clean his teeth and receding gums. "It's on me," I said, returning his money. Hak looked bewildered. No other foreigners had ever paid for him to eat with them.

THE ANGKOR WATS

The French naturalist Mouhot getting credit for discovering the Angkor temples in the 1850s is as specious as giving Christopher Columbus credit for discovering America in the presence of an Indigenous population.[37] But Mouhot's drawings and account of a prosperous monastery with over 1,000 slaves became well known. As an unofficial ambassador to Indochina, Mouhot was wary of colonialism. Soon after he died from malaria in Laos, France annexed territories in Indochina.

With my biological clock still skewed, I did sit-ups and push-ups at 3:30 a.m. Hak showed up on time at 4:30 a.m. to take me to Angkor Wat before sunrise. In the predawn light I was fascinated that the spatial dimensions of Angkor Wat paralleled the lengths of the four ages, or Yuga, of classical Hindu mythology. Walking toward the main tower was a metaphysical trip back in time to the creation of the universe. To respect the Angkor Wat temple's construction as a funerary temple that faced West, the direction of death, and the Hindu deity Vishnu, we circumambulated counterclockwise around the base of the bas-reliefs. Angkor Wat is surrounded by a moat 190 meters wide. From the west, looking down the sandstone causeway that crossed the water, it was difficult to fathom the enormous undertaking to quarry the sandstone blocks many kilometers away and float them down river on rafts, just as it was hard to imagine building the Egyptian pyramids.

The three-meter statue of Vishnu, carved from a single piece of sandstone at the beginning of the causeway, looked like a deity in search of itself with offerings of human hair. Jewelry and cloth from couples about to get married and those who had recovered from illness were draped over Vishnu's eight arms holding a man, a spear, a disc, and a conch.

Walking past *mana naga* mythical serpents that lined the causeway and two libraries with large reflecting pools, I was glad that we had arrived in time to see the sun's first rays rise above the temple before it was inundated with tourists. Three monks in orange-and-saffron robes were as excited as I was approaching the elaborate temple mountain.

Guana from bats clinging to the domed ceiling of the entry tower did not diminish a sense of wonder as we walked past a larger-than-life statute of the standing Buddha into an elaborate courtyard whose walls were covered with stone carvings of *apsaras*,[38] heavenly nymphs with moon breasts, swan waists, and elephant hips that epitomized the Hindu ideal of beauty in service of their God Kings.

The central temple was three stories tall, carved from laterite. Legions of sculpted *apsaras* with polished breasts and loins also decorated the walls of the inner courtyard and baths. Climbing from the earth to the heaven realm, the final steep stone steps to the third tier, offered sweeping views of an ancient civilization. But the awe came with the realization that the Angkor Wats were built with slave labor.

According to the Khmer historiographer George Coedes, King Jayavarman VII ruled from 1181 to 1201 and is credited with building Angkor Thom for a new capital in the thirteenth century.[39] He also built a host of smaller complexes: Ta Nei, Preah Khan, Preah Palilay, Ta Prohm, and Banteay Kdei. To give an idea of the scope of this undertaking, there were 13,500 villages to house the 306,372 slave laborers erecting mausoleums for the glory of their God King. King Jayavarman VII was also a megalomaniac whose foolish prodigality parodied the decadence of his country.

Angkor Wat's construction had an eerie parallel to Pol Pot's Khmer Rouge Revolution, Cambodia's second Indigenous revolution eight centuries later that also used slave laborers to build irrigation canals. By evacuating everyone in the cities to the country to grow rice, the Khmer Rouge used the urban population to fuel their agrarian ambitions, just as the Chinese Communists forced people in cities to work in the countryside during the Cultural Revolution. Standing on top of Angkor Wat, I imagined Pol Pot fancied himself the reincarnation of King Jayavarman VII who had conscripted slaves to reclaim Cambodia's dominance of Southeast Asia.

We stopped for chilled coconuts with straws to sip the best oral rehydration solution in the world. At ten o'clock in the morning, it was already over a hundred degrees. Seeing hundreds of tourists disembarking from dozens of buses that kept running reinforced the benefit of getting up early when a young girl selling packs of postcards for $3 approached me with irrepressible enthusiasm.

"Please buy postcards from me. Three dollars one pack. Two pack five dollars."

"What is your name?"

"My name is Lia."

"*Kinyum chemu Blake* (My name is Blake)," I said. "Pee (two) books, pram (five) dollars."

"Your Khmer is very good," Lia said, taking the money. "*Akun chiran* (thank you)."

"Akun chiran."

"I know the capital of your country is Washington, DC. I know America has fifty states. The capital of Alaska is Juneau. The capital of Hawaii is Honolulu."

"That's right! Did you learn that in school?"

"I learn from tourists. I know America people don't like George Bush. They like Bill Clinton."

"How do you know that?"

"Tourists tell me."

"Which tourists?"

"All tourists say American people don't like George Bush. They like Bill Clinton."

MR. LAND MINE

It is easy to miss Aki Ra's Landmine Museum on the road to Angkor Wat. Since he opened in 1999, Ra has endured threats from the governor of Siem Reap and the Cambodian police who demanded money, tore down his signs and banners, and threatened him with closure. The police had also accused Ra of arms dealing, supporting local amputees, raising money for their education, and scaring tourists from visiting Cambodia.

A short drive from Angkor, an inconspicuous stick fence concealed a makeshift museum with land mines stacked on tables, packed in crates, and piled next to the main house. A path meandering through the compound displayed hundreds of defused land mines, weapons, ammunition, and tripwires hidden behind logs and bushes and under rocks. Even the trees were booby-trapped.

Cambodia has over 10 million unexploded land mines, about the same number as Afghanistan and Iraq.[40] Egypt has the most with 23 million left over from World War II. Angola and Iran have 15 million and 16 million respectively. Every month 2,000 people are killed in the sixty-eight countries infested with the world's 110 million unexploded mines. In Cambodia, 98 percent of the victims are civilians and children.

Hak pushed me toward a stilted house with a thatched roof and half walls overlooking a lily pond that bred mosquitoes carrying malaria and dengue. I introduced myself in Khmer to the bulge in the middle of a green hammock that looked like a python that had swallowed a small pig.

Aki Ra sat up and passed his infant son to his young wife's engorged breast. Swinging both legs onto the floor, Ra replied in English, as he had many times before, how Khmer Rouge soldiers killed his parents when he was five years old. As time passed they let him play with guns. From 1975 to 1979, he laid mines as a child soldier for the Khmer Rouge. When the Vietnamese invaded, he laid mines for the Vietnamese soldiers fighting the Khmer Rouge for another ten years. And after 1989, he worked for the Cambodian Army that continued to fight the Khmer Rouge.

Ra began clearing land mines in 1991 when the United Nations Transitional Authority in Cambodia (UNTAC) assumed control of the transition after a decade of Vietnamese occupation. When he found three mines while clearing the land to build his own house, he borrowed a metal detector from a foreigner. After finding nine more mines on the same small plot of land, Ra decided to dedicate the rest of his life to clearing land mines.

To find the mines, Ra demonstrated how he swept with his foot, a stick, or his hand. In his lifetime he has defused 20,000 mines without a single accident. Five hundred was the most mines that he ever found in one day. Ra was not shy about pointing out that more land mines had been cleared in the past few years because of his video, in addition to substantial financing and personnel from Australia and Japan. The *Landmine Monitor Report 2000* for Cambodia listing 1,019 "casualties" in 1999, one third of the 3,047 victims in 1996, bolstered Ra's claim that fewer people in the Siem Reap area were still being maimed.[41]

According to Ra, land mines were simple. They had five parts: TNT, firing pin, fuse, detonator, and case. The amount of damage they did depended on how much TNT was inside, and the casing. A harder casing made the blast more lethal, so did wrapping the mine with nails or barbed wire, or placing it behind a stone to make shrapnel. Some land mines were meant to kill, others to take off a hand or a leg.

"Cluster bomb," Ra said, tossing an orange ball the size of a lemon to catch. I did not know that the cluster bombs dropped from B-52s in cases of 500 were colored so children would think they were toys. If a child playing found one and picked it up, the child would be maimed or killed, even thirty years later.

"Most people think if you step on a land mine it will not blow up until you take your foot off," Ra said. "Like Rambo in the movies. You have time to transfer your weight to a knife or a rock. This is not true. If you step on a land mine it blows up immediately."

Ra showed us the video of him finding and defusing mines hidden in bushes, trees, jungle, and fields. There was also graphic footage of amputees being treated at the Battambang hospital. The Pailin area near the Thai border had millions of mines. Samlaut had the most. If I ever went to Samlaut and Pailin near the Thai border, where the Khmer Rouge leaders lived in their jungle redoubt, Ra warned, "Do not walk on any path!" I did not realize at the time that I would need his advice.

Noticing an open suitcase under the hammock I asked if he was traveling. Ra replied that he was going on the Fast Boat to Phnom Penh tomorrow for a US visa. He had been invited to speak at the Ohio University. When I congratulated him he said the first time he went to the embassy an alarm went off. His body was covered with TNT dust. I laughed when Ra said that the security guards gave him a bar of soap and told him to wash his hands three times a day for one week before coming back.

"And not touch any more mines."

FAST BOAT

Poverty was at arms' length as we sped past trash-strewn stick huts on both sides of the elevated dirt track into the wetlands that produced Siem Reap's frog legs. I handed Hak $20 when he dropped me off at the gangplank to the fast boat that would take me down the Tonle Sap River to Phnom Penh. Instead of descending into the cramped, smoke-filled cabin crammed with passengers, filthy windows, and no view, I mantled onto the roof and stashed my pack behind a metal shield on the bow that provided some protection from the wind. From my perch I noticed Ra walking across the gangplank.

"You look like a visa coming," I said as Ra waved a hand that still had TNT under the fingernails.

The engine's clatter obliterated conversation with other backpackers who climbed onto the roof before the fast boat navigated narrow channels, past a floating market with stilted bamboo houses and fish drying in large nets over the murky green water. As our rivulet opened into Tonlé Sap Lake, Cambodia's fish basket, a great blue heron flapped its gangly limbs into flight like a prehistoric apparition.

Historically, Tonlé Sap Lake provided Cambodia with the world's richest source of freshwater fish. Tonlé Sap Lake's abundance, with extensive Khmer irrigation, provided enough protein and rice for the Khmer civilization to dominate its neighbors from the ninth to the thirteenth centuries. Today pollution, overfishing, and Chinese damns along the headwaters of the Mekong threaten Tonlé Sap Lake's vitality.

Siem Reap and Tonlé Sap Lake are connected to the Mekong River by a hundred-kilometer channel, the Tonlé Sap River. The Mekong River is best known for its Thai name—*Mae Nam Khong*, "Mother of Waters"—that starts at 17,000 feet in Tibet and flows 3,000 miles through Myanmar, Laos, Thailand, and Cambodia before fanning through the delta of South Vietnam into the South China Sea.[42]

During the rainy season from May to October, the Mekong River backs up with enough water to reverse the direction of the Tonlé Sap River.[43] This yearly influx of water, nutrients, and fish from the Mekong makes the Tonlé Sap Lake the largest freshwater lake in Southeast Asia, swelling from 2,700 to 16,000 square kilometers as its depth rises from one to nine meters. When the monsoon ends and the water level of the Mekong falls, the Tonlé Sap River again reverses course and flows back down to join the Mekong River at Phnom Penh.

The fast boat sped for three hours past sampans and canoes plying the shallow depths. I scanned floating islands of hyacinths but saw no corpses of Cambodian and Vietnamese fishermen, by-products of many Cambodians' deep resentment of Vietnamese coming to "steal their fish." The ethnic tension between the Cambodians and Vietnamese rivaled those in the Balkans. For over five centuries Cambodian and Vietnamese bands have crossed their borders to rape, kill, and steal, perpetuating endless cycles of violence and retribution.

Tragedy marred much of Cambodia's history.[44,45] Following King Jayavarman VII's death in 1218, the Khmer Kingdom deteriorated for the next six centuries of internecine warfare and Siamese and Vietnamese conquests. The extravagance of King Jayavarman VII's throne, and the introduction of Mahayana Buddhism, threatened the preeminence of the king and led to the Siamese invasion in 1431. The

Siamese controlled much of Cambodia for the next 500 years. Vietnam also claimed one of the largest Khmer territories when it annexed what is currently part of South Vietnam, including Ho Chi Minh City.

After a series of battles with the Vietnamese, the French seized Cambodia in 1863 to block Thai and British expansion up the Mekong. In 1864, the French enticed King Norodom to sign a treaty that made Cambodia a French protectorate. For much of the next century the French reduced the king's powers, making Cambodia a colony, but their support of the Cambodian throne is credited for stifling the nationalist activity that plagued their control of Vietnam.

When the Japanese occupied Indochina in World War II, the French were left in nominal control. In 1941 they crowned the eighteen-year-old Prince Norodom Sihanouk king of Cambodia. In March 1945, Japanese troops evicted the French and made Sihanouk declare independence. When the French returned after the war, they kept Sihanouk as the head of state. The withdrawal of French colonial forces in 1953, on the eve of their defeat in Vietnam, enabled Sihanouk to declare independence on November 9, 1953. Sihanouk abdicated the throne two years later and has remained one of the key figures in Cambodian politics to his death in 2012

I did not see the dugout canoe with four children until it was too late. As the Tonlé Sap Lake funneled into the Tonlé Sap River, I was watching children scamper up the steep slippery bank to jump into the turbid water, climb back up the bank, and jump in again. The fast boat could have changed course in time if the teenager steering the large wheel with his feet had been paying attention. The fear on the children's faces etched in my mind as they dove into the water seconds before the fast boat demolished their canoe. As nearby sampans came to search for the children, I realized there was no safety net for dead or wounded children in the Land of Smiles.

PHNOM PENH

One man stood in the shade of a solitary tree behind the taxi drivers waiting for the fast boat to dock in Phnom Penh. Wearing a clean white shirt and dark aviator glasses, Sokha looked like a diminutive extra in a James Bond movie. Sokha welcomed me to Phnom Penh and drove to the Goldiana Hotel, where he got a $2 commission, then as fast as he could to the Foreign Correspondents Club, the only FCC in the world that allowed non-journalists access to its restaurant and computers.

Unlike journalists, who are supposed to be unbiased, follow an unwritten code of ethics, and not pay for interviews, I was not bound by professional constraints. I had always given Tibetan victims of torture and sterilization an offering for "His Holiness." Bribing Chinese soldiers to access restricted minority areas was standard. In Tibet, I benefited from the Chinese police releasing detained foreigners if they wrote a self-criticism. In Cambodia, the Khmer Rouge tortured and killed their captives.

Sokha drove without any regard for the structural integrity of his twenty-year-old white Toyota Camry, or for our safety. He was thirty-seven years old with a six-year-old daughter and nine-year-old son. His father was Chinese, his mother Cambodian. When I asked about his wife, Sokha almost ran over a couple with two children on a moto. His wife had just taken the children to her mother's home near the Laos border. Although we had separation in common I figured it was safer to not ask any more questions while he was driving.

With little sense of lanes, nonexistent stop signs, and the few lights that were ignored, each intersection became a game of chicken and chance. Size and speed determined each vehicle's right of way. Pedestrians, amputees, and bicycle rickshaws vied with mopeds, motorcycles, and open-backed trucks filled with workers wearing faded *kramas*. The irony of two monks in saffron robes smoking cigarettes and talking on their cell phones evaporated when I noticed hundreds of bullet and mortar scars on the colonial facades facing the wide boulevards.

Phnom Penh was a Renaissance in motion with baguettes stacked in pyramids on the sidewalks and women wearing bucket hats in the shade of frangipani trees. Striking a giant pothole that launched our heads to hit the roof, Sokha grumbled about a "Pol Pothole." But he got us to the FCC in time to see an elephant on her way home from having photos taken all day at Wat Phnom, walking past sidewalk cafés, and the man with a racine of bananas tied to his bicycle for diners to feed an inquisitive trunk.

The FCC had a curved mahogany bar on the second floor with thirty-foot ceiling fans and magnificent views of Sisowath Avenue and fishermen in sampans casting their nets into the turgid confluence of the Tonlé Sap and Mekong Rivers. None of the tourists, expatriates, journalists, prostitutes, and embassy staff perused the graphic black-and-white photos on the walls of Khmer Rouge soldiers and their victims.

After Sokha finished every grain of fried rice and shrimp, I asked about his life under the Khmer Rouge. Sokha was twelve years old when "Pol Pot" came to his village, 200 kilometers northeast of Phnom Penh. Sokha remembered Lon Nol soldiers who were backed by the US giving up without a fight, and having to work all day in the fields. "Angkar" woke him up before sunrise to carry "100 waters." At mid-day he got one "small-small" bowl of rice, cupping his hands for effect. Sokha cleared land and worked the rice paddies long after dark. If he was lucky, he got another bowl of rice before his work unit leader extolled the glory of the revolution. Besides his mother who was forty-five, and father who was fifty, Sokha had a seventeen-year-old brother.

"Very hard work," Sokha said. "Every day cannot food, for three years eight months and twenty days."

"How did your family survive?"

"Mama, Papa, Pol Pot cannot kill. If work, not kill. Cannot work, kill. Understand?"

Sokha was grateful that the US military had backed the Lon Nol government when Sihanouk went to Paris in 1970 and helped the Cambodian Army fight "Pol Pot Communists." Sokha also knew that the US had bombed the Vietcong along Cambodia's eastern border with Vietnam, and the Khmer Rouge in the jungle. "America very good," Sokha said, cleaning his teeth with a toothpick.

I put the leftover rice, fish, fresh pineapple, and coconut rice wrapped in banana leaves into a bag. Sokha did not leave leftovers. Stepping into the night with enough food to feed a family, it did not take long to find a young woman carrying an exhausted infant in a sling made from her faded *krama*. When she sat down on the grassy quay next to the riverbank, two toddlers rushed into the huddle.

I was surprised to see so many children this late at night on the street selling newspapers, shining shoes, begging, and picking through garbage for anything they could eat, sell, or recycle. The young mother and her children eating my leftovers also shared the lines of starvation etched around sunken eyes and gaunt faces: snapshots of the suffering on Phnom Penh's decrepit streets.

PHNOM PENH'S NIGHTLY DEATH

"Lock your door," Sokha admonished when I asked him to take me on a tour of Phnom Penh's street prostitutes and brothels. Sokha seemed disappointed when I told him I did not want to have sex. I wanted to see how the prostitutes were faring in the Land of Smiles.

Prostitution was illegal during the Khmer Rouge Revolution from 1975 to 1979, rose during the next decade of Vietnamese occupation, and peaked in the early 1990s during the UNTAC when many of the 22,000 UN personnel frequented Phnom Penh's many brothels.[46] Out of Phnom Penh's 20,000 women and children working as prostitutes, the majority were smuggled in from Vietnam. Brothel owners paid $350 to $450 to traffickers for attractive virgins under the age of sixteen, $150 to $170 for less attractive girls.[47]

Once the girls are sold, they are brought to a hotel room or brothel where their virginity is sold to a "customer" willing to pay $400 to $500 to have sex with her for one week. After this, the girl is considered damaged. With expenses for food, clothing, medical care (abortions), and lodging deducted from the money taken on the girl's behalf, the girls get no money and are forced to have sex for as little as $2 with many men a day, under contracts for six months to one year.[48] If the girls refuse, they are beaten. Because politicians and policemen and their networks own the smuggling rings, brothels are difficult to close.[49]

According to the Cambodian Women's Development Association, the average age of prostitutes in 1992 was eighteen years old. One year later this had dropped to fifteen years old. By 1995 one third of the prostitutes in Phnom Penh and eleven other provinces were between the ages of twelve and seventeen.

"Very dangera," Sokha said driving down a dirt road with girls standing in the shadows of decrepit buildings. Most of the girls were prepubescent teens, with short skirts, thick-soled flip-flops and too much makeup. "How much?" Sokha called out to several girls before reporting, "One fuck, two dollar."

"This house very good," Sokha said as we stopped in the courtyard with neon lights in the windows. "Navy house has Vietnam girls. Cambodian girls no good for yum yum boom boom."[50] Asked to define *yum yum*, Sokha made a crude gesture shoving a banana into his mouth.

An obese *mamasan* escorted us toward a floor to ceiling glass wall that looked onto tiered platforms where dozens of young girls fidgeted, giggled, and talked on their cell phones. One girl who could not have been more than fourteen years old sharpened red lipstick with a razor blade. When *mamasan* clapped, all of the girls sat up and tried to look their best.

"For me?" I asked, pointing to the razor. The girl smiled stained teeth.

"She Vietnam," Sokha said approvingly. "She give good yum yum. Out of ten Vietnam girls, seven can make yum yum. Out of ten Cambodian girls, two can make yum yum."

"How can you tell Vietnamese from Cambodian girls?"

When Sokha went from one girl to the next asking, "Yum yum? Boom boom?" like a broken record, it did not take long to realize why Sokha's wife had left him. I was amazed that Sokha didn't get slapped. After interrogating each girl, Sokha reported that it cost "five dollars for Cambodian man to fuck. Ten dollars for foreigner."

"That's discrimination."

"*Mamasan* says foreigner have big cock. These are new girls."

"Do the girls use condoms?"

"You pay extra, no condom possible."

Sokha drove to another house where girls with numbers on their uniforms were seated in another amphitheater behind glass. Almost as depressing as the listless prostitutes was the stream of drunken men that could have sex with any girl for $5. Under these conditions, it would not take long to get infected with herpes, syphilis, gonorrhea, chlamydia, hepatitis B, and HIV. Many Cambodian men think that having sex with young girls protected them from getting infections. The opposite was true. The girls' young vaginal membranes were much more vulnerable to cuts and infections than women who were physically mature.

TUOL SLENG

Outside the Royal Palace, Phnom Penh has two main tourist attractions: the Tuol Sleng Genocide Museum, and the Choeung Ek Memorial (The Killing Fields). It was a hundred degrees under a cerulean sky at nine a.m. when Sokha drove to Tuol Svay Prey, "hillock of the wild mango," a high school in Phnom Penh that the Khmer Rouge turned into Security Office 21, the largest detention and extermination camp in Democratic Kampuchea. With over 100,000 pages of documentation, the Tuol Sleng Genocide Museum offered a detailed record of the Khmer Rouge's infamous killing machine. Like the Nazis in World War II, the Khmer Rouge kept meticulous dossiers of their victims' names, ages, belongings, photographs, clothes, torture, confessions, and executions.

Coils of rusted barbed and razor wire surrounded the fenced-in compound with five three-story buildings. At first glance, the coconut and frangipani trees and meandering walkways across the well-kept lawn lent a peaceful feel. A billboard outside Building A stated:

. . .

SECURITY REGULATIONS

1. You must answer according to my questions. Don't turn them away.
2. Don't try to hide the facts by making pretexts this and that. You are strictly prohibited to contest me.
3. Don't be a fool for you are a chap who dare to thwart the revolution.
4. You must immediately answer my questions without wasting time to reflect.
5. Don't tell me either about your immoralities or the essence of the revolution.
6. While getting lashes or electrification you must not cry at all.
7. Do nothing, sit still and wait for my orders. If there is no order, keep quiet. When I ask you to do something you must do it right away without protesting.
8. Don't make pretexts about Kampuchea Krom in order to hide your jaw of traitor.
9. If you don't follow all the above rules you shall get many lashes of the electric wire.
10. If you disobey any point of my regulations you shall get either ten lashes or five shocks of electric discharge.

I was speechless walking through Building A's three stories of rooms converted into cells for the interrogation and torture of high officials. Graphic photographs on the walls depicted the room at the moment of Vietnamese liberation. The rooms still had the metal beds that held the victims: corpses bound, gagged, chained, and blood-splattered; limbs twisted in unnatural positions; unrecognizable, swollen faces. The second and third floors had larger cells for mass detention and barbed wire curtains to keep prisoners from leaping off the balconies to commit suicide.

The central building had photographs of thousands of prisoners' faces, mass graves, open pits filled with hundreds of corpses, and a giant map of Cambodia on the wall made from skulls. There were also paintings on the wall by Van Nath, one of seven survivors of Tuol Sleng, depicting the treatment of prisoners shackled in their cells. Standard forms of torture included mutilating children in front of their mothers, beating prisoners whose hands and feet were bound, ripping fingernails off with pliers, lashings, waterboarding, suspension from wrists tied behind the back to dislocate arms and shoulders, and removing nipples with pliers then placing centipedes to excoriate the wound.

David Chandler's *Voices from S-21: Terror and History in Pol Pot's Secret Prison* details how those unlucky enough to end up at Tuol Sleng were interrogated, imprisoned, and killed, along with their spouses and children: bureaucrats, doctors, teachers, students, Buddhist monks, ministers, the Cambodian diplomatic corps, and foreigners.[51] No one was spared, not even Khmer Rouge soldiers and cadre leaders. By trying to abolish all family and social ties, the Khmer Rouge created a revolution with the complete absence of trust. This, coupled with the Khmer Rouge not taking any new recruits after they controlled the country, predisposed the Khmer Rouge to cannibalize their own ranks.

Behind the graphic pictures of torture, the Tuol Sleng Genocide Museum reveals the Khmer Rouge paranoia of foreign intervention. The purpose of torture was not to kill someone but to prolong their suffering as long as possible, and to get signed, detailed confessions of the prisoners' links to the CIA, the US-backed Lon Nol government, and the Soviet and Vietnamese intelligence services. It is impossible to understand the brutality of the Khmer Rouge Communists without appreciating the depth of their paranoia about the CIA and foreign intervention.

CHOEUNG EK

A solitary stupa rises above an orchard littered with excavated mass graves six kilometers from Tuol Sleng. Inside the Choeung Ek Memorial, platforms of fractured skulls are arranged according to categories: children, younger than fifteen; juveniles, age fifteen to twenty; adult, age twenty to forty; mature, age forty to sixty; and senile, older than sixty. Many of the killers were fourteen-year-old boys who, wanting for bullets, bludgeoned their victims to death.

There were no accidental deaths at Choeung Ek. The evidence of blunt force showed in jagged holes on the otherwise smooth surfaces of frontal, parietal, and occipital bones, torn suture lines between cranial plates, and straight, thin cuts from machetes and axes. The Khmer Rouge exterminated 20,000 people at Choeung Ek, sometimes killing hundreds of people in a single day. Although the death toll was not as large as the Nazi death camps, Choeung Ek's brutal efficiency put it in the company of Auschwitz and Buchenwald.

I was clinical asking Sokha to pose with his ankles in wooden stocks that shackled fifteen people; inspecting stacked tables of skulls fractured by blunt trauma from hatchets, rocks, and clubs; a mass grave with 160 headless bodies; the Chankiri tree where adolescent executioners swung children by their feet to smash their heads against the polished trunk. When I found Sokha staring into an excavated mass grave, I asked him to climb down to the bottom of the pit where, without prompting, he knelt on the dirt, put his head down, and folded his hands behind his back.

"Pol Pot time," Sokha replied.

Studying medicine had enabled me to distance myself from another person's suffering if someone needed a painful but lifesaving intervention, like a tracheotomy or chest tube. Witnessing the Chinese police beating unarmed Tibetans like baby seals, and a decade investigating China's torture of Tibetan political prisoners and national policy of coerced abortions and sterilization, had exposed me to the cruelty of China's military occupation of Tibet. Nothing prepared me for Tuol Sleng and Choeung Ek.

Tears streamed down my cheeks in a sudden burst of emotion when I found teeth and bone fragments scattered like pebbles on the ground around the Chankiri tree. Holding a small humerus from a child's arm, the carnage, horror, and total disrespect for human life came into focus. So did hundreds of butterflies fluttering over the small purple, yellow, and white flowers that softened the contours of excavated mass graves. The more I looked, the more the butterflies appeared as apparitions for the souls still imprisoned in this carnal landscape.

It was impossible to miss the shirtless, legless man with a jagged scar extending from his faded camouflage shorts to his sternum who had stationed his wheelchair at Choeung Ek's parking lot entrance. Sokha said the man was a government soldier for the Hun Sen Army who lost both of his legs when he stepped on a land mine in 1990. The soldier pulled the shorts up to reveal a fractured spear of femur protruding from his stump despite six operations at the Battambang hospital.

The soldier's story was typical of many wounded Cambodians who had to beg to support their families. This man had five children to feed. Unable to find work in Cambodia, he went to Thailand to sell "small things" on the street. It did not take long for the Thai Police to send him back to Cambodia. Five dollars raised the soldier's folded palms to a winning smile.

DON'T BREAK

Seated at a table overlooking the pedestrians on Sisowath Avenue walking past a United Nations of flags along the riverbank, with views of boats plying the muddy brown waters of the Mekong, a gregarious, inebriated American smoked a joint after downing a hot Margherita pizza with cold Tiger Beers. Before I could catch up, and against my better judgment, I agreed to "get my head out of my guidebook" and ride motorcycles south to Kampot and see the countryside. According to Bruce, Kampot was world-renowned for its black pepper, and had a great restaurant, the Marco Polo, with a crazy owner. Bruce had exhausted Phnom Penh's genocide tourist attractions. He was also from Long Island. It had been three years since his wife died from ovarian cancer. Bruce was ready for an adventure.

"Cannot," Sokha implored in his unique syntax when I told him that Bruce and I were going to ride motorcycles to Kampot. "Pol Pot in Kampot," Sokha insisted and I persisted, despite knowing that I was an inept rider, and the US State Department's website warned that Khmer Rouge soldiers were still active in the provinces. The State Department also advised against straying off any path for fear of land mines, not to travel alone or after dark, and never take motorcycle taxis, boats, or trains.

I was more worried about having a motorcycle accident than meeting Khmer Rouge soldiers. It was common knowledge that injury in Cambodia was looked upon as a sign of weakness. Accident victims were robbed instead of helped. In exchange for a $20 deposit to Lucky's Motorcycle Rental on Monivong Boulevard, and the promise to pay $6 a day for a 250 cc dirt bike when we returned, Ew Ya locked our passports in a flimsy wooden desk drawer.

"Fastest motorcycle in Cambodia," Bruce exclaimed. "The police have 125 cc bikes, and they carry two policemen." Surveying the maddening street, Bruce admonished to not use the front brake. There was too much gravel on the road and I would fly over the handlebars. I should use the gears to slow down. "Drive like a warrior," Bruce shouted as he accelerated into traffic going in both directions in both lanes that swallowed him whole like a giant Mekong catfish.

Because I had not mastered the clutch, and I was afraid to use the front brake, each downshift became a misadventure off the road. Going too fast and leaning too much into my first turn, I was fortunate to raise my left leg in time to ride the motorcycle on its side surfing into a throng of bicycles and rickshaws that parted without a single shout, curse, horn, or anyone stopping to help me. Standing up, I felt lucky to have no more than a snapped clutch cable, and I limped back to Lucky's with the engine still running in second gear.

"Accident?" Ew Ya asked, inspecting scratch marks along the gas tank.

"Broken clutch," I said, pointing to the clutch curved forward like a banana. Without questions Ew Ya outfitted me with a new 250 cc dirt bike. When I caught up to Bruce he was waiting at the only left turn on National Highway 3 that would take us the 148 kilometers to Kampot. Putting both of his arms out to the side and riding without his hands, Bruce showed off by maneuvering his motorcycle around potholes by swiveling his hips.

I was incapable of riding like a warrior. Riding too fast and downshifting to slow down focused all of my attention to stay on the road. After passing through several Khmer villages, I became more comfortable avoiding dogs, ducks, and chickens, and started to appreciate glimpses of thatched huts, lily ponds, and fallow paddies that stretched to the horizon. This was the dry season. Infrequent stands of palm and coconut trees offered little protection from the sun that seared the Mekong Delta. Bruce almost pissed himself from laughing so hard when I finally caught up to him, stuck my arms out to the side, and wiped out into red earth.

We stopped for lunch at a hut with open walls under a giant mango tree that provided welcome relief from the sun. Bruce played peek-a-boo with an infant girl wearing baggy pants and sunglasses. Uncertain whether to smile or cry, the smile won every time until mom served steaming bowls of Khmer noodle soup.

Fishing two small balls of mystery meat from the brown water with chopsticks, Bruce queried, "Moo?" mimicking a cow. This delighted the woman who said something in Khmer I could not understand. "Bok, bok, bok," and "oink, oink," were met with more laughter. When the woman pointed to a coconut tree, I handed her a pen. She found a scrap of paper and drew an elongated rodent with a big tail.

Bruce picked up two bags of marijuana on the counter and the woman pointed to my soup. "For cooking," a young man wearing pressed pants and a clean, long-sleeved, white shirt said in English and sat at our table. Pauk stood out from the barefoot villagers who stopped to stare at us. "The Khmer people like to put marijuana in their soup," Pauk said. "Only one old man in this village smokes."

I greeted Pauk in Khmer and complimented his English. Pauk had just graduated from the University of Phnom Penh where he studied to be a teacher. He was incensed that the headmaster was corrupt. Because he could not afford the "bribe money" he could not get a job teaching. "Hun Sen does not lead Cambodia," Pauk said. "He presides over a totally corrupt regime."

Asked if he had to be careful criticizing the Hun Sen government, Pauk said that he was the only person in the village who spoke English. Pauk left us to a growing chorus of villagers encircling the *barangs*.[52] I paid 25 cents for lunch, and $2 for two plastic soda bottles of gasoline. Bruce lit a joint and zoomed into the oncoming lane to pass a truck packed with field workers. The men who cheered when Bruce passed laughed when I wobbled around an oxcart.

Obsessed with avoiding collisions with other vehicles and the ubiquitous potholes from land mines and disrepair, three hours passed as I white-knuckled in Bruce's wake to the outskirts of Kampot. Hundreds of children wearing uniforms—boys in blue pants and white shirts, girls in blue skirts and white shirts—yelled, "Hello!" and, "What country you?" The student's voices startled me from a trance. Trying not to hit any students, I noticed but did not stop for a stocky man in a black motorcycle helmet waving muscular arms.

The towering Italian proprietor of the Marco Polo Guest House could not stop scratching the red spots on his hairy arms and chest as my motorcycle nudged a bamboo table at his outdoor restaurant. Eyeing the blisters on my left index finger from desperate downshifting, Davide asked why I did not use the rear brake. When I admitted not knowing there was a rear brake, Davide yelled into the kitchen for cold beers. He seemed eager for company.

Davide yelled several more times before his young Khmer wife arrived carrying a tray of cold beers and a bottle of Loch Lomond scotch. Pith had dark skin from working in the sun for decades. She was, according to Davide, the perfect wife. She spoke no English. She was a great cook. She let him do anything he wanted, and she took great care of their four-year-old son, Tito.

"Fucking backpackers," Davide complained about the few travelers who came to eat at the Marco Polo. He had the best restaurant in Kampot but they wouldn't pay $5 for a room when they could pay $3 at a hotel. Davide's cantankerous demeanor also explained why few travelers stayed at the Marco Polo, but Pith returned with delicious spaghetti Bolognese and venison with mushroom sauce.

"This is the best venison I've ever had," Bruce exclaimed with the surprised palate of a gourmand.

"Actually," Davide said, "it is, how you say, Bambi. Last night I shoot this deer with my M16 and the police take my gun. It is not illegal to shoot a deer. The police took a liking to my infrared scope. Here you can pay $50 for an M16, $25 for an AK-47. This scope cost me $500. Now it belongs to the chief of police.

"A man can do anything he wants in Cambodia," Davide mused.

"Are there still tigers in the jungle?" Bruce asked.

"Last month two Germans pay me $10,000 to kill a tiger. Which means I send Khat Mann into the jungle for $50 to find the tiger, then return with the hunters and he carries the kill. As a Khmer Rouge soldier for twenty-five years, Khat Mann has a PhD in killing."

"If you want to kill a tiger," Davide continued, "you must hunt with an AK-47. If you want to kill an elephant, the best weapon is an RPG. If you shoot an elephant with an AK-47 he will only get mad and trample you."

As Davide recounted how the Elephant and Cardamom Mountains along Cambodia's western border with Thailand had the largest and most undisturbed jungles in Asia, I found myself siding with the elephants, tigers, bears, white rhinoceros and long horned sheep on the verge of extinction.

"Don't ride motorcycles into Phnom Vor," Davide warned as we headed to our rooms. Phnom Vor was still controlled by Chhouk Rin's Gang who killed the last backpackers who came down here.

PHNOM VOR

The next morning Davide said that we should ride along the coast to the Vietnamese border and return through Phnom Vor, which he said had been too dangerous last night. When I asked about the backpackers, Davide said we should be more concerned with villagers trying to throw a small pig or duck in front of our motorcycles to cause an accident: the Cambodian equivalent of winning the lottery. We should also keep a few dollars in our pockets if the police stopped us. After two o'clock the police were drunk and would try to rob us. Davide did not need to warn us to get back before dark, but he did.

Following Bruce on the discombobulated road from Kampot to Kep, and being able to slow down with the aid of the rear brake, instilled a newfound confidence that allowed me to negotiate a herd of Brahman cows with ease, marvel at vibrant rice paddies under irrigation, baked dun of fallow fields, and brilliant salt flats drying along the shore. As soon as we left town, children splashing in lotus ponds yelled, "Hello! Hello! Hello!" So did children walking by the side of the road and playing badminton. "Hello! Hello! Hello!" I replied.

The children were from a Muslim village where women were covered with veils and men wore white skullcaps. The Cham people had migrated from central Vietnam after the Vietnamese defeat of the Cham Kingdom in 1471. Because they practiced an orthodox version of Sunni Islam, the Khmer Rouge targeted them for extermination.

"Hello! Hello! Hello!" to the sound of a beating drum. Unlike other Muslims where the call of the muezzin led the faithful to prayer, the Cham banged on drums. The village of thatched huts and wooden houses on stilts surrounded a mosque dwarfed by coconut and mango trees gave the illusion of bucolic bliss: great sprays of purple, vermillion, and fuchsia bougainvillea covered walkways. Pigs and chickens roamed unattended. Water buffalos walked wherever they wanted, and a bare-chested man waded into a lily pond to cast his net to catch frogs and *trei changvar*, a small silvery fish that lived in the mud.

As we drove along a rocky shore with a few abandoned colonial buildings and more coconut trees than people, I was lulled into a false sense of security with sunlight glittering over turquoise waters to offshore islands. Suddenly dozens of policemen drinking beer in the shade of bamboo huts stood up and waved for us to stop. Bruce accelerated. I followed and did not look back after the first curve that shielded us from the policemen's view.

For once I had no difficulty keeping up as we slalomed along the rugged coastline, then took a small, paved driveway to a one-story house on a promontory overlooking the Gulf of Thailand. To the north we could see the strait that separated Cambodia from Vietnam. The house had once belonged to Sihanouk. Now monkeys roamed the grounds and two families squatted on the land. All of the windows and glass doors in the house were intact and locked. Several women cooked under the garage. Two men checked out our motorcycles as we argued.

I wanted to go back on the road we knew. Bruce insisted that we were lucky to pass the police once. They would be even more drunk on our return and wanting us to pay their bill, if we were lucky. Once again I followed Bruce until the pavement ended and a rutted red dirt path disappeared into the jungle. Every time we passed men walking home with machetes tied behind their backs, I inquired "Kep?" Each time the men pointed in the direction we had come.

Pain from insects hitting my face accompanied the realization that we would not make it back to Kampot before dark. The first grasshopper crash-landing in my throat got me to breathe through my nose. It was too dark for sunglasses so my eyes were forced into a squint. Although the nuances of the trail demanded our full attention, I could feel people staring at us from open restaurant huts in villages without electricity that had a noticeable absence of litter. Women wore stylish, colorful sarongs, their black hair cut straight across the napes of their necks. Bare-chested men wore faded *kramas* wrapped around their waists.

It seemed like hours before the dirt track turned into a freshly graded dirt road that traversed an enormous coconut plantation. Five kilometers after the pavement resumed, I recognized the turn that led to Kep. My elation at heading back to Kampot on a road that I knew vanished when we passed two policemen riding on a 125 cc bike. They were as startled as we were and waved for us to stop. We waved back and kept riding, picking up enough speed to make hitting a pothole more dangerous than the police stopping us. For once, Bruce followed me.

CHILD SOLDIER

A stocky man walked into the Marco Polo wearing a black motorcycle helmet with the visor down. Bruce, Davide, and I were drinking cold Tiger Beers at a teak table under his Cambodian-style house that was elevated on stilts to provide shade and natural air-conditioning. Davide welcomed the Helmet like a brother and yelled for Pith to bring more beers. Davide introduced Khat Mann as a onetime child soldier for the Phnom Vor Gang before becoming Pol Pot's radioman in Phnom Vor. Khat Mann was tall for a Cambodian, with muscular arms and legs. Removing his helmet revealed the matted black hair and intense stare of a madman, or a monk who had meditated in a cave for too many years. Khat Mann boasted that he saw us coming into Kampot yesterday, and in Phnom Vor today.

"That's impossible," Bruce said.

"I know everything that happen in Phnom Vor," Khat Mann said, leaning close to Bruce. "Why you come Kampot?" Bruce leaned back before stuttering that we came to see the Komchi River. I was more than a little amused that Bruce was a lot tougher riding a motorcycle than he was with a Khmer Rouge soldier.

When Davide announced that I was a doctor, Khat Mann grabbed my hand to feel a small piece of shrapnel wedged behind his right upper eyelid.

"You must take out!"

"I need a CAT scan first," I replied.

Khat Mann did not understand my first Khmer joke and stared at Bruce. "When headache come!" Khat Mann said slapping the table for effect.

There was an awkward silence until Davide said that Khat Mann was a very good killer, which inflated him with pride and distracted him from taunting his prey. Davide paused for effect before saying that most afternoons Khat Mann robbed everyone who came down Highway 3 into Kampot. He would have robbed us if we had stopped by the school yesterday. He also killed the last backpackers who came to Phnom Vor. Davide paused to monitor the concern registering on Bruce's face before continuing.

In 1994, the Australian, British, and French embassies told three backpackers not to go from Phnom Penh to Sihanoukville by train.[53] Even the ticket sellers at the station told them it was not safe. The backpackers did not know that Chhouk Rin and his Phnom Vor Gang had stopped the train from Phnom Penh six times in the previous eighteen months, robbing everyone before they let the train pass. This was the first time three Westerners were kidnapped. Cambodia's Prime Minister Hun Sen wanted to break up the Khmer Rouge in Phnom Vor and loaded a flatcar in front of a train with sandbags and troops and orders to not stop for any reason.

"Chhouk Rin plan ambush," Khat Mann said. "We kill seventeen Hun Sen soldiers, and capture thirteen Vietnam." When I asked what happened to the Vietnamese nationals, Khat Mann referred to Vietnamese as *"you'en,"* which I later learned meant ants. Khat Mann's laugh reached a manic crescendo before flashing serious. "I hate Vietnam. Must kill all."

As Davide described the three backpackers sitting on the roof, smoking ganja, and enjoying the view at six kilometers an hour before they were surprised by Chhouk Rin's Gang, I realized that Bruce and I could have been on top of that train. I wanted to know the backpackers' names and how the Khmer Rouge treated them. As a child soldier for the Khmer Rouge who spoke English, Khat Mann offered a remarkable opportunity to understand how he participated in the Khmer Rouge killing machine. He was also fascinating from a psychiatric perspective.

Davide explained that during the Khmer Rouge time everyone had someone above them and someone below them. Khat Mann worked in Chhouk Rin's Gang. When they kidnapped the backpackers, Khat Mann telegraphed Nuon Paet, their commander of Phnom Vor, who telegraphed his commander, Sam Bith, who telegraphed Pol Pot, the president of the Democratic Republic of Kampuchea. Because Pol Pot wanted to use the backpackers to get the Cambodian government to allow the Khmer Rouge to be represented in a coalition government with the UN, he ordered Chhouk Rin to hold the backpackers hostage.

"The ransom was Chhouk Rin's idea," Davide said. "You have to understand that Chhouk Rin is a soldier. He is not political. He has never read a newspaper. He did not know you can't get money for hostages from any embassy. You have to contact the family directly. Chhouk Rin also did not know that Hun Sen had just signed cooperation agreements with France and Britain."

Bruce was visibly upset when I bought Khat Mann another beer and inquired about the backpackers' treatment. According to Khat Mann, foreigners were treated the same as everyone else in Cambodia. If you worked in the fields all day, you got one bowl of rice at night. If you did not work, you did not eat. After two months the Australian tried to escape. "I know jungle very well!" Khat Mann said. "I catch Australia man and bring back." Khat Mann described the long talk their gang had that night at their camp in Phnom Vor to prevent their hostages from escaping again.

"Chhouk Rin give order to cut here," Khat Mann said, slicing his index finger across the back of my Achilles tendons with the same emotion one might have cleaning a fish. "After that, they not run away."

Suppressing the sick feeling in my stomach, I was determined to not show any emotion as Khat Mann kept talking and Davide kept translating. For one month while Chhouk Rin bargained with Hun Sen, the backpackers crawled to work in the field or they did not get any rice to eat. Then Hun Sen became impatient and sent troops down to Phnom Vor.

When Hun Sen's soldiers reported that the backpackers had been "crippled," he said they had a "big problem." Returning cripples to their countries would look bad for the Cambodian government so Hun Sen made a deal with Chhouk Rin. If Chhouk Rin laid down his arms along with 10,000 men under him, he would receive amnesty for everything he had done during the Khmer Rouge time. He would also become a colonel in the Royal Cambodian Armed Forces (RCAF).

When Khat Mann killed the backpackers on September 28, 1994, Chhouk Rin became the first Khmer Rouge officer to surrender to the Hun Sen government. Khat Mann reassured me that he took each man into the jungle and shot him in the back of the head so they did not feel any pain. I doubted this was true. Khmer Rouge soldiers were known to kill their prisoners with blunt force from clubs or machetes. No matter how Khat Man killed the backpackers, I shuddered imagining how each man must have felt before being executed.

Khat Mann put his helmet on and left as quickly as he came. Davide broke the silence, "Mann has a headache. He wears his helmet to warn people not to talk to him."

"What happens if anyone talks to him?" Bruce asked.

"He will kill them without thinking," Davide replied with a soldier's certainty. "Don't ever go into the jungle with Khat Mann."

"How could you buy him a beer?" Bruce protested.

. . .

Seven beers later Bruce stood up to go to the bathroom and stumbled, his right hand moving gracefully out to the side. A woman in the kitchen with charcoal skin and short black hair cut straight across her neck followed Bruce perfectly, a Khmer Ginger Rogers to his Fred Astaire. When Bruce grunted sitting down, she reproduced his eructation.

"Koki is pure Khmer," Davide said. "She is straight out of the rice fields. Two months ago, she had never seen a mirror. Now she can copy Bruce like a monkey."

Bruce jumped up and screamed. Koki ran terrified behind a wooden stilt, then peered around and mimicked Bruce's yelp. Bruce stretched his arms out to the side. Koki did the same. Bruce scrunched his face into an inebriated visage with wagging tongue. Koki followed. Bruce grabbed her hand to dance. Koki screamed and ran behind the stilt.

"How old do you think she is?" Davide asked. Bruce guessed twenty-two. I guessed thirty. "She is forty-four," Davide exclaimed. When I asked Koki's name in Khmer, "Neak chmou ei?" she returned a blank stare. Davide explained, "She can't understand you. Even if you speak perfect Khmer, she does not expect you to speak Khmer, so she will never understand you."

Bruce coaxed Koki from behind the pole to further their repertoire of facial expressions and animal noises that entertained us into the night. Before retiring, Bruce reached into his wallet and handed Koki $10. Koki looked at Davide, who nodded for her to take the money. Koki took the money and ran into the outdoor shower.

"She is yours," Davide said before Bruce could protest. "Lock your door if you don't want her."

MERCENARY

The next morning while Bruce snored out of his second-floor window, Davide recounted his renegade career as a mercenary in Thailand after he participated in a failed attempt to overthrow the Italian government when he was nineteen years old. Thailand was extending its northeastern border into Laos to the Mekong River, the only part of eastern Thailand not defined by the river. After Thai and Laotian soldiers launched grenades at each other in the morning, they took siestas during the hottest part of the day. That's when Davide's men used elephants to remove the gargantuan hardwoods that they had cut, which the Thai military considered stealing.

"You see this?" Davide said, pointing to the jagged scar on the right side of his neck. "I had 120 commandoes working for me. One day the government found out that I am harvesting teak wood and they shell my home, which kill my girlfriend. This was pretty shocking for me. Without any preparations I decide to get the bastards who killed her. That night I take my commandos and cross enemy lines. But I am late. Normally you have to be in position before daylight, and 120 commandoes are not that quiet. So the enemy hears or sees something and begins to fire mortars.

"My radio man was hit in the head right next to me. I had a cask helmet so no shrapnel could go through. I felt something hit my neck. I knew I was hit but I was more concerned about my radioman. So I tied my scarf around my neck to stop the *hem-orr-ha-ging*. The next thing I know I am on the ground and one of my men is pulling the scarf as tight as he can.

"This is funny," Davide continued. "Just the previous day I had given my men a lecture on tourniquets. 'Stop,' I yelled at him. You can put a tourniquet on an arm or a leg, not on a neck. HE WAS FUCKING KILLING ME!" Davide succumbed to deep, rapacious laughter before recounting how he met Khat Mann for the first time in 1994 when he came to the Marco Polo to sell the backpackers' traveler's checks. Khat Mann was wild. He had never been in a house before and squatted on a chair. As a child soldier for the Khmer Rouge, Khat Mann had filled many of the mass graves at the nearby Kep Killing Fields. He was also intelligent and had an affinity for languages. When he saw older child soldiers being killed, and men fighting and dying on the front lines, he became a telegraph operator. That way he stayed with the Khmer Rouge officers behind the front lines. Davide was impressed with Khat Mann's accomplishments and respected him as a soldier.

"When you go into the jungle with Mann, don't pay him too much! He will just want more."

Listening to Davide's stories reminded me of the mercenary I treated in New York who was part of the 31,000 American and 43,000 South Vietnamese soldiers that Nixon ordered to "clean up" the Vietnamese sanctuaries in Cambodia in 1970.[54] The US ground invasion of Cambodia also coincided with the beginning of Cambodia's five-year civil war where the US-backed Lon Nol government would be beaten by an obscure band of Communists that would come to be known as the Khmer Rouge.

"I find you!" Khat Mann exclaimed, startling me. Khat Mann was in full manic phase and demanded that I go into the jungle with him immediately. I offered to buy him breakfast and was encouraged when he said he would like to try Western food. As Davide yelled into the kitchen, I tried to think of ways to avoid going into the jungle with Khat Mann.

"Maybe tomorrow."

"Tomorrow!" Khat Mann confirmed.

When Davide instructed that I step exactly in Khat Mann's footsteps when we went into the jungle, Khat Mann boasted that he knew all the land mines in this area. "You should!" Davide said. "You planted most of them."

"I also know spitting cobra," Khat Mann said with the air of a seasoned tour guide.

The spitting cobra rose up in the tall grass and spit in your eyes before you knew what was happening, blinding you and giving the cobra time to strike. Most people died in two or three days. Davide said that he knew five people who had died from the spitting cobra. As Davide and Khat Mann tried to out regale each other, I was struck by Khat Mann's enthusiasm. When Pith served Khat Mann a plate of scrambled eggs, baked beans, and toasted French bread, Khat Mann ate in large bites like a wolf and swallowed without chewing.

"I want to *hope muon American chiran*," Khat Mann said between gulps.

"But you are married!" Davide chided.

"I want to *hope muon American chiran*," Khat Mann repeated ad nauseum before Davide explained that *Hope muon chiran* literally meant to "eat one chicken." *Hope muon chiran* was a metaphor for sex. Khat Mann had two children with his Khmer wife in Kampot. He wanted to have an American wife because American women were the most beautiful and rich. I did not interrupt Khat Mann's fantasy. Any sway over him would be helpful. Pointing to my crotch, I told Khat Mann that if he wanted an American wife, he had to kiss her there.

"Cannot," Khat Mann exclaimed, sounding like Sokha and leaning back in his chair like Bruce. "Cambodia man cannot kiss." It was fun laughing with Khat Mann until he ordered me to go to the jungle with him again like a child having a tantrum.

"I'm taking him to the Kep Killing Fields," Davide said.

Once again, Khat Mann left as fast as he came. Davide said that we would never see Khat Mann at the Kep Killing Fields. He was fourteen years old in 1975 when Pol Pot evacuated Phnom Penh's 2 million inhabitants to the countryside. The 100,000 "New People" who were sent to Phnom Vor were distrusted by villagers who had been ravaged by years of war and US bombing. Under the Khmer Rouge, New People became slave laborers to dig irrigation canals and grow rice. Anyone who refused was killed. As a child soldier for Chhouk Rin's Gang, Khat Mann had killed thousands of New People, including some of his own relatives.

KEP KILLING FIELDS

Bruce claimed the front seat of Davide's Land Rover, which he affectionately called "the Defender," that was much larger than most vehicles on the road. I was thrilled to sit in the spacious back seat, free from worrying about accident or injury. Cars and bicycles in town parted as Davide drove around potholes big enough to swallow motorcycles. When we got to a statue where the road continued along the coast to Kep, we veered north onto a dirt track through dry scrub toward the jungle-covered Kep Mountains. This was Chhouk Rin's land where they had held the backpackers hostage.

It seemed a long time before we stopped at a small *wat* where a group of acolytes guided us to the main stupa. Most of the acolytes had only been at the *wat* for a few months to fulfill their religious obligation and could not read. Inside, a series of murals depicted the Buddha's life, from his privileged upbringing leaving his palace for the first time as a young man and seeing the utter poverty, disease, and despair that surrounded him, to his enlightenment and first teachings under the Bodhi Tree in Sarnath. The murals were simplistic and helped illiterate monks and farmers visualize the Buddha's life.

In the sixth century BC, an Indian prince named Siddhartha Gautama traveled as an ascetic until he took the title of Buddha and preached the four noble truths: Existence is suffering. The cause of suffering is desire. If you can eliminate desire you can transcend suffering. And the eight-fold path is the way to enlightenment. In essence, the Buddha's teachings were heretical to India's Hindu Brahmans who believed in an eternal, blissful self.

Theravada Buddhism ("Teaching of the Elders") spread south from India to Burma, Laos, Thailand, and Cambodia, where it tried to preserve the early Buddhist canons. At the same time, Mahayana Buddhism spread north into Nepal, Tibet, China, Mongolia, Korea, Japan, and Vietnam. The Mahayana Buddhists considered themselves "the Great Vehicle" because they expanded on the Buddha's original teachings to reflect the needs of the people.

Theravada Buddhism prevailed in Cambodia until the ninth century, when Mahayana Buddhism suffused the reign of the Khmer God Kings for the next four centuries. With the fall of the Khmer empire, Cambodia reverted to Theravada Buddhism for the next 1,200 years. When the Khmer Rouge took over Cambodia in 1975, in their attempt to extinguish all religions, they destroyed or damaged over 3,000 *wats* just as the Chinese Communists destroyed over 6,000 monasteries in Tibet.[55] Buddhism again became Cambodia's religion in 1980, as evidenced by the abundance of acolytes at the Kep Wat.

Hearing that we wanted to see the Kep Killing Fields Memorial, the tallest monk ran to his room to retrieve a hatchet that seemed incongruous in his hand as he led us down a path to a red wooden shed where a large termite mound blocked the door. It took ten minutes for the monk to chop at the mound and pry nails from the shuttered boards before the door creaked opened. Two piles of human bones came into view. On the left, long bones from arms and legs rose to the ceiling. On the right, a smaller pile of skulls. Many of the skulls had been smashed and fractured. Gaping holes in the craniums bore the distinct marks from blunt trauma.

"Chhouk Rin's soldiers told people with education to come to this place for teachings," Davide said. "If they were identified as having any intelligence they were killed. Most had their heads smashed. Some were tortured and killed with machetes."

The monk explained in Khmer that this memorial held the remains of 500 skeletons from one mass grave. There were 200 more mass graves around Kep Mountain. Even if each grave did not hold 500 people, thousands of people died in this region alone. The monk led us to an excavated pit in a nearby field that produced all of the bones for the Kep memorial. Seeing this one mass grave in Kampot disturbed me more than Tuol Sleng and Choeung Ek, where 17,000 people had died. The Kep memorial represented the 100,000 people killed by the Khmer Rouge in Phnom Vor alone.

"Money go to school?" from a boy behind a barbed wire fence. As I got closer pleading hands thrust between the rusted wires. "Money go to school?" the boy pleaded. As if on cue, seven other urchins with runny noses and wearing tattered shorts tied with string belts materialized. The youngest child was naked and began to wail.

"How do you count to ten?" Bruce asked in English to more pleas.

Bruce raised his right hand. Counting out loud in English from one to five, starting with his thumb, stopped the wailing and the children fell in step behind the oldest child who led everyone on a count of one to ten in Khmer. "*Mui, pii, bei, buan, bram,*" the children sang, counting from one to five, then, "*Bram mui, bram pii, bram bei, bram buan, dawp.*"

I tried to copy the children's excellent pronunciation as we counted from one to ten several times. The Khmer number system was based on counting from one to five. Six was five plus one. Seven was five plus two. When the children counted to "*dawp*" (ten), Bruce gave each child 500 riel, about 9 cents. There were 5,800 riel to the dollar.

"*Akoun chiran* (Thank you)," from the oldest.

"Not much!" from the wailer who resumed his desperate pleas as we walked away from the barbed wire that separated us from their misfortune through no fault of their own.

HERMAPHRODITE BEACH

When Davide offered to drive us in his Toyota pickup truck for a swim in the ocean at a village of hermaphrodites near the Vietnamese border, Bruce claimed the front seat. Davide's son Tito stood in the open back jousting with a bamboo stick in his hand. I did not pay any attention to Tito's swordsmanship as offshore islands came into view. When we turned off the paved road a deranged teenager started chasing us down the dirt track. Tito raised the stick to strike the older boy each time he came close to catching us until we arrived at a fishing village with a pristine beach of yellow sand that stretched for six kilometers along the tranquil Gulf of Thailand.

With a sweep of his hand Davide said we could buy the beach for $10,000. Club Med had just bought the only other beach on Cambodia's coast near Sihanoukville. There was an abandoned airstrip nearby. Cambodia was about to open its southeastern border with Vietnam. According to Davide, people only came to Cambodia to visit the Angkor Temples and Phnom Penh. If we built a few bungalows we could make a fortune.

As we waded into the waveless, shallow, piss-warm water, Bruce asked if foreigners could get title to the land. Davide said to never mind that foreigners were not allowed to own land in Cambodia. For some "small money" we could evict the hundred families living along the beach and own the last undeveloped beach in Cambodia for $10,000. One hundred meters into the still knee-deep water, Davide assured Bruce that he could get one of Sihanouk's nephews to be the titular owner.

The teenager was standing next to the pickup when we returned to the village. "*Akrok* (Crook)," Davide yelled at the boy who followed us to an outdoor restaurant. The boy cowered when Davide raised his arm to strike him, then snapped to attention when Davide handed him 500 riels to protect us from the gathering crowd. Within minutes of sitting down at an outdoor table, the entire village surrounded the three strange white men and their iron horse. Children pulled the hair on Bruce's arms while an old woman hacked a pineapple into wedges for us to dip into chili salt.

"Like a monkey," Bruce said, mimicking a chimpanzee to the children's delight.

Despite Akrok glaring at anyone who approached, children continued pulling the hair on Bruce's arms and pointing to his big nose. I was as fascinated by the villagers as they were by us. A young girl with Down syndrome who was accepted by everyone made me miss my son. Zachary may have been chromosomally challenged, but he was an ambassador of goodwill and would walk up to anyone and say, "Hello! Hello! Hello!"

The first year went by quickly after Zachary was born in Southampton Hospital and whisked into emergency surgery at Stony Brook University Hospital for an intestinal blockage. During Zachary's first week of life a cardiologist informed us that Zachary would need to gain ten pounds before he could have open-heart surgery to repair his AV canal, an endocrinologist discovered hypothyroidism, and a nephrologist reassured us that his one kidney would not pose any significant problem.

"Didn't anyone tell you?" the geneticist asked. "Your son's mongoloid features. His slanted eyes and heart defect. The Mongolian crease in his palms and bifid scrotum are all typical of children with Down syndrome."

I thought Zachary's almond eyes were adorable. It took five weeks to liberate Zachary from the neonatal intensive care unit. After convincing his physicians that I could tube feed Zachary as well as anyone, Kate and I were allowed to go home to fatten him up before an operation to reconnect Zachary's intestines that did not go well. Zachary perforated hours after the surgeon went on vacation. Any medical student would have seen the elevated white blood cell count of 30,000 and crescent of free air under the diaphragm on the X-ray, clear indications of perforation and sepsis.

The lowest point of my life was not wanting to exact revenge on the surgeon, but thinking that Zack would be better off dying than "failing to thrive." But Zack would have none of it. He withstood hundreds of needle sticks for blood and the ephemeral intravenous lines. During the first eleven months, Zachary survived five abdominal operations and open-heart surgery, Kate and I helped each other in and out of cars, walked down sterile corridors holding hands, and stood vigil amid the technological bustle of expensive care units. Three years later we had a beautiful daughter, Kaley.

Davide laughed when I asked if Chhouk Rin spoke any English. The backpackers taught him some English before Khat Mann killed them. During the Khmer Rouge Revolution Chhouk Rin was responsible for carrying out Pol Pot's orders to eradicate all foreign influence in Phnom Vor. I could not stop thinking about Khat Mann leading the three backpackers into the jungle one at a time and shooting them in the head. Humane treatment, compared to how most of his victims fared.

"I understand how Khmer Rouge could kill Lon Nol soldiers and anyone who supported the US-backed Lon Nol government," Bruce said. "Why kill people performing valuable services to their own communities? Why eradicate all ties with civilization?"

Davide did not answer the question and said the previous month, in January 2000, Hun Sen's agents had come to Kampot and invited Chhouk Rin to go drinking. Because of Chhouk Rin's legendary capacity for alcohol consumption, it took a case of beer before Hun Sen's men could get Chhouk Rin into their car and drive him to Phnom Penh. The last order Chhouk Rin gave to Khat Mann was to find his "Freedom Letters." It took Khat Mann seven days to find the letters that Chhouk Rin had received from Hun Sen and King Sihanouk absolving him of crimes committed as a Khmer Rouge officer, and for killing the backpackers. When Khat Mann took the letters to Phnom Penh, Chhouk Rin's lawyer said that he would have freedom. Although Chhouk Rin had been in prison now for several months, Judge Mong Mony Chariya had not charged him with any crime, which was not unusual by Cambodian judicial standards.

After I paid for the warm beers and pineapple, Davide charged an extra $20 for the gas and transportation. Seeing Bruce's displeasure, Davide complained we would not have seen the Kep Beach without him, and he had a lot of expenses. Bruce paid the $20 and Davide resumed his pitch for us to buy Kep Beach. When Bruce said there were too many problems buying the beach, Davide offered to send a container of Burmese teakwood to New York for $10,000, for a 6 percent commission. He could sell the wood for five times the price in New York.

The price was rising faster than the sun was setting.

LARIAM DREAMS

Sunday was Lariam day when we swallowed our first weekly pill to prevent malaria which infected over one third of the Khmer population. It was no coincidence that taking Lariam spawned vivid, violent dreams: gouging eyes, hand-to-hand combat, dismembering limbs with a machete, shooting people at close range with an AK-47, fighting to the death again and again until I was killed and thrown back into the melee. Bruce dreamed he was running through the jungle, trying to escape from Khat Mann cutting his Achilles tendons.

By morning both of us vowed to never take Lariam again.

The engine *put-put-putting* accompanied our two-hour venture north up the Komchi River to villages without electricity. After leaving Kampot, the river narrowed into a canyon of skyscraping ferns that blocked our view of heavy cumulus clouds sitting on the 3,000-foot Elephant Mountains. Men on both sides of the river filled dugout canoes with sand retrieved from the bottom until the gunnels almost touched the water. Lone fishermen standing in canoes had the remarkable ability to paddle with one leg so both hands could cast and retrieve their nets.

According to a world demographic report by the US Population Reference Bureau, and the 1998 census carried out with UN assistance, the Cambodian government spent 40 percent of its budget on the military and police.[56] After the remains were divided between the different ministries, little was left over for vital areas like basic medical care, education, and clean water. Although Cambodia had the second highest birth rate in Southeast Asia, with 38 births for 1,000 people, this was offset by the second highest infant mortality rate, with 103 children out of 1,000 dying before they reached the age of one. Cambodians also had the second lowest life expectancy at fifty-three years. In 2000, 85 percent of Cambodians lived in the countryside, 36 percent lived below poverty level, and 20 percent suffered from malnutrition.

Dozens of children were waiting for us when the boat stopped at the riverbank where a man was washing a white ox in the turgid water. Bruce climbed the bank first and transformed into the Pied Piper with the children following him along dirt paths between rice paddies, mimicking his whistles and barnyard epithets. Once again, I was struck by the abundance of rice, sugarcane, bananas, papaya, tomatoes, manioc, mango, coconuts, cows, pigs, water buffalos, and flocks of chickens. The village seemed well-off. The children shared the same rotten teeth of most Cambodian children before their adult teeth grew in like ivory, but no one appeared malnourished.

Bruce found a woman in a hut frying sticks of dough in hot oil and dusting them with powdered sugar and bought one for each child, which ignited another frenzy. At 100 riels for each child, the bill came to 3,000 riels, about 50 cents. For his next act, Bruce entertained the children by showing them pictures on his digital camera. Bruce became an instant hit when a village elder gave a two-capped gold tooth smile of approval. After I took a group picture of Bruce surrounded by thirty children, an old woman led me by the arm to take a picture of her cow. Laughter rippled through the villagers who enjoyed our exhibit in their zoo.

When I picked up an apricot-colored fruit on the ground, a scrappy child scampered up the trunk and dropped handfuls for everyone to share. I followed the children's lead, biting off the end, squeezing out the pit, and sucking the piquant, sweet-tasting orange flesh, until a helicopter flying low over coconut trees scattered everyone.

At the Marco Polo that night Davide said the helicopter belonged to a CIA agent who paid Khmer Rouge village chiefs to stop growing marijuana and lay down their weapons. With the DEA's help, the Cambodian Army was making a big deal eradicating sixteen hectares of marijuana along the Komchi River.

When asked what the Khmer Rouge did with the money, Davide explained that the Khmer were dirt poor once you left the riverbank and walked inland. They had no access to electricity, medical care, or other villages. The Khmer were even more vulnerable than other impoverished people around the world because so many people with skills had been killed. "So the Khmer Rouge take the money and continue to grow marijuana."

"Pax Americana!"

I could still feel Lariam's after-effects the next day when Khat Mann insisted that Bruce and I follow him on motorcycle into the jungle. Bruce graciously declined. Davide surprised me again by saying that this was a good idea. I did not trust Khat Mann, but I did not think he would kidnap or kill me, and I wanted to see where the backpackers were killed. Khat Mann took the lead off-road on paths through dense underbrush.

Following Khat Mann on foot through high grass, stepping exactly in his footsteps, I didn't know if I was more afraid of spitting cobras, stepping on a land mine, or Khat Mann killing me. The Australian didn't have a chance of escaping through this terrain. I felt sick to my stomach remembering Khat Mann's sterile rendition of slicing the backpackers' Achilles tendons and killing them two months later.

I tried to convince myself that Khat Mann wasn't barbaric. He was a soldier following orders, which meant he would kill me if ordered.

Khat Mann stopped at a large depression whose contours were softened by grasses, vines, and licuala bushes. Noting the similarity between the hole and a vagina, Khat Mann told me about one night in Battambang when he and Chhouk Rin took two karaoke girls to a hotel. Chhouk Rin could not get an erection so Khat Mann took Chhouk Rin's chicken. Khat Mann cackled as he descended twelve feet into a pit large enough to fit four tractor-trailers.

When Khat Mann pried an arm-length piece of metal from the dirt, fashioned a knife within minutes, and demonstrated how he used it to kill Vietnamese soldiers, I realized that we were standing over a bomb crater. Khat Mann's ingenuity to fashion a weapon out of US bomb fragments was impressive.

Gesticulating with his arms and whipping the air around him, Khat Mann mimicked bombs exploding. "You not see B-52 before bomb," Khat Mann yelled. "Only after. There was no warning." Khat Mann threw his arms up in the air in another mock explosion. "We dig the bunker to hide under ground. When I was ten years old, I hide in bunker many times."

Khat Mann showed no emotion when he said that an American bomb killed his mother. I remembered when the loudspeaker called my brother and me to the principal's office and he drove us home without saying a word. We knew that our father had just died in the hospital. It would have been nice if he had said something, anything, a simple acknowledgment. Although I was too young to serve in the military during the Vietnam War, I felt guilty for the devastation that my country had wrought on the people of Southeast Asia.

As a direct result of US bombing and other military actions in Indochina, 60,000 civilians died in Laos, 300,000 civilians died in Cambodia, and over 2 million civilians died in Vietnam.[57] These statistics do not include 10 million refugees created from US bombing. Nor do they address the immediate and long-lasting health consequences from exposure to a wide range of toxic chemicals that would have profound, debilitating effects on nursing mothers, infants and children, the elderly and infirm, for generations.

Khat Mann did not respond when Bruce said that he was sorry that an American bomb killed his mother.

HOW CAN YOU BE MAD AT A SPIRIT?

On our last night in Kampot, Davide recounted how he met his wife. Riding his motorcycle "like a crazy" through the countryside seven years ago, Davide inadvertently ran over a woman and knocked her out. Davide said that she was beautiful and that he was afraid he had killed her. When she came to, he asked her to marry him. Now they had Tito. Davide yelled into the kitchen until Pith returned with a plate of homemade french fries. Pith was not the least intimidated by Davide and yelled back at him.

When his first wife divorced him and got full custody of his Italian son, Davide vowed to never be with another Western woman again. Pith did all of the cooking and cleaning. When he went out of town for a few days to Phnom Penh on "business," he never called. When he returned the house would be clean and Pith would be "extra affectionate." The whole time Davide was gone Pith would be thinking, *What have I done wrong?*

According to Davide, Pith knew that he had other women while he was away, but she never asked. As long as Davide did not bring any prostitutes to Kampot, where Pith knew everyone, she did not care if Davide was with other women—as long as she did not lose face. Davide turned rapturous describing his favorite opium den in

Phnom Penh that he liked to go for one or two days a month to "smoke the finest black opium, not that red shit you get in Laos."

Basking in the light from a crescent moon, Davide recalled one day after he got married when an old man came unannounced to his house. Pith served tea while Davide talked to the man about the weather, the crops, and the family. After he left, Pith said that when she was six years old that man grabbed her younger brother by the ankles and swung his head against a tree, killing him.

Bruce looked at Davide, incredulous.

"In Cambodia," Davide said, "if you lose a leg from a land mine, if anything bad happens to you, it is because you did something bad in a past life. This is your karma. Anyone can be possessed by a spirit that makes them do evil things. You can commit murder and be forgiven. But if something bad happens to you, people will shun you. Once you understand this, you understand the Khmer."

"How can you not hate the man who killed your brother?" Bruce asked.

"How can you be mad at a spirit?"

Standing with his hands to his sides as though expecting a tip, even though I had given him $20, Khat Mann did not believe that I would come back to Kampot next year. When I said I wanted to meet Chhouk Rin, Khat Mann boasted that he knew him well. Khat Mann was visibly worried about his commander's health, and that he was not being treated with respect in prison. I tried not to smirk at the Khmer Rouge commander who had killed thousands of people not getting respect. I complimented Khat Mann on his English and asked if he would be my translator when I met Chhouk Rin, if he got out of prison. Khat Mann agreed and promised to study English every day. He also offered to build me a nice house for $5,000.

"If you have that kind of money," Davide said, "you should buy Kep Beach."

"Next year in Kampot," I said, bidding farewell to the Khmer Rouge soldier and Italian mercenary.

Bruce and I took turns in the lead, around oxen carts, potholes, and incoming traffic, driving as fast as we could on open stretches of road from Kampot to Lucky's Motorcycle Rental in Phnom Penh. Bruce had a night flight to Vietnam to see a woman he had met in Ho Chi Minh City and could not stop thinking about.

BEGGAR IN THE
LAND OF SMILES

After wading through the beggars, bumpkins, newspaper boys, and rickshaw drivers accosting everyone who went into or out of the FCC, I looked forward to a quiet dinner. A small girl pushing a wheelchair with a boy missing both arms and his left leg, his right foot sticking unnaturally from his hip, looked up with forlorn eyes. They could be orphans from an impoverished village who came to scavenge food and shelter in Phnom Penh's burgeoning streets. I did not like giving money to beggars and would look for them with an FCC sampler after dinner.

Before going up the long wooden stairs to the second floor bar and restaurant that would insulate me from the bustle and misery on the street, I bought a *Phnom Penh Post* from an enthusiastic boy carrying a large bundle under one arm. When I waved off the 3,800 riels change, the boy flashed a lottery-winning smile that made me feel good for a moment, thinking he would get a good meal, until an older boy punched his arm and stole the money. There was nothing I could do to change my good deed that got punished.

Eating red snapper and sauteed vegetables at a table overlooking ragged children picking through garbage strewn along Sisowath Avenue, I read the lead article in the *Phnom Penh Post* with pictures of police raiding a garment factory along the road where thirty-four Vietnamese and seventeen Chinese all wanted to stay at the factory even though none of them had been paid. According to the factory records, all foreign guest workers were allowed to leave once their debt from factory expenses that exceeded their salaries had been paid.

Being in Cambodia less than one month, I was struck by how little I knew about the Khmer people and their Land of Smiles, and how much I wanted to return to Cambodia. Interviewing the Tibetan victims of torture and forced sterilization taught me the importance of meeting the perpetrators of their crimes, whenever possible. Pol Pot's Khmer Rouge regime committed one of the largest genocides of their own people. I was afraid of Khat Mann. He was a psychotic soldier who followed orders, cunning, and remarkably free of guilt. But he could introduce me to his warlord who was responsible for killing the backpackers. Chhouk Rin also had direct knowledge of the 100,000 New People executed in Phnom Vor, survived three decades of warfare, and was the first Khmer Rouge officer to surrender to the Hun Sen government.

Like a Lariam dream, each time I imagined asking Chhouk Rin a question I was hacked, bludgeoned, stabbed, burned, and beaten before he killed me. Like the children scavenging Phnom's streets, I would become a beggar in the Land of Smiles.

JEAN-MICHEL BRAQUET, MARK SLATER, AND DAVID WILSON

My obsession with the backpackers ballooned when I returned to New York and found an article from the Agence France-Presse about Jean-Michel Braquet from Nice, France, age twenty-seven; Mark Slater from Corby in Northamptonshire, Great Britain, age twenty-eight; and David Wilson from Melbourne, Australia, age twenty-nine, traveling by train from Phnom Penh to Sihanoukville on July 26, 1994.[58] This led to a video that the Khmer Rouge had used to get a ransom for Mark Slater. "I am very weak from stress and bombings," Slater said, "It is as if they were bombing to kill us. The government should pay the ransom directly to the Khmer Rouge. There is no way for us out of here if the ransom is not met."[59]

A confidential cable from the Australian Embassy in Phnom Penh to Canberra noted that the Australian government paid $150,000 to the Cambodian military as ransom for the backpackers.[60] The British journalist Tom Fawthrop confirmed that an initial ransom request for $50,000 for each hostage was complicating Pol Pot's desire to "keep the long noses quiet and in good condition" in order to force the Hun Sen government to stop France and Australia from training the Cambodian military.[61]

In mid-August of 1994, the Royal Cambodian Armed Forces laid siege to Phnom Vor to free the hostages. A translation of an intercepted transmission from Chhouk Rin to his immediate superior, Noun Paet, to his superior, Sam Bith, on September 25, stated that: "According to the instructions of #99 (Pol Pot), the recommendations are that these three have no further use. Suggestion to #37 (Sam Bith) is that they be destroyed . . . After the execution keep it strictly secret." Fawthrop put the backpackers' executions between September 28 and the end of the month.

When Chhouk Rin defected to the Cambodian government on October 15, 1994, with 200 of his men, he gave General Nhek Bun Chhay, the deputy chief of the RCAF, handfuls of radio reports scribbled on Cambodian exercise books. Translations of the radio reports confirmed Pol Pot giving direct orders to Sam Bith, then Nuon Paet, then Chhouk Rin to kill the backpackers. Chhouk Rin received amnesty for future prosecution in January 1995, and the rank of colonel in the RCAF.[62] The backpackers' graves were discovered on October 30, six days after the RCAF captured Phnom Vor.

PART II

MY ENEMIES, MY FRIENDS

THE ELEPHANT BAR

Davide's emails kept me abreast of Chhouk Rin's legal odyssey. In January 2000, Chhouk Rin was arrested and charged with murdering David Wilson from Australia, Jean-Michel Braquet from France, and Mark Slater from Britain. Six months later, at Chhouk Rin's trial on July 18, 2000, Judge Mong Mony Chariya acquitted him of all charges.[63] When Davide emailed in May 2001 that Chhouk Rin would meet me in Phnom Vor, I flew from New York to Seoul to Bangkok to Phnom Penh in forty-eight hours.

Torrential rain and lightning heralded the beginning of the monsoon as I landed at Phnom Penh's Ponchetong International Airport. Greeting the first customs official in Khmer, I watched my passport leapfrog the line of no less than nine officials perusing passports and visa applications. "How much you pay?" from a disgruntled backpacker waiting in a line of his own choosing. "Fuck America!" when a female customs officer returned my passport for $25. The backpackers did not care that I was trying to meet Davide at the Elephant Bar in time for happy hour when the savings from one drink surpassed a Khmer family's monthly income. After immigration I put on sunglasses and waded into the cluster of taxi drivers.

Sokha appeared from my left flank holding a white paper with **MR BLACK** written in bold letters. He was pleased to have snuck up on me. I missed my Cambodian brother until Sokha drove too fast down the airport road under an ochre sky, challenging incoming motorcycles, bicycles, and cars before swerving to avoid head-on collisions. Two monks leapt for their lives in front of Phnom Penh's premier luxury hotel, Le Royal, where a skeleton of a boy with his younger brother—whose stumps did not reach the edge of the wheelchair—watched us enter the guarded parking lot. The boys seemed like regulars. Although the hotel's security protected guests from any contact with beggars, I would have something to eat for them when we came out.

Parked under a jasmine tree, Sokha confided that he had a "police problem" while I was gone. One night a playboy stole his car. The next day the police found his car with a man in the passenger seat who had been shot in the head. The police took Sokha to Dola Ka, the central police station near the stadium. "Very bad," Sokha said, looking down in shame. "Dola Ka very dangera." But Sokha was lucky. His mother came to the police captain with $1,000 and bailed him out before he was subjected to the indignities of a Cambodian jail.

The Elephant Bar was an auspicious oasis to meet Davide in the company of billionaires and movie stars, businessmen, dignitaries, generals in the Cambodian Army, Hun Sen goons, and stunning women in silk evening dresses. Before the Khmer Rouge took over in 1975, and during the Vietnamese occupation from 1979 to 1992, journalists and international workers enjoyed the hotel's opulent suites and pool garden. Reopened to the public in 1996, Le Royal Hotel continues to set the standard for elegance.

A Black woman at the piano with an Australian accent introduced herself as Rozalyn, and, if that was too difficult for Americans to pronounce, we could call her Roz. Registering the second jibe against Americans in half an hour, I was no stranger to anti-American sentiment while traveling overseas. I had my own reservations when the US Supreme Court designated George W. Bush president on December 12, 2000, and he abandoned his campaign promises of compassionate conservatism. Instead of being "the unifier" Bush embarked on an unprecedented concentration of executive authority and infused his administration with right wing, "neoconservatives" courting Evangelical Christians.

Davide had lost weight. Dark circles hung under his eyes, and he was still scratching his chest. Between guzzles of Coke, Davide said that I would like staying at the new Marco Polo, an old colonial building on the Komchi River that he had renovated in the last year. Davide was proud of the Marco Polo's listing in the Lonely Planet's Cambodia guidebook and serving the best food in Kampot Province.[64] Business was good, but he looked exhausted.

"Two weeks ago, I take a girl from Phnom Penh to Kampot. It was late at night. Normally my wife is at the old Marco Polo. I leave the girl in the car and go inside the restaurant to get some money. Suddenly I hear a terrible scream. I run outside and see my wife trying to kill this girl with a kitchen knife. I mean, *WHAAAH*, she is trying to stab this girl to death. Pith is small but I could barely get the knife from her."

Davide waited a few days before trying to go back to his house. When he did, Pith attacked him again as soon as she saw him. It was all Davide could do to get away without injury or hurting her. Davide looked distraught. There was no way he could talk to her, and he did not want to lose his son, Tito. So Davide bought a gold necklace for $1,000 and had Penya take it to her. He would give Pith a few more days to calm down, then meet me in Kampot.

Davide warned me to be careful around Khat Mann. After a German woman gave him $2,000 to build her a house, he took the money and disappeared. Davide last heard that Khat Mann had a new motorcycle. I asked about Chhouk Rin, and Davide resumed his pitch for me to buy Kep Beach. Because Davide was married to a

Khmer woman, he was considered Khmer and entitled to 51 percent ownership of a business. Thirty percent of the corporation would go to one of Sihanouk's nephews who would buy the land and hold the title. With $10,000 from me, and some backing from "millionaire friends," we could get the land and the airport and flip this to a five-star hotel and make a lot of money!

"Chhouk Rin does not want to talk to you," Davide said before I asked. "He is in Phnom Vor with his men. After seven months in prison, Chhouk Rin does not want to talk to anyone, especially a foreigner."

Davide paused to monitor my reaction. The possibility that I had traveled all this way on a ruse reminded me that every encounter with the Khmer Rouge was a slow dance with extortion. Davide was testing me. The more eager I appeared, the more he set the hook. Before I silently counted to ten in Khmer, Davide asked if I would pay $100 to meet Chhouk Rin. When I nodded, Davide dialed a number on his cell phone, talked for a few seconds, and hung up. This had been rehearsed. I would go down to the Marco Polo and stay in the "nice room" upstairs for $25 a night. Penya would take care of me. He had just gotten married and Davide warned me not to get him into any trouble.

"Khat Mann will take you to meet Chhouk Rin tomorrow," Davide said. "Do not go anywhere with Khat Mann if he is drunk. Do not go to Phnom Vor after dark. And remember to look at Chhouk Rin's foot. He lost his left foot in a land mine. One hundred dollars is a lot of money. I don't want him ripping you off. I don't have to tell you what Chhouk Rin and Khat Mann did to the last foreigners they met."

I had no shortage of worries about meeting the warlord who ordered Khat Mann to kill the backpackers. From the US perspective, Chhouk Rin was an officer in the Khmer Rouge Army who had committed crimes against humanity and genocide of his own people. I had no doubt that Chhouk Rin had committed atrocities of war, and that I needed to have an open mind. From the Khmer Rouge perspective, Chhouk Rin helped free Cambodia from foreign aggression and spent the last twenty-two years fighting the Vietnamese occupation. He was a soldier following orders, a hero to his people.

Davide made me promise to call him from the Marco Polo that night when I met Khat Mann. If I did meet Chhouk Rin, Davide warned me not to ask any questions about the Khmer Rouge time and not to give Khat Mann any money until after I talked with Chhouk Rin. Khat Mann was a soldier. If Chhouk Rin gave the order to kill me, or Davide, Khat Mann would do it without hesitation.

I knew going to Phnom Vor was dangerous, but times had changed for the low-level Khmer Rouge who had "liberated" Cambodia from US hegemony and survived the killing fields. As a *barang* trying to meet Khmer Rouge officers, I knew that atrocities were committed on both sides of conflicts, and that the victors assigned the lions' share of crimes to the vanquished. I also believed that on some level the survivors of all wars yearned to return to their families and previous lives. Whether or not this was possible for Khat Mann and Chhouk Rin remained to be seen.

OFF THE ROAD
TO KAMPOT

Fast-moving banks of dark clouds spewing bolts of lightning and violent rain galloped eastward across the rice paddies on the Mekong Delta. Leaving as fast as they came, brilliant wakes of late afternoon light electrified verdant rice fields. The landscape looked flat, but the fields stretching to the horizon were no less terraced than those clinging to any mountain slope, only here a few centimeters distinguished each vibrant paddy.

Sokha honked his horn at incoming bicycles, stray dogs, mopeds, oxen carts, pigs, pedestrians, chickens, and ducks. Sokha also honked at inanimate objects, like coconuts and hundred-year-old kokum trees. Even on a clear day with no rain or traffic, Sokha slammed into potholes that could dent rims and rip wheels from their axels. I wondered if his mother paying $1,000 for him to buy a new used car, with none of his own money, diminished his respect for the car.

The Nissan in front of us bucked into a gaping concrete hole. Instead of learning from the other driver's experience, Sokha drove straight ahead while gnarled asphalt ravaged the undercarriage. At that moment I felt that Sokha was the worst driver in the world and that this was my arrogance manifest. Traditional Western culture mandated that every group had a scapegoat. In a pair, Sokha inherited my wrath. Although I wanted to flog him each time he slammed into potholes and my head hit the roof, Sokha was loyal and honest. Applying the same logic to Chhouk Rin's Gang, I would be their goat.

A man in faded camouflage fatigues and sunglasses watched a child throw a piglet onto the road, forcing an oxen cart carrying a dozen monks in saffron robes into our path. Instead of slamming on the breaks or trying to avoid a collision, Sokha locked his elbows and honked the horn, tempting fate. To the amusement of the monks and onlookers, the ox turned its head and gored a motorcycle, which launched three men over the handlebars into a puddle. When the men stood up drenched but without injury, I let down my guard.

"Fucking eh, Sokha. You're making great time!"

The rain wiped out the bridge to Takeo on Route 2 from Phnom Penh to Kampot where a gaunt woman walking with the aid of a bamboo staff, the left side of her face drooped from paralysis, watched Sokha drive off the road into a ravine, scattering a flock of ducks with clipped wings. Fortunately, neither of us nor any foul were injured. Sokha was driving too fast, as usual.

For once I was grateful for Sokha's driving. Without this detour we would not have passed the tall, leafless samrong trees along the riverbed whose pods released a fetid stench, and giant thickets of clacking bamboo. Although it took hours to get to Route 3, the ribbon of asphalt pockmarked with land mines that the Americans built in the sixties to connect Phnom Penh with Cambodia's southern coast, it was worth realizing that the many small ponds that people used to catch fish and frogs were reincarnated bomb craters.

NOT MEETING CHHOUK RIN

Pith watched Sokha's Toyota pull up to the newly painted white, three-story colonial house with ten-foot ceiling fans and wooden shutters that opened to views of the Komchi River. Pith looked self-conscious adorned with a gaudy, gold, rapper necklace. We had arrived in time to watch the sun sink into the jungle-covered ridge across the river. Penya was an easygoing twenty-year-old, comfortable with his pot belly, glad to be married. Before finishing our first cold Tiger Beer, Khat Mann drove up too fast on a new Honda 250 cc motorcycle and banged into the potted palm separating our table from the street. Khat Mann's drunken dismount and trouble extracting his key from the ignition reminded me of my entrance to the old Marco Polo last year when I was sober.

"Nice bike," I said to an inebriated Khat Mann.

"Germany friend give me," Khat Mann said, then demanded, "If you want to meet Chhouk Rin, we must go now."

Sokha stared at the maroon tiles on the floor. Child soldiers like Khat Mann had killed people like Sokha and their families throughout Cambodia. I felt sorry for Sokha but I was hungry and offered to pay for Khat Mann's dinner. Khat Mann insisted that we go to meet Chhouk Rin right away. When flattery that Khat Mann's English had improved failed to stimulate his appetite, I called Davide on his cell and said that our friend was intoxicated. Davide replied that this was unusual. I gave the phone to Khat Mann and watched the jugular veins on his neck distend before he threw the phone back at me. It was settled. I would not go into Phnom Vor with Khat Mann at night when he was drunk. We would wait until morning to meet Chhouk Rin.

Khat Mann was furious. I depended on Khat Mann to take me to Chhouk Rin and to translate. Realizing what a dumb, stupid idea this was turning into, I ordered a Tiger Beer for Khat Mann, which further terrified Sokha. Khat Mann's beer arrived with my spaghetti Bolognese and French bread. I ate as fast as I could with Khat Mann protesting that there was no time. His bloodshot eyes loomed closer as he kept insisting that we leave immediately.

Khat Mann's logic was impeccable. Chhouk Rin and his gang were in Phnom Vor surrounded by the Cambodian Army. Chhouk Rin did not want to go back to prison while his acquittal for murdering the backpackers was on appeal. Khat Mann said that he told Chhouk Rin that I was a "doctor friend" of the Khmer Rouge. Chhouk Rin said that he would meet me but we had to go at night. If Hun Sen's secret police saw me with Khat Mann it would be dangerous for both of us.

I had not felt this close to danger for a long time. Twenty-five years ago, caught in a rainstorm at 18,000 feet on a snow-covered ridge in Peru's Cordillera Blanca, I almost froze to death before daylight. The following year, rappelling twenty pitches off The Nose on El Capitan through a blizzard, I almost died twice: once from freezing to death and once climbing up the rope without an anchor to free a knot that had gotten stuck. Fourteen years ago in Tibet, I was prepared to die running with rocks in my hands toward Chinese police armed with AK-47s, but the police turned and fled at the last second. I was not ready to die now.

Sokha refused to let me borrow his car and insisted that Pol Pot was still in Phnom Vor. I knew that Sokha referred to all Khmer Rouge as Pol Pot, and that I could not convince him, or myself, that this was safe. When Sokha stood up from the table, Khat Mann lunged for Sokha's car keys in his hand, but I snatched them first.

Khat Mann looked nervous as I drove too fast into the pitch-black night without any stars, slamming into potholes with a speed and frequency that would have made Sokha proud. We drove past the statue at the fork to Kep and the Kep Killing Fields Memorial. A few kilometers after the pavement yielded to grass, two stone pillars marked the entrance to Phnom Vor with a muddy track that disappeared into dense brush. Knowing this was where Chhouk Rin's Gang had kidnapped and killed the backpackers, I could not stop imagining the Australian David Wilson trying to escape, being caught, hamstrung, and having to crawl to work in the fields for two months before Khat Mann killed him.

When the headlights went out, I could not see my hands in front of my face. Fear surrendered to paranoia. I was as surprised by the sudden flood of headlights when I wiggled switches on the dash as I was by the freshly graded dirt road through banana and coconut trees. As we approached a ridge and turned to the east, Khat Mann explained that this plantation used to belong to Lon Nol, the Cambodian Army general backed by the CIA who overthrew King Sihanouk in 1970. After Chhouk Rin got amnesty from Hun Sen, Chhouk Rin assumed stewardship of 16,000 hectares of land in Phnom Vor and was responsible for every hut and well. He built this road for himself. Khat Mann said that Chhouk Rin was a "Big Man" in Phnom Vor with 10,000 armed men who were loyal to him.

Thuds from the front and rear tires accompanied the car running over a log spanning the road. Khat Mann jumped out, grabbed a stick, and beat the twelve-foot log on the head. Another thud as a giant snake landed in the trunk.

"Python," Khat Mann smiled.

"Tastes like chicken."

"You eat python!"

Khat Mann shrieked when the headlights went out again and the car skidded off the road. In the darkness I became even more nervous thinking of questions to ask Chhouk Rin. What was it like fighting the Lon Nol soldiers? How did the Khmer Rouge defeat the US-backed Cambodian government? What was it like during the Khmer Rouge Revolution?

Khat Mann yelling, "I feel safer as Khmer Rouge soldier than riding in this car with you," raised my spirits. Khat Mann was terrified of not being in control.

A welcome burst of moonlight illuminated two families using a hand pump to propel a small platform along the train tracks. Hopping freight trains across the US during a break from college with John Ackerly, I could appreciate their smiles as they enjoyed an uninterrupted view of the country. This was also the cheapest and most dangerous way to travel anywhere in Cambodia. When a train came, the people had little or no warning to get the platform off the tracks before they were run over. There were no statistics on how many people died from this each year.

After Khat Mann pushed Sokha's car out of the ditch by himself, I tried to stay in the center of the dirt road whose sides were rutted by the rain and large wooden wheels from *phoeks* (oxen carts) carrying loads of wood to be sold at the Kampot market. The average worker on Chhouk Rin's land made 50 cents a day. There was no electricity in the thatched huts that we passed. I lost any sense of time before we pulled up to a large teak house elevated on cement pillars with cement footings.

Khat Mann said that this was Dr. Noun's house, pronouncing *Dr. Noun* like "high noon." Dr. Noun was Chhouk Rin's doctor. A similar, stilted house across the road belonged to Chhouk Rin. This was all planned. I had to gain Dr. Noun's approval before Chhouk Rin would meet me. Khat Mann brought plastic chairs from under the house for us to sit in the driveway. There was no breeze to keep the mosquitoes away or dull the sound of my heart pounding both eardrums.

WHAT DO YOU CALL A DOCTOR WITH ONE LEG?

Dr. Noun's above-the-knee prosthesis on his right leg was in full view as he descended the stairs with a new red-checkered *krama* wrapped around his waist. Dr. Noun's wife followed in black pants and a stylish orange print shirt. In contrast to Dr. Noun's portly countenance, Bopha was lithe and agile and had a radiant face. Khat Mann translated my questions to find out that they had three healthy children, two boys, eighteen and sixteen, and one girl, thirteen. According to Khat Mann, everyone in Phnom Vor loved Dr. Noun.

When I asked about the health needs of the Khmer living in Phnom Vor, Bopha responded that she worked as a midwife delivering babies in the jungle. Many children died before they reached their first year. Many women also died during childbirth. They had no immunizations. One third of the people living in the jungle had malaria. Typhoid and tuberculosis were rampant.

"Everyone love Dr. Noun for help when they sick," Khat Mann said. "Dr. Noun no money for medicine."

Khat Mann repeated ad nauseum that everyone in Phnom Vor loved Dr. Noun, and that he had no money. After the Khmer Rouge "liberated" Cambodia in 1975, Pol Pot sent Dr. Noun to China to study medicine for five years. When Dr. Noun returned to Cambodia in 1979, after the Vietnamese routed the Khmer Rouge to the Western border of Cambodia, Dr. Noun worked as a combat surgeon for the Khmer Rouge who fought their Vietnamese occupiers. Dr. Noun had two things going for him. Because his uncle was Ta Mok, Pol Pot's most feared general in the Khmer Rouge Army, Dr. Noun had a Pure Biography. Only the highest-ranking Khmer Rouge leaders and their families had Pure Biographies. Khat Mann had a Good Biography because his family grew rice. New People, referring to the people in Phnom Penh who were forcefully evacuated to the countryside, had Bad Biographies.

"Angkor say all people in Phnom Penh rich and fat," Khat Mann said. "Angkor say Phnom Penh people steal rice from village people who do not have enough to eat. Angkor say Phnom Penh people not know how to grow rice. They enemy Khmer Rouge. The runway behind Kep Beach built by a hundred New People with Bad Biography. After runway finish, must kill all." The megalomaniac who craved attention laughed inappropriately. Dr. Noun did not smile.

A sad irony underlay Pol Pot's labeling all of Phnom Penh's population as *neak thmei* or "New People," which marked them for slave labor and death. Before the US bombing of Cambodia in 1969, Phnom Penh had a population of 800,000. Five years later, when the Khmer Rouge overran the capital, Phnom Penh had grown to 2 million people. This meant that 1.2 million of Phnom Penh's 2 million people were villagers who went to Phnom Penh to flee the effects of US bombing. They knew how to grow rice and would have been sympathetic to the Khmer Rouge.

"Angkor say all New People bad," Khat Mann said. "Must kill all."

"What kind of biography would I have had during Pol Pot time?"

"You *barang*, you Bad Biography."

"Must kill?"

"Must work! Not work, kill."

After Dr. Noun's wife went to bed, he looked forlorn and spoke in pathetic tones. Khat Mann repeated that Dr. Noun could not work with one leg, and that I was a rich doctor and had to give him money, which infuriated me. Dr. Noun was a professional. Losing his leg had affected his self-esteem but it did not prevent him from practicing medicine. I knew that I was rich compared to Dr. Noun and Khat Mann, but I resented Khat Mann begging. It was time to invite Dr. Noun and Khat Man to karaoke.

Shafts of moonlight breaking through the clouds punctuated the drive back to Kampot and Khat Mann's persistent pleadings. Sokha was pacing back and forth in front of the Marco Polo in his underwear, worrying about his American brother.

"Serpent!" Sokha shrieked when I opened the trunk.

Davide drove Khat Mann, Dr. Noun, Sokha, and me to a karaoke bar on the first floor of the Phnom Khieu Hotel. When we entered the dingy, windowless room that smelled of sweat and stale beer, six hostesses seated us on couches facing a television. After bringing plates of sliced green mango, chili peppers, jackfruit, and buckets of ice, the hostesses poured mugs of warm Tiger Beer that were refilled after each sip.

Dr. Noun looked dapper in a clean shirt and long pants that concealed his prosthesis. Sitting next to Sokha on a couch, Dr. Noun and Sokha looked like two shy teenage boys at a prom. Khat Mann sat next to the hostess with the largest breasts and a boy's hips. Makeup covered a black eye. When Khat Mann pinched her arm, she slapped his shoulder, initiating rounds of Khmer foreplay.

Davide slumped in the farthest chair from the television, smoking a joint laced with opium. He considered himself lucky that Pith had not attacked him in the four hours that he had been home, and that he left before she changed her mind. I was distracted with the profile of the hostess sitting next to me. Her almond eyes, wide nose, and full lips rivaled any apsara. Returning my greeting in Khmer, she raised her glass and downed the entire contents in one giant slurp.

"You look like your chicken!" Khat Mann cackled.

Poin turned to face me for the first time, revealing a scar from her right ear to her cheek that missed the corner of her mouth and stopped short of her chin. Instead of being repulsed I was even more attracted. What left-handed beast had done this? Without my asking, Davide explained that the crimes against prostitutes came from every part of their lives. Poin's father cut her face after she was raped by an army captain. Prostitutes were outcasts from society. During the day no merchant or pedestrian would talk to her. She had to pay a higher price for vegetables and rice at the market. She would never be allowed to buy land or a house. But at night every man wanted to talk to her.

Khat Mann pinched his hostess. The hostess slapped Khat Mann's face. Dr. Noun sat bolt upright staring at two teenage wallflowers trapped inside women's bodies. Sokha was terrified of Khat Mann and stared at the television with the vacuous gaze that helped him survive Pol Pot time.

"Dr. Noun cannot work," Khat Mann said. "He need money."

"Cambodian girls are very shy," Davide said with glazed eyes. "Not like Vietnamese or Thai girls. They don't have technique but they have heart. If you take your time, you can do what you want, and she can really enjoy it."

"Dr. Noun cannot work. He need money."

"What do you call a doctor with one leg?" I blurted. Unable to suppress my anger, I asked Dr. Noun what he called a doctor with one leg between every warm beer and karaoke song. Just when I thought Khat Mann would hit me, he grabbed the microphone and sang karaoke songs subtitled in English at the bottom of the television screen. With the hostesses fighting for the microphone after each song, a pattern emerged. Every Khmer karaoke video started with a handsome couple walking along the beach in Sihanoukville with the man serenading the woman into the sunset. After they embraced, the man tried to leave for another woman. Then she slapped his face.

"Cambodia is a very macho culture," Davide said. "If you don't want this girl, you take another. Tonight, a minister from Phnom Penh arrived with his bodyguards and drivers, maybe a hundred men. He is a Big Man so the local police rounded up the best girls. Other nights you can find pretty girls everywhere."

"Dr. Noun need money," Khat Mann insisted. "He cannot work with one leg!"

"What do you call a doctor with one leg?"

"Dr. Noun cannot doctor with one leg! You must give money!"

"What do you call a doctor with one leg?"

Desperate to distract Khat Mann, I motioned for a hostess Dr. Noun was eying to sit next to him. When her hand brushed his prosthetic and did not retreat, Dr. Noun grabbed the microphone from Khat Mann and turned out to be a great singer.

"Dr. Noun tiger not strong," Khat Mann announced to the room and grabbed his groin when Dr. Noun finished his third song. Dr. Noun looked self-conscious. I would be, too, if I couldn't get an erection and Khat Mann told everyone.

"*Kla at klang* (Tiger not strong)," Dr. Noun confirmed.

Khat Mann was incapable of not giggling while explaining that Dr. Noun could not get an erection after losing his leg. A vascular injury from stepping on a land mine made sense because Dr. Noun did not have any of the primary causes of erectile dysfunction: smoking tobacco, high blood pressure, diabetes, or drinking to excess. I complimented Khat Mann on his translation and was glad that he still responded well to flattery, but I was about to lose my mind if I had to spend five more minutes with Khat Mann. It was time for my secret weapon.

When Davide nodded off in his chair, I motioned for Khat Mann, Dr. Noun, and Sokha to follow me into the bathroom. Khat Mann and Dr. Noun held hands like schoolgirls as they entered the malodorous chamber with a streaked, porcelain hole in the floor. Sokha kept a respectful distance from Khat Mann as I slipped $5 into everyone's pocket.

"For chicken?" Khat Mann asked, counting his money.

With the stealth of a magician, I rotated my right hand over my left fist three times before revealing four blue, diamond-shaped pills.

"What this!"

"This is a magic pill! If it does not kill you, you will have the biggest tiger of your life."

As a physician I felt duty-bound to explain that anyone taking nitroglycerine would die if they took Viagra, and that it would not work as well if they drank a lot of alcohol or ate a fatty meal. I also gave everyone condoms and made them promise that they would use them if they had sex.

"I must try," Khat Mann said and looked at his watch.

After Khat Mann, Dr. Noun, and Sokha agreed a second time to use a condom if they had sex—they would have agreed to anything—we took the magic pills together. Back in the Karaoke room, Khat Mann tallied the pieces of paper that listed every beer and snack. The total came to $38. When I paid with a $50 bill, Khat Mann demanded $6 for him and Dr. Noun to get a room upstairs. There was no sense in getting cheap now. I left $6 on the table and gave $6 to an ecstatic Khat Mann. For the first time in days, I was not worrying about Khat Mann killing me or taking me hostage.

The next morning an elated Khat Mann and Dr. Noun appeared in time for me to buy them breakfast. "Last night I see your chicken leaving the Marco Polo," Khat Mann said, grabbing his left forearm. "She say you have BIG TIGER. Same donkey. Then she say, 'I fuck an American!'" As a late-blooming Caucasian teenager, I was not used to having more than an average tiger but appreciated any sway over Khat Mann. I also worried that my desire to meet the Khmer Rouge leaders had compromised my judgment, and that this was going to get worse.

I did not need to ask Khat Mann what happened to him before he volunteered, "Last night, after I fuck my chicken, she run away." Laughter was intoxicating to Khat Mann. "When I get home, my wife grab my tiger and she say, 'Oh! What happen you! Then I fuck second time! *Kla klang*! (Tiger strong)."

"Did you use a condom?"

"Yes!" Khat Mann said with a straight face and I believed him. "Dr. Noun also use." Dr. Noun's face radiated happiness. "This morning his wife also told him to get more magic pills."

"What do you call a doctor with one leg?"

When Dr. Noun replied, "A doctor!" in English we went to Kampot's largest pharmacy to buy medicines. At first Dr. Noun chose two large plastic bottles of 1,000 paracetamol for $3 each, then two more bottles of paracetamol. Dr. Noun was happy to have this mild, non-narcotic pain reliever, but he did not understand. I ordered stock bottles of penicillin, erythromycin, and doxycycline, enough antibiotics to treat people with malaria, typhoid, and infectious diseases. Understanding, Dr. Noun selected injectable chloramphenicol, gentamycin, kanamycin, streptomycin, and Ceftin, all life-saving antibiotics. We also stuffed packages of sterile syringes, needles, intravenous bags with tubing, and vials of sterile water into a large black satchel. For $38, the same price of our karaoke evening, a clinic was born in Phnom Vor.

WARLORD

I packed a cooler with Tiger Beers and ice before driving Sokha's car with Khat Mann and Dr. Noun into Phnom Vor to meet Chhouk Rin. Driving on the rutted dirt road into Phnom Vor distracted me from worrying about meeting Chhouk Rin. Khat Mann laughed every time I slumped behind the wheel when we passed a thatched hut or someone walking along the road. When I reminded him that last night he said it would be dangerous if anyone saw me during the day, Khat Mann assured me that no harm could come to me while I was with him. He also nodded toward a man on a bicycle who was an intelligence officer and joked that I might have a problem at the airport. After what seemed like hours, Khat Mann ordered me to stop at an intersection with four huts and people mingling on the road.

"Everyone in Phnom Vor love Khat Mann," Khat Mann said. "I help build one fence here. I do many small jobs."

Dr. Noun and I sought the shade of a thatched restaurant with open walls while Khat Mann inquired about Chhouk Rin's whereabouts. I sympathized with a turtle hanging upside down on a cord of twisted grass, its extremities and head retracted. I envied the turtle's shell as we ate sliced green mango with chili salt. In stark contrast to Khat Mann, I felt relaxed around Dr. Noun even though we had little language in common. He was gentle, softspoken, and kind.

Khat Mann returned to report that many people had seen Chhouk Rin earlier in the morning. We continued another ten kilometers on the newly graded road that we had traveled the previous night. During the day I could see that the road was elevated above the floodplain that brimmed with many small lakes and lily ponds.

Chhouk Rin's wife and two teenage daughters were sitting in the cool shade under his house when we drove into the driveway. Like Dr. Noun's wife, she was fashionably dressed in black pants and a yellow print shirt. Like Dr. Noun's house across the road, Chhouk Rin's house was on stilts ten feet above the ground, with cement columns supporting the teak floor and walls and a tin roof. Seated in plastic chairs, unable to say more than basic greetings, it was reassuring to see that my presence amused the whole family.

Khat Mann took off on a motorcycle in search of Chhouk Rin and left me with the quiet rumble of adrenaline awaiting their return. I tried to not think of Chhouk Rin as an evil Khmer Rouge commander. I was the enemy. When Chhouk Rin arrived on the back of Khat Mann's motorcycle, he had the tanned, leathery complexion of someone who had spent his entire life outdoors. He wore black pants, sandals, and a plaid shirt. Despite his diminutive stature, his reptilian stare made me feel like an inferior being. He barked for Khat Mann to seat me at a card table in the yard under the midday sun and yelled at Khat Mann for long minutes. Chhouk Rin reminded me of a petulant surgeon deriding anyone within range. Stretching time, he put a loaded revolver on the table with the barrel pointed at my chest.

"Chhouk Rin wants to know why you are here." Khat Mann said. "Chhouk Rin says he is a Big Man. He will kill you if you ask about Pol Pot time. He will kill you if you ask about backpackers. He will kill you and me if anything bad happen because of this meeting." Khat Mann was deadly serious. Dr. Noun did not show any emotion.

When Khat Mann translated my asking Chhouk Rin if he had any health problems, he nodded toward the satchel of medicines on top of the stairs to his house that I had bought for Dr. Noun. Chhouk Rin grabbed his groin and reiterated his threats to kill me if I asked about "Pol Pot time," if I asked about the backpackers, or if anything bad happened because of our meeting, which would not take long.

When Chhouk Rin noticed my peering under the table to confirm the absence of toes sticking through his left sandal, he put his left foot on the table with the stump, and pistol, both aimed at me.

Then Chhouk Rin swelled with pride as Khat Mann recounted how Chhouk Rin lost his foot to a land mine. During a battlefield operation, Dr. Noun replaced the torn femoral artery on Chhouk Rin's left leg with the saphenous vein on his right leg. At first Khat Mann did not understand when I asked about anesthesia. When I asked about "medicine to kill pain," Khat Mann said Dr. Noun had one vial for injection, which he only gave when Chhouk Rin screamed loud enough to give away their position. I complimented Dr. Noun's battlefield skills, Chhouk Rin's will to live, and said that I wanted to work with Dr. Noun in Phnom Vor.

Beads of sweat streaked my face as I said that I was interested in Chhouk Rin's story. He said that he was a soldier in the Khmer Rouge Army that "liberated" Cambodia on April 17, 1975. He loved the Cambodian people. For the first time since the Khmer Kings the Cambodian people were free from "foreign devils." After the Vietnamese Communists took control of Phnom Penh in 1979, Chhouk Rin was a hero who fought the Vietnamese occupation. Even now he still fights the Vietnamese.

I sensed that Chhouk Rin was a man of principle who loved his country. His threats to kill me were understandable for a Khmer Rouge colonel who had just been acquitted of killing three backpackers. His threatening to kill Khat Mann and me if anything bad happened confirmed that my presence was also threatening to him. He must have known that outsiders considered the Khmer Rouge soldiers barbaric, their revolution failed.

So began our game of chicken and chance. There was no turning back. I needed to find common dialogue before the threats stopped. Khat Mann translated my asking what it was like before the Khmer Rouge time? How did the Khmer Rouge come to power?

Chhouk Rin's face softened as he talked about 1969 when the US started bombing Cambodia's eastern border where the Vietcong had taken refuge from the US bombing in Vietnam. When I asked how he knew the bombs were American, Chhouk Rin scoffed. Everyone knew that US president Nixon was bombing Cambodia, and that "America" wanted to stop Communist China and the Vietcong. He also knew the B-52 bombers came from bases in the Philippines and Guam. In 1970, when the CIA gave weapons to the Lon Nol government to kill the Khmer Rouge, Chhouk Rin started to fight Lon Nol soldiers and America. From 1970 to 1973, the Pathet Lao and Vietnamese Communists in Hanoi also helped the Khmer Rouge fight the Lon Nol government.

"Chhouk Rin want to talk to you about this but he afraid for his life," Khat Mann said.

"That makes two of us!"

Chhouk Rin, Khat Mann, and I laughed together for the first time. Everyone watched as I opened my notebook and drew a crude map of Cambodia, Vietnam, and Laos.

"Look like pussy!" Khat Mann exclaimed.

Chhouk Rin took the pen and made a series of X's along Cambodia's eastern border with Vietnam where the US started to bomb Vietcong sanctuaries. When the Vietcong moved farther into Cambodia to avoid the bombs, more bombs followed. In essence Chhouk Rin had summarized and confirmed what I had read in William Shawcross's *Sideshow: Kissinger, Nixon, and the Destruction of Cambodia*. Khat Mann gesticulated with his arms as he mimicked bombs exploding.

I had found common dialogue.

Chhouk Rin described what it was like walking into a village after American bombs killed men, women, and children. Parts of bodies and animals were everywhere. And bombs kept coming. Because of this many "countryside people" moved into the jungle and began to hate the Lon Nol government, and America, and everyone who lived in cities. After a B-52 bombing, people came up to Chhouk Rin and volunteered to help the Khmer Rouge fight the American foreign devils.

Khat Mann feigned obsequiousness when Chhouk Rin yelled again. "America is a great country but had bad ideas," Khat Mann translated. When I asked what Lon Nol soldiers were like, Khat Mann did not need to consult Chhouk Rin to reply that Lon Nol soldiers were lazy and afraid to go outside Phnom Penh. By 1973, the Khmer Rouge controlled all of the countryside. When the Lon Nol Army came to Phnom Vor, the Khmer Rouge slept close to them at night so the American bombs did not kill them. One day before dawn, Khat Mann killed three Lon Nol soldiers and stole their chickens. Recounting that "chicken look like pussy," reduced Khat Mann to childish fits.

I was surprised when Chhouk Rin said that American bombs helped the people in Phnom Vor. There were not many people living in the area. Only a few water buffalos were killed. And the bomb craters gave them many wells and ponds for frogs. I laughed with Chhouk Rin and Khat Mann for the second time. Even Dr. Noun, arms folded across his chest, cracked a smile.

"Today Chhouk Rin like America people. Chhouk Rin want America to help Cambodia."

I brought out the first round of cold Tiger Beers from the cooler. Chhouk Rin toasted, "Kla klang," and guzzled his beer. Khat Mann, Dr. Noun, and I followed. After downing our second round, Dr. Noun talked excitedly in Khmer. I did not need him to translate Chhouk Rin grabbing his groin while Dr. Noun described our exploits the previous night. Chhouk Rin stood up abruptly, apologized that he had a "small meeting" to attend, and ordered me to take him out tonight in Kampot, like I had done with Dr. Noun.

Giving Chhouk Rin a $100 handshake and saying that it would be his pleasure lifted a weight from my shoulders. I had been in Chhouk Rin's yard for four hours and not noticed the Caryota palms and bougainvillea along the driveway, an enormous mango tree shading the house, and the bucolic groves of coconuts, cashews, and bananas on the old Lon Nol plantation rolling down to the Gulf of Thailand.

KAMPOT KARAOKE

On his first trip to Kampot since the Khmer Rouge Revolution, Chhouk Rin met me at a karaoke restaurant after midnight. Two men with pistols sitting at the entrance watched the street. Two more bodyguards sat inside with their backs to the wall where they could see the door. For the duration of the evening the bodyguards drank sodas and kept their vigil. It seemed telling that twenty-two years after Chhouk Rin supervised the purge of New People in Phnom Vor, he still needed armed guards to go into town. While the people living in Phnom Vor may love him, there were many people in Kampot who could still recognize him and the murders committed under his name.

Chhouk Rin presided over hostesses who refilled our mugs after each sip of warm beer and served plates of dried fish, chicken fat, lungs, intestines, eggs, testicles, mystery organs, mushrooms, and a selection of greens to put into pots of boiling water lit by cans of Sterno. The Phnom Vor Gang was a long way from their wives. Contrary to best medical practices, I took a Cipro before my chopsticks joined the procession retrieving everything that did not move from the pot and spitting our bones on the floor.

"You like?" Chhouk Rin asked, pointing to a shy, generously proportioned sixteen-year-old. "Small woman, small water. Big woman, big water!"

"Very beautiful," I said, not wanting to offend Chhouk Rin or the girl or have "big water" translated. Cramps and sharp pains followed by the urge to defecate roiled my intestines. The hostesses were depressing. I felt claustrophobic. My heart was pounding. My chest felt tight. And I did not want to get stuck squatting over a filthy porcelain hole.

"Chhouk Rin want to know if you like communism?" Khat Mann asked.

"No," I replied instinctively, alcohol having liberated my tongue.

"Good," Khat Mann said, "either does Chhouk Rin."

I was so relieved that my inebriated, unfiltered mouth had not offended Chhouk Rin that I felt a fleeting kinship until Khat Mann grabbed his groin and announced that Chhouk Rin's tiger was not strong. Besides the operation on his legs, one day a Vietnamese soldier shot Chhouk Rin in his penis. Once again, Khat Mann succumbed to adolescent insensibilities.

"Dr. Brake," Chhouk Rin said in English, unable to pronounce the *l*. "You Dr. Number Two."

Chhouk Rin toasted "Dr. Number Two" with another Tiger Beer. I was flattered by Chhouk Rin's compliment. Dr. Number Two referred to Nuon Chea, the Khmer Rouge's second in command after Pol Pot, who was called Brother Number Two. I told Chhouk Rin that having two doctors could be a problem. What if each doctor had a different opinion? Chhouk Rin insisted that I stay another week. Big Men from Phnom Penh were coming down to celebrate the completion of his road. Chhouk Rin smiled like a diplomat and placed my hand on the obese teenager's thigh. The boys were getting randy. The cramps were coming more frequently. I needed to escape.

"Dr. Brake cannot leave," Khat Mann said, businesslike. "Chhouk Rin want to have karaoke with you, another two or three hours, perhaps thirty dollars."

Khat Mann checked everything on the bill to make sure I was not being cheated before we moved to a windowless room to sing karaoke with no bathroom. After singing his inebriated heart out, Chhouk Rin insisted that we join him in the *romvong*, the traditional Khmer dance where everyone moved counterclockwise in a circle, repeating the same footsteps, the body erect as the hands made graceful, repetitive motions like birds flying in slow motion. When two women tore at Chhouk Rin's shirt and pinched his stomach, I gave Khat Mann $20 for doing a "great job" translating with Chhouk Rin that afternoon. Khat Mann asked why I had said that and did not laugh when I said that if he had not done a good job, we would both be dead.

Chhouk Rin saw Khat Mann and me laughing together and embraced both of us. If I was going to escape, it would have to be soon. I needed a Western toilet to ride out waves of intestinal eruptions that threatened anyone within range. I slipped a magic pill into Chhouk Rin's, Khat Mann's, and Dr. Noun's hands. Chhouk Rin was wild-eyed when I thanked him for allowing me to take him out to dinner. I made sure he was not taking any nitroglycerine and made him promise to wear a condom if he had sex. If Chhouk Rin got an erection, Viagra would be more valuable than money. If it did not work, his good will could backfire or worse. I did not know at the time that Chhouk Rin had HIV and worried having unprotected sex with prostitutes could infect his wife.

Chhouk Rin did not let go of my hand when I said that I was about to have "big water" exploding out of my ass and kept talking in a drunken, affectionate tone.

"Chhouk Rin want you to know one thing," Khat Mann said. "When Hun Sen send army to get backpackers, and they see cripples, Hun Sen say they cannot take back cripples. Hun Sen give the order to kill backpackers. Not Chhouk Rin."

MY LAND

The next day Chhouk Rin received me at his wife's restaurant in Phnom Vor. We sat at the only outdoor table drinking cold Elephant Beers while she served chicken soup with basil and lemongrass, pork sautéed with hot chilies, sautéed mango shoots whose long stems and white bell-shaped flower kept their crunch, buffalo soup with cabbage, and shredded green mango with dried fish. As was his custom, Chhouk Rin washed everything down with copious amounts of beer. He did not volunteer any details about the previous night, and I did not ask.

After lunch Chhouk Rin's driver drove us a few kilometers to a stick house on a hill. Khat Mann said that Chhouk Rin was giving me this land from the road to the top of the ridge, and from the cashew orchard on one side of a small, thatched house to the banana grove on the other side. Asked about getting title to the land, Khat Mann said that title was not possible. If I built a house, I owned the land. I laughed at the idea of my building a house for Chhouk Rin before noticing an attractive woman in a hammock under a mango tree.

With a handshake, Chhouk Rin gave me land to build a house in Phnom Vor to plant coconuts, bananas, mangoes, and vegetables. That way when I came back to Phnom Vor, I would have a place to stay. I thanked Chhouk Rin in Khmer and he said that I was his Cambodian brother. The next time I came to Cambodia Khat Mann would build me a house, just like Dr. Noun's and Chhouk Rin's houses, for $5,000.

A hawk swooped down from the top of the ridge and carried a four-foot snake into a jackfruit tree. I asked if Khat Mann ate the python that I had run over the other night, and he said his wife cooked it and they had enough leftovers for days. Khat Mann had eaten snake many times when he lived on this land for one year. During the day he killed Vietnamese soldiers. At night he went to people's homes to ask for a handful of rice, some meat, a pinch of salt. Khat Mann said that people thanked him for fighting the Vietnamese and covered his tracks. When I asked if anyone ever reported him to the Vietnamese soldiers, Khat Mann swatted the air.

"Must kill," Khat Mann said. "Same Vietnam."

Pointing up at the steep ridge covered with dense vegetation, Khat Mann recalled how he had seen monkeys many times, along with deer and a small striped cat. Once he saw a tiger. In the evenings he liked to climb to the top of the ridge and watch birds catching insects above the canopy. For $7,000 Khat Man would build me a house like Chhouk Rin's and Dr. Noun's house.

Although the price had gone up $2,000 in a few minutes, I liked the idea of building a house on this land. Three house-sized mango trees, an enormous jackfruit tree, and dozens of papaya, banana, coconut, and orange trees provided enough fruit for an extended family. Imagining a house and garden surrounded by a perimeter of cashew trees, I asked Khat Mann if there was any spring or water on the land.

Chhouk Rin nodded lasciviously toward the hammock. His mistress was also available for marriage. When I said that I had a wife in New York, Chhouk Rin said that she would be my Phnom Vor wife. I told Khat Mann that I could never sleep with Chhouk Rin's mistress. Khat Mann reassured me by saying that Chhouk Rin had another child with his Pailin wife. I laughed thinking about building a house for Chhouk Rin and his mistress and the ubiquitous Chhouk Rin retaining his executive privileges. Khat Mann took laughter as confirmation.

Suddenly serious, Khat Mann said that the previous night Chhouk Rin and Khat Mann took two *chirans* to a hotel. Chhouk Rin could not get an erection so he watched while Khat Mann had sex with both women. I explained to Khat Mann that Chhouk Rin could have permanent neurological damage from alcoholism, smoking, and war injuries that would each prevent him from getting an erection. Because Khat Mann was good with numbers and perused every bill, he knew that Chhouk Rin had drunk over twenty beers before they took the hostesses to the hotel. When I explained that Viagra did not work if you drank a lot of alcohol, Khat Mann looked somber.

"Maybe magic pill not possible for Chhouk Rin."

AIDS IN THE JUNGLE

Chhouk Rin ordered his driver, Thuch Sombo, to tell me about a vision that he had had. Dr. Noun was polite but did not appear interested in the forty-four-year-old man with no formal education in medicine, AIDS, or horticulture who said that he had six boys with his wife and still wanted a girl. One night last summer the spirits came to him in a dream and led him into the jungle. The spirits told him to pick two kinds of bark and dark green leaves to make a tea for AIDS patients that would stop diarrhea and allow them to eat again. In the last month the spirits and word of mouth had drawn thirteen families to his land in search of his cure.

Thuch Sombo drove us a few hundred meters from my land to a banana grove. We did not have to walk far to the first makeshift lean-to that sheltered a skeleton of a twenty-year-old man lying on a straw mat. His cherubic wife nursed their infant son on her breast, and then cleaned her husband's intractable diarrhea that left him with sunken eyes and the look of death. Opening his parched mouth revealed a tongue colonized by the white plaques of a fungus. Given his emaciated state, the oral candida constituted an opportunistic infection that anyone with a healthy immune system could fight.

This qualified him for the diagnosis of AIDS, which meant that he may have been infected by the HIV virus for a decade or more.

Grandparents sitting on the ground under a plastic tarp looked after their emaciated daughter and her eight-year-old son. The boy did not have the strength to raise his head from his adoring mother's chest. His eyes were close to blinking for the last time. Like the first man, the mother and child had just arrived, their mouths coated with white plaques.

Moving farther into the banana grove we met a group of people who had been there for one week: a striking teenage girl with a gaunt face sat next to her sister who was all smiles; a policeman with a syphilitic chancre on his lip; and an emaciated man with a deep, tuberculous cough. Everyone was eating rice and vegetables. After drinking the tea for one week, their diarrhea and oral thrush had improved enough to relish their first solid food in months.

Sombo stopped at a small fire with a teakettle perched over three rocks. Like Dr. Noun, I was skeptical of the boiled concoction of bark and leaves. When Sombo added sugar to the kettle, which would only encourage a fungal or yeast infection, I became incredulous.

"Mr. Sombo is going to need a lot of money to feed people," Khat Mann said. When I suggested selling bags of the medicine, Khat Mann said the spirits told Sombo that the power would go away if he tried to make money from the tea.

I distracted Khat Mann by hiring him to help me record each person's name, age, and medical history. Chhouk Rin smiled at my surprise when Khat Mann opened the trunk that held the bag of medicines I had bought for our clinic. Chhouk Rin had not confiscated the medicine. He had taken control.

Dr. Noun looked nervous. He had never seen "AIDS people" in Phnom Vor. We returned with pockets full of medicines and followed Sombo on a tour from one makeshift shelter to the next. People who had just arrived slept on the ground. Those who had been here for a few days had erected small platforms under banana leaves or makeshift tarps. At the end of each interview, I distributed a one-dollar bill to appreciative smiles.

Sem Charon was a twenty-nine-year-old woman who had been here for ten days. Her two-year-old daughter was scratching a nasty diaper rash. After one week of the tea, Sem's diarrhea stopped and her appetite improved. Nothing would get rid of her daughter's rash. I gave her a tube of antifungal cream for the rash, which was easy to cure. I had nothing for the herpetic blisters on her lips.

Tao Kuncham was a twenty-seven-year-old man from Kep with thinning hair. He had been sick since 1996 and lived with his mother. He found out he had HIV when he applied to go to the US and his visa was denied. Tao had been on the land for ten days. He complained of diarrhea and a wrenching cough for four months. He was too weak to lift himself from the mat. I asked Dr. Noun if he thought Kuncham had tuberculosis and bronchitis.

"He think the same," Khat Mann said without asking Dr. Noun, and I realized that I had committed a faux pas. In Khmer society Dr. Noun would not say anything to contradict me so that neither of us would lose face. Dr. Noun stood with his hands at his side, afraid to talk or touch anyone. I inquired if Tao had any allergies to medicines and gave him a course of penicillin.

Chhouk Rin talked with everyone, shook hands, and tickled babies, even people with advanced signs of AIDS. Instead of worrying that he was witnessing a burgeoning AIDS colony on his land, Chhouk Rin welcomed everyone and offered encouragement. Chhouk Rin, having overcome his fear of death decades ago, stood in stark contrast to Dr. Noun who was afraid to interact with anyone.

Nough was a forty-two-year-old grandmother. Her seven-year-old granddaughter had been sick for ten months. The girl's mother had died of AIDS six months ago. Nough reported that the girl's abdominal pains had improved in the eight days that she had been drinking the tea, although it had given her a headache.

Flies infested the sores around Roskong's mouth. She was thirty-eight years old and cradled Rosi, her infant son shriveled from diarrhea. Roskong beamed as Khat Mann said that Rosi's diarrhea was 100 percent better after fifteen days of drinking Sombo's tea. Rosi was also feeling better and could eat. I inquired about Rosi's family and learned that her husband and two older boys had all died from AIDS. As I cleaned the sores on Roskong's face, I knew that I was putting Band-Aids on an abyss. Even if the sores healed, she was dying from a virus her husband had given her from having unprotected sex with prostitutes. But giving Roskong a tube of antibiotic cream and $1 made her smile and both of us feel better.

Wat Keang was a plump thirty-nine-year-old woman who reported having diarrhea for one week. After four days of the tea, she felt better but still could not eat solid food. Before we got to the next shelter, a frail woman arrived on the back of a moto driven by a one-eyed man in black pajamas. Sonso Paun was nineteen years old. Her husband helped lay her down on a woven mat. She had become sick after the Cambodian New Year. Her main complaints were months of weakness and being covered with a rash. She also had frequent headaches.

Dr. Noun put three-inch squares of cloth tape on her temples for her headaches and handed her paracetamol folded in paper to take one tablet every four hours. Seeing the woman cupping her hands in prayer and Dr. Noun talking to the next patient made me proud of my Cambodian colleague. In the next hammock, a skinny, young man named Than was attended to by his wife who played peek-a-boo with their twenty-five-day-old son. After ten days of drinking the tea, Than's stomach was much better and they named their son Cham Ka Bye. Than relished his wife and son, and eating a small bowl of rice and boiled squash.

Sombo had twenty-seven people with end-stage AIDS and their families living on his solitary acre of land. As word of his medicine spread, more people would come. The HIV virus did not discriminate between infants and single mothers, children or adults. All the people who had come to Sombo's land were malnourished and came in search of a miracle. Although I was skeptical at first, I was impressed that everyone who had come with oral and intestinal candida seemed to have improved after drinking the tea for several days to a week.

"If you have diarrhea and drink the tea," Khat Mann said, "it stops diarrhea. If you don't have diarrhea, the tea gives you diarrhea."

I asked if Sombo had had any more dreams, and he pointed to the jungle-covered ridge above my land. Sombo had a second dream to look for another well. Every day more people came to his land who did not have water. It was a long walk to the well. Khat Mann said that he had lived on this land for one year and never found a spring.

The hope shared by those who were too weak to clean themselves, and their families who coped with their relentless diarrhea, was so inspiring that I gave Thuch Sombo a $50 handshake. I did not cry until later when I was alone. I cried for the spirits radiating from sunken eye sockets and seeing starving people eat again, happy to be surrounded by their extended families for a little longer before their disease took their lives. I also cried because much of the world's suffering could be addressed if industrialized countries freed themselves from their addiction to oil, war, and the disproportionate consumption of the world's resources.

The physical affection and closeness of Phnom Vor's AIDS patients and their family members stood in marked contrast to Westerners who, upon hearing tales of death in Asia, remarked that Asians did not feel the loss of a child. Poverty was so rampant with so many people dying from preventable diseases that Asians valued an individual's life less than someone living in the West. My experiences had convinced me that the opposite was true. Unlike industrialized countries where the nuclear family has been reduced to one or two people, where divorce has left most children growing up with single parents, the average Asian family had parents, grandparents, uncles, aunts, and cousins living in close proximity, often under the same roof. This resulted in a level of intimacy not seen in the West.

* * *

"If you want to know the truth," Davide said back at the Marco Polo, "the fucking UN bastards brought AIDS to Cambodia. After ten years of Vietnamese occupation, the UN ran Cambodia during the nineties. So you have all these HIV-positive men coming from Africa who like to go out into the villages and fuck young boys and girls without condoms. Now you see AIDS everywhere in Cambodia."

Prime Minister Hun Sen and King Norodom Sihanouk agreed with Davide. In 1992, Hun Sen publicly blamed the UNTAC for spending $2 billion over a decade to run Cambodia and leaving AIDS in its wake.[65] Sihanouk had profound reservations about how the massive UN presence would defile the Cambodian women and lead to an increase in prostitution.[66] Cambodia had 6,000 prostitutes in 1991. One year later, with the arrival of 22,000 UN personnel, Cambodia had over 20,000 prostitutes. By 1995, the World Health Organization estimated that between 50,000 and 90,000 Cambodians were infected with AIDS.[67]

Cambodia has the highest HIV infection rate in Asia, in large part due to the commercial sex industry where 42 percent of sex workers are infected with the virus, half of whom regularly don't use condoms.[68] Cambodia has 120,000 people infected with HIV, approximately 2 percent of the population.[69] For the 100,000 children who have lost their parents to AIDS, most come from families that are poor and unable to care for an AIDS orphan who is cast into the streets. Although Western sex tourists are widely portrayed in the media with fueling the sex industry, the majority of clients in Cambodia's brothels, karaoke bars, and massage parlors are Asian men.

DOCTOR KROH AND AMERICAN BOMBING

When I told Khat Man that I wanted to learn more about the American bombing before the Khmer Rouge came to power, he offered to take me to Dr. Kroh, the Khmer Rouge doctor who had amputated Dr. Noun's leg. Dr. Kroh had a story about American bombing for me. For $20 Khat Mann led us on motorcycles for two hours under cumulous clouds heavy with rain. As we wound our way into the jungles of Kho Sola, red mud kicked up from Khat Mann's tires covered my clothes and bike. Dr. Kroh's one-room concrete clinic with a cot and small wooden table was barren, but Khat Mann found him down the road in a hammock under his stilted house, enjoying his three spirited sons while his young wife nursed a baby girl.

Dr. Kroh looked younger than his forty-seven years, with no wrinkles on his forehead and a full head of black hair. He was a loving family man with a gentle demeanor, in stark contrast to Khat Mann, and had four children ages one, eight, nine, and twelve. Dr. Kroh said he was proud to have his children grow up with more than he had. Like Khat Mann, he had a Good Biography. He was a Khmer Rouge soldier for three years before his gang leader sent him to China in 1976 to "study doctor."

According to Dr. Kroh, the main health problem for people living in Kho Sola stemmed from the lack of medicines. Six people in ten had malaria. Three people in ten had typhoid because of bad water. When I told Dr. Kroh that we could get some medicines from Kampot, he rejected having to pay money when he could get medicine in the forest for free.

Describing Dr. Noun's operation, Khat Mann laughed like a heavily armed fourteen-year-old on steroids. One morning Dr. Noun got up to wash in the river. On the way back he stepped on a land mine. His leg was "finished." Khat Mann made a slicing motion below my knee where Dr. Kroh amputated Dr. Noun's leg with a saw. During the half-hour operation, Dr. Kroh had two medicines: one pill for infection and one vial of injectable anesthetic. He also had two kinds of Chinese plasma: one reconstituted with water, another in a bag.

Dr. Kroh spoke of the day his father was plowing his fields and asked him to get some water. Khat Mann interrupted, shouting, "BAAAH BOOOOOM," and jumped into the air with raised arms. "BAAAH BOOOOOM," Khat Mann shouted again loud enough to make the baby cry. "His father dead," Khat Mann exclaimed. "Half body ten-meter one direction. Half body ten-meter other direction."

As an American whose country had bombed Cambodia, I felt sad that American bombs had killed Dr. Kroh's father and Khat Mann's mother. I was also interested to learn that Dr. Kroh joined the Khmer Rouge the next day, in 1971, after many American bombs fell in Takeo Province. Dr. Kroh was eighteen years old. Like Chhouk Rin, Dr. Kroh knew the bombs were American. Everyone did. After his father was killed, he wanted to fight and joined the Khmer Rouge with his brother. Dr. Kroh said that in 1971 and 1972 he fought Lon Nol soldiers. In 1973, when the US bombed Cambodia every day for months, people could not talk or sleep. Eight hundred people from Kho Sola joined the Khmer Rouge at this time, including every able-bodied man in his village.

According to Shawcross in *Sideshow,* the bombing of Cambodia was not just illegal: it was a crime. Henry Kissinger's refusal to admit any wrongdoing in Cambodia has not changed since his interview with Henry Kamm in 1991 where Kissinger said, "Journalists keep saying 'bombing Cambodia.' We were bombing four Vietnamese divisions that were killing 500 Americans a week."[70]

A former Khmer Rouge leader from northern Cambodia, Chhit Do, agreed with Shawcross and argued that the American bombing of Cambodia helped the Khmer Rouge rise to power. Chhit Do described the after-effects of US B-52 bombings. "Every time after there had been bombing, they would take people to see the craters, to see how big and deep they were, to see how the earth had been gouged out and scorched. The ordinary people sometimes shit in their pants when the big bombs and shells came. Their minds just froze and they would wander around for days. Terrified and half-crazy, the people were ready to believe what they were told. That was what made it so easy for the Khmer Rouge to win people over. It was because of their dissatisfaction with the bombing that they kept on cooperating with the Khmer Rouge, joining up with the Khmer Rouge, sending their children off to go with them."[71]

KHAT MANN STORIES

On the ride back from Kho Sola, Khat Mann stopped to show me a three-kilometer irrigation ditch. After digging for six months, he was selected to become a soldier for the Khmer Rouge. I complimented Khat Mann that his English was *klang* (strong) and gave him $20 for translating for Dr. Kroh. Khat Mann preened like a tufted titmouse.

"Before I soldier Khmer Rouge. Now I soldier you."

Asked what life was like when he was a Khmer Rouge soldier, Khat Mann said he preferred to sleep on a hammock or in a bed of wood and banana leaves. He only slept on the ground when he was fighting for several days and couldn't move. Cambodia has a lot of poisonous snakes. Sometimes sleeping on the ground was more dangerous than the Vietcong. For water, if there was no rain or river nearby, Khat Mann wrapped a cloth around cut bamboo at night and squeezed a few drops in the morning. Some vines in the jungle also gave him a good drink.

The closest Khat Mann came to getting killed was when his friend fired an AK-47 that made a buffalo stampede. Khat Mann hid behind a lone papaya tree, certain that he would be trampled. Another time he threw an American grenade into the water to fish, but the grenade blew up on land. Khat Mann laughing when he described near-death experiences reminded me of Tibetans who sometimes laughed when they described their torture by Chinese police. For Tibetans this was a testament of the human spirit rising above human cruelty and suffering and forgiving their captors. Khat Mann had the psychotic humor of a soldier who enjoyed killing.

A few kilometers later Khat Mann stopped at a metal bridge spanning ten meters of stagnant green water that disappeared into the jungle. One day fighting with Sam Bith's gang against the Vietcong, he had to cross this river and encountered a large snake. He got out of the water and shot at the snake, missed, then shot again. The snake was difficult to shoot in the water. Khat Mann shot twenty bullets before he hit the snake in the back of the head. When the water turned red from the snake swimming in a circle, Khat Mann pulled a ten-meter python out of the river.

"I very happy, but Sam Bith very angry with me. He say, 'Why you waste bullets on snake? Why you not kill Vietnam?' Then Sam Bith say I have Bad Biography. Everyone must hit me." Khat Mann looked pitiful, like a child who had misbehaved and was going to be punished. I felt sorry for him until he recounted "four fucking stories."

One time in Kho Sala, after his gang had killed all the Vietnamese soldiers in the village, Khat Mann found a water buffalo in a trench with a stool behind the animal. "For fucking!" Khat Mann exclaimed. "Vietnam soldier fuck water buffalo!" An old Khmer woman in the village thanked him for killing Vietnamese soldiers. The woman said when the Vietnamese soldiers first came to her village, they cleaned the yard while people slept and left fresh firewood and water before people woke up. One day when the Vietnamese soldiers raped her, she protested that she was too old. She had no teeth. The Vietnam soldier said, "That's what you said last year."

Khat Mann said that Angkor did not allow Khmer Rouge soldiers to have sex that Angkor did not sanction. If a soldier was discovered having unauthorized sex, he would be killed. One time a Khmer

Rouge soldier killed a deer and made a hole in the buttock with a knife. Pointing to his buttocks, Khat Man said, "He fuck deer here," and dissolved into laughter.

Another time, retreating from the Vietcong, a virgin woman soldier in his gang was shot. Khat Mann hid in the bamboo and watched Vietnamese soldiers rape her until she died.

That night the sheer volume and weight of the rain seemed to threaten Davide's recently renovated French Colonial house. Rain beating down so hard on the tile roof convinced me that returning to Phnom Penh would be delayed. Even if the rain stopped now the road would be flooded for days. Smoking an opiated hash joint, Davide explained the command structure of the Khmer Rouge.

The Khmer Rouge had two main factions, political and military. Pol Pot was the main architect of the Khmer Rouge genocide. He was political, not military. Khieu Samphan, the president of the Khmer Rouge, was under Pol Pot. Nuon Chea, known as "Bother Number Two" was third in command. Ieng Sary was fourth. Son San was the highest-ranking general in the Khmer Rouge military. Ta Mok was the next most powerful general. He was also Dr. Noun's uncle and had been in prison since his capture along the Thai border in 1999, one year after he killed Pol Pot. I told Davide there were two subjects I could talk to the Khmer Rouge about without getting killed: before the Khmer Rouge came to power and American bombing.

Waxing poetic, Davide said that he admired the Khmer Rouge. "They are excellent soldiers. No one has ever tried to tell their story, only the crap you hear about the killing fields. Under Pol Pot, the Khmer Rouge Revolution was the first true Khmer movement since the God Kings who constructed the Angkor Wats. For Khmer people, for most Cambodians in the villages, the Khmer Rouge freed Cambodia from 800 years of foreign domination when they ousted the US-backed Lon Nol government.

"Yes, I know the Khmer Rouge made everyone leave the cities to grow rice, but they mainly killed rich people. They have been fighting Vietnamese occupation for the last twenty-six years. You think Hun Sen is the head of the government? He is a Vietnamese puppet. Did you know that all of Hun Sen's bodyguards are Vietnamese!"

I asked Davide if he would drive Khat Mann, Dr. Noun, and me to Pailin to try and meet Khieu Samphan and Nuon Chea. Davide liked my idea of trying to understand the Khmer Rouge from their perspective and offered to help. Dr. Noun was the linchpin. Besides having a Pure Biography and being Ta Mok's nephew, he was Nuon Chea's and Khieu Samphan's doctor.

"There is a saying in Asia," Davide said. "If you show up at a man's house bearing gifts, even your mortal enemy will invite you in and serve tea."

The next morning when the rain stopped, Khat Mann said that he did not think I would come back to Cambodia. I reminded him that he said the same thing last year, and that next year I had land to come back to. When I told Khat Mann that I appreciated his help translating and wanted him to work for me next year when we went to see the Big Men in Pailin, he offered to build me a "nice house" for $10,000.

"Next year in Pailin," I said, bidding farewell to the child soldier who had become my translator and bodyguard.

MY ENEMIES, MY FRIENDS

Sokha was so anxious to leave Kampot that he barreled into the flooded road where puddles the size of football fields concealed potholes. Not far from Kampot the Toyota's engine exploded in a cloud of steam. When Sokha raised the hood, I saw but did not have time to stop him from unscrewing the radiator cap and being blinded by a geyser of scalding water. But there was no eruption. Unaware that he had just risked his eyesight, Sokha reconnected a rubber hose to the radiator next to a severed metal fitting. With open fields in all directions, I looked for any vehicle to hitch a ride. Sokha wrapped his belt around the radiator hose and started the car. I was impressed by Sokha's ingenuity, and by how quickly I wanted to abandon him.

The main street in the next town was one gigantic pond. Four children splashing each other accepted 5,000 riels each to run shrieking with delight in front of the car. Sokha followed the child whose knees stayed above water, turning when a child sunk waist-deep or disappeared under the surface. When we reached the other side of town, the children waved. It seemed miraculous that Sokha's Toyota had not gotten an electrical short on our return to Phnom Penh. As soon as the road permitted excessive speed, we hydroplaned over an Olympic-sized puddle and almost hit a minibus.

An article in the *Phnom Penh Post* described one monk at Wat Botoum throwing acid on another monk over the use of the toilet, and a bride who had acid thrown on her face. It was the middle of May and already fifteen women had reported having acid thrown on their faces. One account stood out from the rest. Hundreds of people witnessed the jealous wife of a government minister, whose husband was having an affair with a younger woman, get out of her chauffeured Mercedes on Monivong Boulevard. With her bodyguards holding the mistress down, the minister's wife poured acid on the woman's face, waved to the crowd, and drove off knowing that she would never be prosecuted. The violent undercurrents swirling through Cambodian society scared me. So did my interest in the backpackers. I hoped meeting the judge who acquitted Chhouk Rin of the backpackers' murders would not complicate my relationship with the Phnom Vor Gang.

The *Phnom Penh Post* newsroom had rows of reporters working on computers at their cubicles. Bill Bainbridge was busy but gave me directions to Judge Mong Mony Chariya's office at Dola Ka, the police station near the stadium. He also told me not to stop for the soldiers at the gate and walk straight up to the second floor. Judge Chariya never answered his phone. I put on my only white button-down shirt and blue blazer in hundred-degree heat and humidity. Sokha drove me to the police station and stayed in the car.

"Dola Ka very bad," Sokha said, holding his wrists together and recounting his trip to Dola Ka after the police found the dead playboy in his car. If Sokha's mother had not brought money in time, he could have been beaten to death. Sokha was terrified when I got out of the car amid columns of light that burst through indigo clouds blanketing the city.

Walking past the guardhouse into the office of the United Nations Human Rights Mission, I introduced myself to a young man who had completed a human rights assessment of Cambodia. It Sath said that he went to Phnom Vor in 1995 to talk to Chhouk Rin about integrating the Khmer Rouge into the government. It Sath remembered Chhouk Rin saying that he had some problems with higher up Khmer Rouge in the Khmer People National Liberation Armed Force (KPNLAF).

Asked if I could meet Judge Chariya, It Sath informed me that the judge was a very busy man. Asked if I had an appointment, I replied that the judge never answered his phone. "You know him!" It Sath said and made a call on his cell phone. In a few seconds It Sath said the judge was at the Supreme Court. He would meet me in his office upstairs in twenty minutes.

"Akoun chiran (Thank you)."

The judge introduced himself as Judge Mong Mony Chariya and welcomed me into his small office with peeling paint and a toothless ceiling fan. The bright red robes hanging behind his metal chair provided the only color in the office. Judge Chariya seemed nervous. Beads of sweat poured down his forehead before I inquired about the backpackers.

At the trial of the foreign backpackers, Judge Chariya said that witnesses testified that three foreigners were killed, but not by Chhouk Rin. Chhouk Rin testified that he had helped the backpackers and provided them with food. Judge Chariya had two main problems with Chhouk Rin's trial. First, no one would testify against him. Second, Chhouk Rin had signed amnesty papers from Hun Sen and King Sihanouk. When faced with the judgment of Chhouk Rin, he had to take the "middle path" and acquitted Chhouk Rin of the backpackers' murders.

Judge Chariya moved his chair back as I described how the backpackers had to work in the fields every day for one month to get one bowl of rice at night. He moved his chair back again hearing how Khat Mann had severed their Achilles tendons after the Australian tried to escape, and how they had to crawl to work in the fields for another two months before Khat Mann killed them. When I mentioned that Chhouk Rin said that Hun Sen gave the order to kill the backpackers when he found them "crippled," the back of Judge Chariya's chair hit the wall.

The silence was deafening. It was not a good idea to go into any Southeast Asian police station and accuse its prime minister of murder. In Cambodia, this could have foreseen consequences. Asked if there were any other cases pending for the backpackers' murders, Judge Chariya retrieved a four-inch-thick red folder filled with depositions for the Sam Bith case. Judge Chariya had been gathering evidence against Chhouk Rin's commander for years. He was ready to bring charges against Sam Bith for the murder of the backpackers but could not because of a tactical problem.

"We don't know where Sam Bith is," Judge Chariya said. "We can't serve him with papers if we don't know where he is. We must follow procedure."

"Have any Khmer Rouge officers ever been prosecuted?"

"We have had some success. Nuon Paet was convicted in 1999 for the backpacker murders."

"Are there any cases pending against the leaders of the Khmer Rouge for crimes against Cambodians?"

"There are many high-ranking Khmer Rouge soldiers in the government. They do not want to make trouble. They do not want to amend or change the Cambodian constitution to include the death penalty."

I felt it was my duty to report the information that I had learned about the backpackers' murderers to the Australian embassy as I went through their security check. After explaining to a consular officer that I was an American physician who had direct knowledge of David Wilson's murder, I did not have to wait long to be led to a locked room with bulletproof glass and a one-way mirror. A man about my height introduced himself as Ian McConville, first secretary of the political and economic sections.

"I have a great interest in the case of David Wilson," McConville said after I explained how I had come to meet Chhouk Rin and learned the details of David's captivity, attempted escape, hamstringing, and death. "I remember the coroner's report noting the severed Achilles tendons. I did not know why, but it turned my stomach. I'd like to talk with you more about this but I have a meeting. Call me tomorrow on this number." McConville handed me his card and showed me to the door.

The next morning when I called McConville, he said that he had come down with the "flu" and could not meet. He did not sound sick. I assumed that he did not want to open any scabs that might hamper economic cooperation between Australia and Cambodia. Before hanging up I asked what effect the American bombing had in Cambodia. McConville hesitated but said that he knew of one British academic who claimed that the US bombing of Cambodia had fanaticized the Khmer Rouge.

Leaving Australia's embassy in Phnom Penh, I realized that I would return to Cambodia the following year to try and meet Khieu Samphan and Nuon Chea. Khat Mann and Chhouk Rin still scared the hell out of me, but Khat Mann had overcome being a child soldier for the Khmer Rouge to become Chhouk Rin's telegraph operator who communicated regularly with Pol Pot. He was also studying English to become a better translator. Although Chhouk Rin supervised the deaths of over 100,000 New People in Kampot, he had also resisted Vietnamese occupation for twenty-six years, given me land, and called me "Dr. Number Two." Dr. Noun was inspired to start working as a physician again and, Buddha-willing, would be grateful to his American colleague. And Davide, the cantankerous mercenary who had a genuine interest and respect for Khmer Rouge soldiers, had a Land Rover. With a little help from the Phnom Vor Gang, I could meet the architects of the Khmer Rouge Revolution and ask them how they rose to power.

Street children in Phnom Penh

Women selling fried insects at Phnom Penh's Central Market

The Chankiri tree at Choeung Ek where bone fragments and teeth are scattered like pebbles beneath the tree where adolescent executioners swung children by their feet, smashing their heads against the polished trunk.

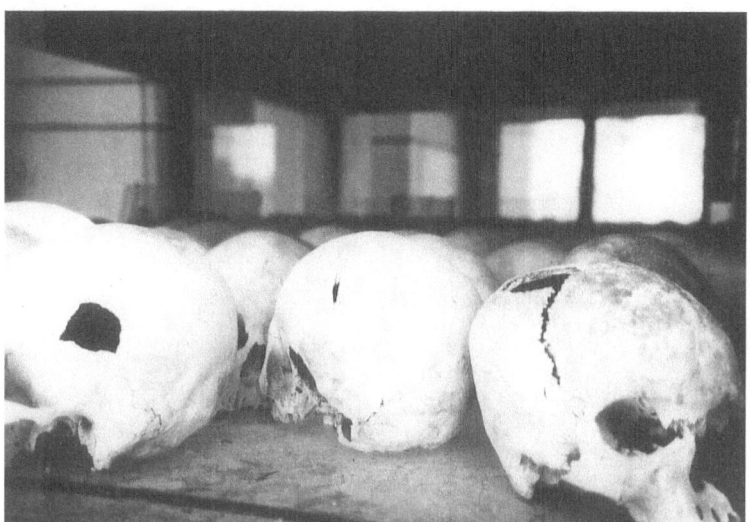
Skulls with evidence of blunt trauma at Choeung Ek Killing Fields Memorial.

Dr. Kerr on the road to Kampot

Kep Killing Fields Memorial for one mass grave with 500 corpses.

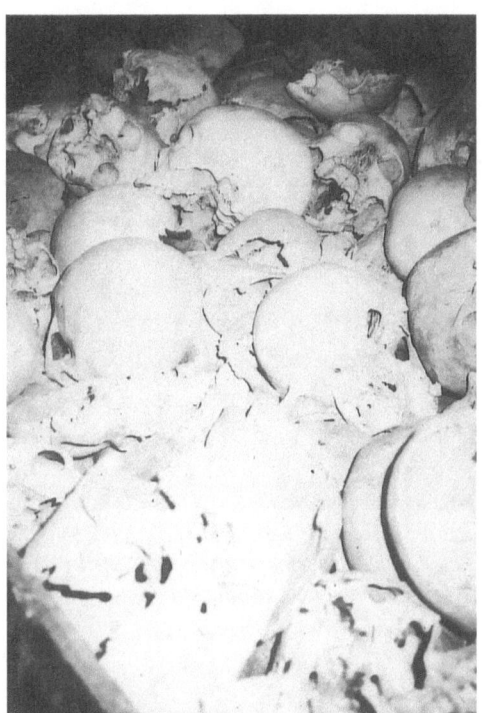

Pile of skulls at Kep Killing Fields Memorial.

Khat Mann and Dr. Noun inspecting an overgrown crater from a bomb dropped twenty-five years ago by an American B-52.

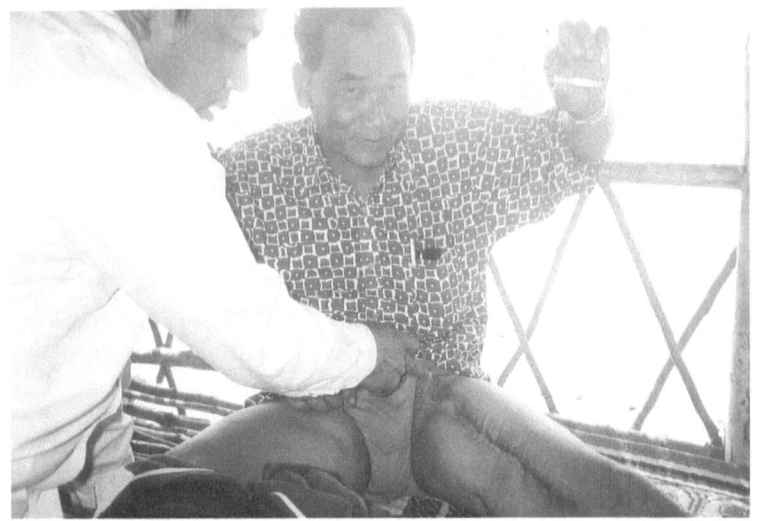

Khat Mann exposes Chhouk Rin's scar from the battlefield operation where Dr. Noun replaced segments of Chhouk Rin's torn femoral artery on is left leg with the saphenous vein from his right leg, under local anesthesia.

Ouch Nim (Dr. Noun's sister and Mr. Muhn's wife), Dr. Kerr, Mr. Muhn (Pol Pot's telegraph operator with a "picture mind" at his home in Samlaut), and Dr. Noun.

Remnants of a tank in the smoldering hills outside Pailin.

Nuon Chea (Brother Number Two) at his home in Pailin sitting next to Dr. Kerr.

PART III

SEARCHING FOR THE TRUTH

SEARCHING FOR THE TRUTH

At the end of a busy summer 2001, a well-groomed man in his fifties came into my office and identified himself as a colonel in the US Army when the Sihanouk government fell in 1970. He did not have to say that he was in the CIA, but he did. Wearing a tweed jacket, the colonel had the amiable persona of a college professor, not the least burdened by the emotional baggage of my previous two patients who fought for the US military in Cambodia. The colonel was aware of my interest in the Khmer Rouge and did not discourage my working with Dr. Noun. He warned me to be careful.

"You cannot trust the Khmer Rouge!"

The colonel reminded me of my grandfather who worked undercover in Germany for the OSS to support the armistice after World War I. Besides stories of kill-or-be-killed, he made fun of his German: more than once while auctioning horses he kept lowering the bid. Throughout my childhood I heard my grandfather reiterate, "The only good Communist is a dead Communist." Captain Jack Doorty was weaned in a military camp on the Mexican border while his father fought Pancho Villa. Too young to serve in World War I, he lied about his age and fought under General Pershing. Too old to serve in

World War II, he lied about his age and served with General Chennault's Flying Tigers ferrying men and supplies over the "Hump" (Himalayas) from India to China.

A decade of documenting the underside of China's military occupation in Tibet had given me a favorable impression of the CIA. After China invaded Tibet in 1949, The CIA supported the Tibetan resistance in the early fifties.[72] After the Chinese Communists brutally suppressed independence demonstrations in Tibet's eastern provinces in 1957, the CIA trained eight Tibetans at the Saipan Training Center to parachute into Kham and Amdo and assess the Tibetan resistance. Armed with muskets, the Tibetans were vastly outnumbered by soldiers in the People's Liberation Army armed with AK-47s. In 1959, when China consolidated its military occupation of Tibet by crushing the Lhasa Rebellion, the CIA helped the Dalai Lama flee to India.[73]

In the 1960s the CIA trained 2,000 Khampa fighters at bases in Mustang, Nepal, Guam, and Colorado to conduct cross-border guerilla raids.[74] Once again the Tibetan resistance was crushed, this time by world politics. Nixon stopped supporting the Tibetans in 1969 as a precondition to normalizing relations with China.[75] At the same time the US increased its bombing of Cambodia to counter China's support of the Khmer Rouge.

Tibet and Cambodia were both caught in proxy wars between the long arms of China's and US foreign policies. From my New York clinic 12,000 miles and twelve time zones from Cambodia, I felt nostalgia for the Phnom Vor Gang. I knew I was obsessed with meeting the leaders of the Khmer Rouge Revolution. How did a ragtag group of communist guerillas defeat the US-backed Lon Nol government? Did US bombing help the Khmer Rouge recruit? Did US bombing fanaticize the Khmer Rouge before 2 million people perished from starvation, torture, and execution? If so, were there parallels to the US bombing in Vietnam and Laos, and the current US wars in Iraq and Afghanistan?

POL POT

Traveling to Phnom Penh in January 2002, I read David Chandler's *Brother Number One, A Political Biography of Pol Pot*.[76] Saloth Sar was born into a prosperous farming family in central Cambodia in 1925 and raised by a cousin in Phnom Penh who worked with the royal ballet. Saloth Sar's privileged background enabled him to enroll in the prestigious College Sihanouk in Kampong Cham, where Sihanouk granted him a scholarship to study radio-electricity in Paris from 1949 to 1952.

Saloth Sar and his fellow Khmer students living in Paris became Communists at a time when it was popular to support the communist resistance to French colonial rule. Working at a labor battalion in Yugoslavia in the summer of 1950 gave him a positive impression of Tito's rise to power. Stalin was also at the apex of his influence as communism was sweeping through China.

Unlike Ho Chi Minh's legendary intellect and organizational skills, Pol Pot was intellectually challenged. In 1952, Saloth Sar published a paper in the local Khmer magazine, *Khmer Nisut*, "Monarchy or Democracy" under the pseudonym *Khmer daom* (Original Khmer). Inspired by Sihanouk's coup d'état in Phnom Penh, the article attacked the Cambodian monarchy as a "doctrine which bestows power on a small group of men who do nothing to earn their living so that they can exploit the majority of the people at every level. Monarchy is an unjust doctrine, a malodorous running sore that just people must eliminate."[77]

After the article, Sihanouk sent an advisor to Paris to terminate the scholarships of all Cambodians associated with the offensive issue of *Khmer Nisut*. In 1953, after failing his exams, Saloth Sar joined the French Communist Party before returning to Cambodia to become a teacher and begin to organize in secret. On November 9, 1953, France granted independence to Cambodia after King Sihanouk agreed to not fight with or against the Vietnamese Communists. Four months later, on March 7, 1954, Ho Chi Minh's Vietnamese nationalists defeated the French at Dien Bien Phu.

Pol Pot worked in Phnom Penh as a schoolteacher and communist organizer from 1954 to 1962, when the Cambodian Communist movement found natural allies in peasants and students. In 1955 Sihanouk appointed his father king, swept national elections, and started taking money from the US. Lon Nol, Sihanouk's military chief, tried to wipe out all Communists who registered to vote. By September 1960, when Pol Pot helped draft the constitution of Cambodia's Communist Party in empty boxcars in Phnom Penh's railway yard, Lon Nol and Sihanouk had wiped out 90 percent of the communist cells.

The year 1959 marked the beginning of the Ho Chi Minh Trail, where China sent arms to the North Vietnamese Communists fighting the US-backed government in South Vietnam, and the Pathet Lao Communists fighting the US-backed government in Laos. After the student revolt in Siem Reap in 1963, Pol Pot and most of the fledgling Cambodian Communists left Phnom Penh and fled into the countryside fearing death threats from Sihanouk's police. Sihanouk continued to receive money from the US and weapons from China and coined the term *Khmer Rouge* for the Communists' wearing red-and-black-checkered *kramas*.

On March 18, 1970, after one year of US covert bombing in Cambodia, Sihanouk flew to Paris and Lon Nol staged a coup d'état, with the CIA's backing, and took control of the country.

Reading Chandler helped me understand how the Khmer Rouge espousing Khmer socialism, with free education and health care and nationalized businesses, appealed to Cambodia's agrarian population. The Right, who were in power, withheld payments to peasants for their rice, and this inspired a rebellion.

YOUK CHHANG AND THE DOCUMENTATION CENTER OF CAMBODIA

Sokha was ecstatic to see his New York brother again. Phnom Penh was crowded with 2,000 delegates for the 2002 ASEAN conference who, according to Sokha, were "no good," the same as the UN delegates who paid "small money." If Sokha could not find a hotel for me he said I could stay at his house. He also said that his wife, eight-year-old daughter, and 11-year-old son were well and they were all living together again. His father had died, but this was expected. His family had gone to the temple and made special prayers for Papa's spirit.

Depositing my passport, cash, and plane tickets into the safety deposit box of the Goldiana Hotel, where I would be charged $100 if I lost the key, came with tremendous relief. The box allowed me to safeguard money while I learned more about the evidentiary weight of evidence against the Khmer Rouge before enlisting the Phnom Vor Gang in a road trip to Pailin.

Youk Chhang cofounded the Documentation Center of Cambodia that had collected detailed biographies from 34,000 Khmer Rouge soldiers and hundreds of thousands of individual accounts of torture, rape, and murder by the Khmer Rouge. They also published a monthly magazine, *Searching for THE TRUTH*, where I found Youk Chhang's address.[78]

Sokha drove me to his office on Sihanouk Boulevard near the Independence Monument. When I knocked on the metal door in the large black metal gate, two men in pressed blue jeans and dark glasses stationed across the street took my picture as I waited to enter a busy office with a dozen Cambodians writing, faxing, and working at computers.

Youk Chhang wore dark slacks and a pressed white oxford shirt. He spoke fluent English and seated me across from him at his desk, the epicenter of activity from the bustling staff. In response to a recent *New York Times* article that Hun Sen had agreed to a tribunal in Cambodia with Cambodian judges and UN participation, Youk Chhang said that whether the People's Congress ratified this was another matter. Nuon Chea had stated in public that he would rather have a Truth and Reconciliation Commission, like in South Africa.

According to Youk Chhang, Nuon Chea did not even know what the truth was. He was not eligible for a Truth and Reconciliation Commission because he was a leader of the Khmer Rouge. If there were a tribunal to try the Khmer Rouge leaders for crimes against humanity, Nuon Chea threatened to mobilize the Khmer Rouge.

"To this day no Khmer Rouge leader has ever admitted that he made any mistake," Youk Chhang said. "Nuon Chea says he does not know about any killing. When Pol Pot evacuated Phnom Penh, he appointed uneducated people to head the communes. The Khmer Rouge taught villagers to hate everyone in Phnom Penh because they were rich. They hated capitalists and used uneducated people to kill educated people."

Youk Chhang decided to do human rights work after he was caught picking mushrooms and wild grass for his favorite sister who was pregnant and had nothing to eat. Picking mushrooms was a crime, so the Khmer Rouge soldiers hit him with an axe and beat him. Youk Chhang begged for his life. He admitted that he knew picking mushrooms was a crime and promised that he would never do this again. Youk Chhang did not care if they killed him, but they tortured him in front of his mother. And every time his mother cried the Khmer Rouge beat her. Under the Khmer Rouge, crying was also a crime.

"We must remember that every single person in the country was in one way or another victimized by the Khmer Rouge," Youk Chhang said emphatically. "Many Khmer Rouge soldiers and officers were killed at Tuol Sleng during the Khmer Rouge purges. Every family in Cambodia has at least one victim."

When I inquired how the Khmer Rouge recruited child soldiers, Youk Chhang replied that when he was a boy, he also wanted to be a soldier. Soldiers got food when there was not much to eat and many Cambodians were starving. Soldiers didn't have to work, and they got to carry a gun. This was every boy's dream. It was not difficult to teach a thirteen- or fourteen-year-old boy to kill. Child soldiers committed most of the Khmer Rouge executions.

According to the Documentation Center of Cambodia, over 2 million Cambodians perished as a direct result of the Khmer Rouge. A few years ago the number was 1.5 million people. The death toll kept increasing as more killing fields were discovered. Youk Chhang said that every town in Cambodia had a killing field. To date his organization had documented over 19,000 mass graves. Unlike the memorial at Choeung Ek, most of the mass graves in Cambodia had not been excavated.

Youk Chhang also said that more than 20,000 people were killed in Tuol Sleng, the high school the Khmer Rouge turned into a torture center. Out of the 20,000 who perished, seven survived. Before leaving, Youk Chhang gave me the names and addresses of Van Nath and Chum Mey, two remaining survivors of Tuol Sleng.

"Why would anyone join the Khmer Rouge?"

"Some people say they joined because an American bomb killed a member of their family. Others joined because King Sihanouk appealed to them on the radio. After Lon Nol took over, Sihanouk set up a government in exile in Beijing and asked people to join the Khmer Rouge to fight the Americans. Before Sihanouk went into exile, he fought the Khmer Rouge. There are many factors so if you choose only one, I think you may miss the point."

Youk Chhang acknowledged that he received frequent death threats from the Hun Sen police and the Khmer Rouge, and that he was monitored by Hun Sen's secret police. But he did not fear for his life. Youk Chhang believed that publishing *Searching for THE TRUTH* helped protect him. Even if the Khmer Rouge killed him, they could not kill the truth.

"Could the Khmer Rouge ever return to power?"

"After what the Khmer Rouge have done, no one in Cambodia would let them come back. If they came to my door right now, I would fight."

The plainclothes policemen photographed my exit into the street. "Hun Sen CIA," Sokha whispered, wary of the men on motorcycles following us. "Very dangera." Sokha took his hands off the wheel and put his wrists together for a second. "Maybe prison. Maybe kill."

TUOL SLENG SURVIVORS

Hun Sen's undercover police followed us from the Independence Monument to the Royal Palace, then raced ahead when Sokha stopped to park. When the policemen were out of sight, I asked Sokha to arrange a meeting with Van Nath and dialed the number Youk Chhang had given me. Sokha talked for a long time on my cell phone before hanging up, pleased with himself.

"Can we meet Van Nath?"

"Yes."

"When?"

"His wife say he out."

"You just said we could meet."

"Cannot."

Sokha's tendency to say yes even if he did not understand just so he would please me spawned violent thoughts. I asked Sokha to drive me to the UN Human Rights Office at the police station where he had been taken the previous year after a "playboy" stole his car, which was recovered with a corpse. Sokha was terrified when we stopped outside Dola Ka, but I figured it was the last place the police would look for us if we were being followed. I also needed It Sath to help arrange an interview with Van Nath.

It Sath was working at his desk and did not seem to mind my intruding. He remembered our meeting last year, and within minutes he arranged back-to-back meetings with two men who were freed from the Khmer Rouge's most notorious extermination prison when the Vietnamese Army liberated Cambodia in 1979. I looked for and did not see any Hun Sen police before getting into Sokha's car.

Van Nath answered his cell phone and told us to park on a side street under the shade of a large Banyan tree. After we waited for ninety-seven minutes, a student in school uniform appeared and led us on a circuitous route to a house hidden by high walls. Inside, Van Nath looked healthy but wizened beyond his years. His white hair matched his clean long-sleeved shirt.

I greeted Van Nath in Khmer. It Sath introduced me as a Western doctor who wanted to ask about his experience in Tuol Sleng, which he had chronicled in his 1998 account, *A Cambodian Prison Portrait: One Year in the Khmer Rouge's S-21*.[79] Van Nath stared at the wall for a while before he talked without stopping. My anxiety that It Sath would only be able to translate part of what Van Nath said and forget crucial details soon dissipated. It Sath turned out to be an excellent translator.

Van Nath was fifty-six years old. He married in 1971 and lived in Battambang, where he had two sons before the Khmer Rouge controlled the entire country in 1975. During "Pol Pot time" Van Nath had another son in 1977. Van Nath was not sure why he was arrested on December 30, 1977. Before he was sent to Phnom Penh, the Khmer Rouge in Battambang beat him.

When he arrived at Tuol Sleng, the Khmer Rouge used a lot of electric shocks when they asked if he knew any rich people who had betrayed the Khmer Rouge. He did not know how long his torture sessions lasted. He was shocked so many times he often fell unconscious. The Khmer Rouge interrogated Van Nath again and again like this.

As far as he could tell, the Khmer Rouge wanted him to confess that he worked for the CIA, the KGB, or the KVB. Tuol Sleng became a paranoid inquisition to root out all American, Soviet, or Vietnamese agents that had infiltrated Cambodia. Under extreme duress, most victims signed confessions that are still on display at the Tuol Sleng Museum.

After one month a guard learned that Van Nath was a painter. Ill from torture and exhaustion and eating two or three spoons of gruel a day, Van Nath was too weak to walk. The guards carried him to a clean room and told him to paint a picture. He had not painted for years and could barely hold the brush. He had no energy. His mind could not concentrate. Van Nath smiled when he said the Khmer Rouge did not like his first picture. But after he tried two or three, they found one they liked—of Pol Pot. After that, Van Nath painted the same picture of Pol Pot every day.

To keep his spirit, Van Nath thought about his wife and family. He did not know where his wife was or if she was still alive. She thought he was dead. When the Vietnamese Army freed Van Nath from Tuol Sleng on January 7, 1979, it took a few months for him to get strong enough to return to his village. When he found his wife in Battambang in May, he could not say anything. His wife was also speechless. She was alive but their three children had died from starvation and illness.

Van Nath allowed another smile when he said that he had three more children with the same wife, two daughters and a son. And today his paintings of torture and prisoner treatment hung on Tuol Sleng's walls, graphic reminders to the world of the Khmer Rouge's cruelty. I said that my stepfather and mother were painters and sculptors and thanked him on behalf of my family and ancestors for talking with me, and for his valuable work. After saying, "*Akoun chiran* (Thank you)," I extended a $50 handshake.

Waiting for hours on the side of a busy street to meet Chum Mey, I was speechless after hearing Van Nath's story. I had interviewed hundreds of Tibetan men and women in Tibet and at refugee camps in India, recorded their stories of torture and rape, forced abortion, sterilization, and infanticide. Although there were shared smiles and brief moments of levity during their accounts of abuse that took hours to tell, they left me exhausted and haunted my dreams every time. I was impressed by Van Nath's quiet inner strength that enabled him to survive.

A truck pulled in front of Sokha's car and we followed it to Chum Mey's house. It was well after dark when we parked a hundred meters from a two-story cement house with a feeble metal gate. Chum Mey was shorter than I expected, with wisps of black hair combed over his tanned, bald head. His eldest son opened the gate and led us through another metal door. A cement floor and marble facade on the first four feet of the ten-foot walls gave a sterile appearance to the house. Chum Mey's children appeared in procession with heads bowed and palms folded upright. Chum Mey had six children from his second wife, three daughters and three sons. "Pol Pot" executed his first wife and their three-month-old baby.

Waves of anger washed over Chum Mey when he opened a wooden box and retrieved a color headshot of Duch, Kang Kek Leu, the director of the Tuol Sleng Prison. With short-cropped hair and dilated pupils, Duch looked like a deer caught in the headlights. Chum Mey was adamant that Duch was responsible for his torture and the guards trying to make him confess that he worked for the American CIA. Chum Mey's eldest son produced a picture of seven people standing before Tuol Sleng. Vietnamese soldiers took the picture when they liberated Tuol Sleng from the Khmer Rouge. Out of 20,000 people who entered Tuol Sleng, this picture showed the seven sole survivors.

Chum Mey pointed to a much younger Van Nath, whom I recognized, and himself when he had hair on his head. Chum Mey pointed to the remaining four men and one woman and pronounced each dead. Leaning close he demonstrated how the Khmer Rouge shackled and beat him with anything they could find: chairs, sticks, machetes, rocks. Oftentimes he was shackled to five or more prisoners who were also tortured. Unlike Van Nath, Chum Mey could not separate himself from his mistreatment.

"The Khmer Rouge time may be over," It Sath translated, "but many of the Khmer Rouge are still in positions of power. They still haunt the hearts and minds of the Cambodian people." Chum Mey said that his name and honor remained, but his body may be killed. He is very concerned about his security. He is still in hiding. The Cambodian government does not provide security for people like Chum Mey.

"Since 1963, Chum Mey has come to know the Khmer Rouge government very well. The Khmer Rouge always spoke to him with sweet words, but their hearts were very bad. Chum Mey says he is not safe. He wants to testify at a tribunal, but he is afraid the Khmer Rouge will kill him. If he dies there will be no one to support his family. Then people will believe the Khmer Rouge lies because there will be no one left to tell this generation what really happened during Pol Pot times."

"At money (not money)," I said in Khmer giving Chum Mey a Ulysses S. Grant handshake. This elevated his mood but would not protect him or his family. Chum Mey's and Van Nath's hopes and fears epitomized a generation of Cambodians who had survived the Khmer Rouge genocide and Vietnamese occupation and now struggled to make better lives for themselves and their families. I hoped this would happen in their lifetime.

VICTORY COCONUTS

That night Davide emailed from China:

> Chhouk Rin lost his appeal for killing the backpackers and was sentenced to life in prison. He is in Phnom Vor with his gang, surrounded by Hun Sen soldiers. Do not talk with anyone about interviewing Khmer Rouge. If you have to go anywhere, you can trust my driver, Po. Be careful of Khat Mann. He was badly beaten and just got out of the hospital. Mann is furious that Chhouk Rin did not intervene. Do not go anywhere with Khat Mann!
>
> I am leaving soon. See you in Kampot.
> Ciao

The next morning Sokha tasted a puddle of fluid under the engine, and said that we needed a new water pump that would cost $20. I was grateful that he had noticed the leak and we had not broken down on the road to worry. Driving to Kampot I worried about Khat Mann's state of mind after being beaten, Chhouk Rin surrounded by Hun Sen soldiers, and how I could get Dr. Noun to travel with me to Pailin to meet the Big Men.

Sokha's reentry into traffic parted a sea of bicycles and pedestrians, and a *SCREECH* from the right front bumper. "Bad road," we both agreed. When the car bounded through another pothole, Sokha veered right onto a dirt path to avoid the head of a white ox from smashing my passenger window. When a herd of cows lumbered across the road, Sokha did not flinch. He leaned on the horn and aimed straight for the lead cow's head. When the cow backed down at the last second, Sokha was ecstatic. He had outwitted the cow, this time.

The game of chicken and chance continued on our drive down Route 3 to Kampot. Between villages Sokha drove with the right two wheels on a dirt path parallel to the road to reduce our chances of losing a tire to the jagged breaks in pavement. Giving my sunglasses to Sokha, who needed them more than I did, littered pieces of paper, cans, and plastic came into view that diminished the luster of the Elysian paddies bordered by palm and coconut trees.

When we arrived at the Marco Polo, Sokha refused my offer for dinner and a room. "Cannot," Sokha said, scanning the street for signs of Khat Mann and begging me to return to Phnom Penh with him. I promised to be careful and gave him $100. Sokha did not look at the money. He was genuinely concerned about his New York brother and left Kampot as fast as he had come.

It did not take long for Khat Mann to find me. He was livid. When I asked about his being in the hospital, he pulled his sleeves back to reveal fresh circular rope burns around his wrists and ankles from being hogtied. Khat Mann looked so pathetic describing how "Bad Men" had tied him up and beat him for four days, I felt sorry for him.

"I very angry no one come to rescue me," Khat Mann said. "I very angry Chhouk Rin not help me. After I am in hospital one week, I tell judge I want Bad Men arrested. The police bring Bad Men to the judge, and the judge say they must pay $2,500. But the Bad Men pay some money to the judge and offer $700. The judge say OK. But I not take small money. I want justice!"

The irony of Khat Mann wanting justice from the Cambodian courts was astounding. How much justice had Khat Mann dispensed to the thousands of people he had killed as a child soldier, or to the Western backpackers? How much justice did the Khmer Rouge give to anyone who perished during their reign of terror? I asked about Dr. Noun, and Khat Mann repeated that he was very angry that Chhouk Rin had not helped him. Chhouk Rin knew everything that happened in Phnom Vor. He could have helped him get out of the house. Khat Mann was madder than pissed-on hornets, devouring his plate of spaghetti.

What a difference one year had made. Penya was proud to take my order in English. Khat Mann was still manic but his English had improved, demanding $15 to rent two motorcycles. I knew that motorcycles were $6 each for a full day, and not to sweat the insignificant daily extortions, to think of them as tips. A good captain covered his crew. If Khat Mann's hatred of me overcame his daily calculation of my worth, I would be cannibalized.

That night I escaped from Khat Mann to read "Ho Chi Minh" by William J. Duiker, a superb chronicle of a great man's determination to free his people from colonial oppression.[80] Ho Chi Minh, "he who enlightens," was first used as a pseudonym by Nguyen Van Hoan while traveling as a Chinese journalist in 1940. Unlike Pol Pot, Ho Chi Minh was an intellectual. Whether he was living in Paris or the Soviet Union, with the Kuomintang or in Communist China, Ho wrote plays, started newspapers, and organized. More than his affiliation with any brand of Soviet or Chinese Communism, Ho was devoted to the Vietnamese people and their struggle to free themselves from French colonialism and American hegemony.

Khat Mann was in full manic phase when he found me reading in my room the next afternoon. "In Cambodia, if read too much, must kill." Khat Mann was serious and lured me into a game of volleyball in a brick-walled courtyard next to a church built by the French. With four players on each side, and dozens of spectators, I enjoyed a tremendous height advantage.

Everyone wanted to be set up for the big spike at the net. Even little guys who could not reach the top of the net tried to spike the ball. When I set them up, they spiked the ball into or under the net. Khat Mann was the best player and played every day, weather permitting, for 5,000 riel ($1) a game. Khat Mann was used to winning, and bathing in the center of attention. He also had a sledgehammer spike. When I could get the ball to him, he scored.

After we won the first three games, our opponents recruited a Chinese soldier who had settled in Cambodia after "advising" the Khmer Rouge. The Chinese soldier shared Chhouk Rin's reptilian eyes and laser stare. When Khat Mann blocked his first spike, the pinkie on his right hand stuck out at a right angle like a flag. Khat Mann did not show any pain at his digit's dislocation or when I pulled the finger straight out to approximate a normal alignment. The middle knuckle looked like a ripe plum and could not bend, but it did not affect Khat Mann's play.

I had no excuse for missing several easy shots and failing to set Khat Mann up, which infuriated him. With my height I should have been more coordinated. Then I blocked a spike from the Chinese soldier and heard a snap from my right knee when I landed. It did not hurt at first, but I could not jump or move quickly and we were trounced.

Sipping the cool, clear milk from our "victory coconuts" through a straw, Khat Mann was upset to have lost one game even though he pocketed a profit of 10,000 riel. It was refreshing to see the other men tease Khat Mann for losing a single game. What they were afraid to say alone was allowed in a pack. Khat Mann regained his dominance by embellishing his pinkie's demise.

Khat Mann also made sure that I did not get ripped off more than 1,000 riel for the coconuts. Before going home to his wife and three children, Khat Mann confided that if he did not win at volleyball every day, his family did not eat. Although I was still afraid of Khat

Mann and did not trust him, I asked if he would be my bodyguard on the road to Pailin with Dr. Noun.

Uncharacteristically serious, Khat Mann said, "Before I soldier for Khmer Rouge. Now I soldier for you."

THE GOOD DR. NOUN

My fear of the Khmer Rouge evaporated trying to keep up with Khat Mann on a motorcycle. I had forgotten how uncomfortable I was on the iron horse. My feet were unfamiliar with the footrests and shifting. The muscles in my legs and back ached as we sped through villages where children still yelled, "Hello! Hello! Hello!" The villages and rice paddies were beautiful, but I was on the lookout for people trying to throw a small pig or duck in front of me. Even without provocation I skidded on eroded sections of pavement.

Dr. Noun received me in his Spartan office at Kep Hospital. His demeanor had noticeably improved. He stood taller and looked me in the eye. Wearing a soiled, full-length white coat, Dr. Noun seated us in plastic chairs. The walls and desk were bare but Dr. Noun looked happy. Khat Mann translated that after we met last year, Dr. Noun started working at Kep Hospital in the mornings. In the afternoons he made hut calls to people in the jungle, treating malaria, typhoid, and tuberculosis. He also stopped by the ever-expanding colony of AIDS patients on Thuch Sombo's land. Dr. Noun's wife still worked as a midwife delivering babies in the jungle.

Dr. Noun was proud to lead me on a tour of the forty-bed hospital with four buildings facing a central courtyard. There were separate rooms for trauma, illness, maternity, an X-ray and ultrasound that did not work, and a kitchen. None of the rooms had any medicines, food, or supplies. Family members sitting with patients had to provide reed mats to cover the metal bed frame and all of the patient's food, clothes, blanket, and medicines.

Bloody gauze partially covered infected lacerations on the first man's forehead and extremities. A suspicious green dextrose solution dripped from an IV line into his arm.

"Motorcycle accident," Khat Mann said.

The woman in the next building looked gaunt and febrile as her husband played with their three-year-old son. Dr. Noun pointed to her as though she were on display and pronounced "*ty-phoid*," emphasizing each syllable. The next patient, a young boy with a deep, rattling cough that made me hold my breath had "*pneu-mo-ni-a*."

A very pregnant twenty-five-year-old woman who looked forty and her five-year-old daughter stood outside the maternity ward. The woman looked exhausted, ready to deliver at any second. I gave her $10 and got two big smiles. When Khat Mann said that his wife delivered their third child at the Kep Hospital maternity ward four months ago, I slapped the proud father on the back. For a moment we were bonded like brothers from a different mother.

The TB ward was next, a large room with ten empty beds. When Dr. Noun said that Phnom Vor had a lot of people with TB, and I gestured to the absence of patients in the room, Dr. Noun said their TB was too contagious to treat in the hospital so they were treated at home. Dr. Noun showed me a black ledger with dozens of names and addresses of patients, when they started their medicines, weekly hut calls, and when they had or would complete nine months of treatment.

Asked if he could have anything from the West, Dr. Noun replied that the Cambodian people needed training in Western medicine.

This was more important than money or medicine. As we posed for a picture at the main gate, I asked Dr. Noun how much he made working at the hospital. Khat Mann replied that for working every morning in the hospital seven days a week, Dr. Noun received $8 a month from the World Bank.

I told Dr. Noun that I was proud of my Khmer colleague for practicing medicine again and helping the people in Phnom Vor and told Khat Mann that I was proud of his learning more English. With both men beaming appreciation, I asked if they would travel to Pailin with me to meet Khieu Samphan and Nuon Chea. I would pay all expenses, plus $10 and one "magic pill" a day. Dr. Noun nodded solemnly. Khat Mann surrendered to adolescent jubilations.

THE PHNOM VOR GANG

At the Marco Polo later that night, Davide placed another sticky black wafer of opium over a bowl of marijuana and made frequent rhythmic inhalations until he exhausted the coal. I had not previously connected this to the dark circles and bags under bloodshot eyes, red palms, and the rash that he was still scratching on his chest. Without blood tests and a complete physical exam, I suspected that Davide had liver failure or cancer.

As far as I could discern through Davide's haze, Chhouk Rin's immediate superior in Phnom Vor, Nuon Paet, received a life sentence and was in prison for killing the backpackers. Chhouk Rin would be in prison if he did not have to sell 16,000 hectares of his land in Phnom Vor to the corrupt tribunal judge. Chhouk Rin was currently at his home in Phnom Vor with his soldiers, surrounded by Hun Sen soldiers.

"Did I tell you about fucking Mann?" David said. "Mann got caught trying to sell land that did not belong to him. Chhouk Rin is furious. They have not talked for three months. Khat Mann will try and use you to get back with Chhouk Rin tomorrow. Getting around Hun Sen's soldiers won't be easy." When I asked why we had to meet

Chhouk Rin in Phnom Vor, Davide said that Chhouk Rin wanted to go to Pailin with me.

"By the way, a man from the US embassy came by asking what you are doing in Cambodia with the Khmer Rouge. He gave me his card." Davide produced a card from Joseph R. Fraley Jr., defense attaché, which meant that he was CIA.[81] I worried more about evading Ieng Sary's checkpoints and Chhouk Rin than any interest our CIA had in my morbid fascination with the Phnom Vor Gang.

The next morning driving the Defender into Phnom Vor, Davide was amused by my looking for absent Hun Sen soldiers. "Hun Sen soldiers are afraid of the Khmer Rouge. They only man their checkpoints between ten a.m. and two p.m." Davide stopped to take a young man carrying four fish on a wooden skewer to his stilted, one room hut with a thatched roof. When I asked Davide to inquire if the man had any direct experience with American bombing, Davide became irritated but spoke with the man in Khmer.

"This is a simple man," Davide said sarcastically. "He is a farmer with six children to feed. He does not remember the year but he remembers hiding in bomb craters while the bombs fell. There are not many people living in Phnom Vor so the bombs did not kill many people."

"I find you!" Khat Mann exclaimed in a well-choreographed entrance as we left the fisherman's hut. Davide did not appear surprised or annoyed as Khat Mann got in the back. No one spoke as we drove.

Chhouk Rin was sitting with five armed men at a table littered with beer cans outside his wife's restaurant where a dozen men with AK-47s watched the wide-open perimeter. Chhouk Rin was awaiting my arrival. His hardened face sprang to life when he saw me. "I think of you many times," Chhouk Rin said, offering a firm handshake.

"*Su serei* (Hello)," I said, flattered that Chhouk Rin had missed me. "*Hope bai bong*? (Have you eaten rice today, uncle?)"

"*Hope bai*," Chhouk Rin said and talked with Khat Mann like old friends with no hint of animosity. Chhouk Rin did not even mind my asking about his court case. Although the appeals court had sentenced him to life in prison, the Kampot tribunal judge promised that he would not go to prison if he got everyone in Phnom Vor to vote for Hun Sen's Cambodian People's Party (CPP) in all future elections.

Chhouk Rin's wife and two daughters brought a bucket of ice and another case of elephant beer. Out of respect they served Chhouk Rin first who, in turn, insisted that I drink with him. After the first ceremonial gulp and glasses were refilled, I lost track of how much beer I was drinking as we enjoyed piles of grilled squid, chicken, and fish on thin bamboo skewers wrapped in banana leaves. We ate Khmer Rouge style, like dogs or surgeons, tossing our bones on the ground.

Picking his teeth with a toothpick, Khat Mann said that Chhouk Rin wanted to write a book. I showed Chhouk Rin my journal and explained that if he wrote a little bit every day, he would have a book within a few months. Chhouk Rin nodded and asked what the first story should be. I did not have to think before asking about the number of times he had been wounded. Chhouk Rin enjoyed this question and took a long time, as though counting, before replying that he had been wounded more than thirty times.

Without asking, Khat Mann unbuckled Chhouk Rin's belt and yanked his pants down to reveal a lightning-bolt scar running from the inside of his left groin to his ankle, and a grotesque serrated scar on the inside of his right thigh. Chhouk Rin smoked a cigarette in his clean, white Speedo underwear while Khat Mann became a tour guide of his injuries. "Sorry to touch your head bong," pointing out scars of varying sizes on Chhouk Rin's scalp, neck, shoulders, and arms. Chhouk Rin did not seem to mind Khat Mann lifting his shirt to show multiple scars on his back and abdomen that were puny compared to those on his legs.

"Sometimes when I angry with him," Khat Mann said, digging his thumb into the stump of Chhouk Rin's left foot. "When I hungry, I take a bite." Khat Mann made a chopping gesture over Chhouk Rin's stump, then pretended to chew. Both men laughed like cannibals until Khat Mann insisted that I paint my hair black. Chhouk Rin painted his hair black. Khat Mann did not think he needed paint until I plucked a solitary gray hair from his temple.

"Must kill all," Khat Mann exclaimed before reporting that his wife grabbed his tiger last night but it did not stay strong. "What happen you?" she said, and told him to get more magic pills. Dr. Noun's wife also wanted more.

Chhouk Rin barked at Khat Mann in Khmer, and I did not need translation to know that I was taking him out to the disco tonight to celebrate our going to Pailin. Chhouk Rin, Dr. Noun, and Khat Mann had all been in Pailin fighting the Vietnamese in 1980 for eight years. Chhouk Rin still had many friends in Pailin.

Once again, our conversation descended to the lowest common social denominator when I gave each man three 100 mg Viagra pills. Noticing the absence of pain in my right knee, I inspected the Chang beer can and found 6.4 percent alcohol beneath the elephant in small print, twice as strong as the beer I was not used to drinking in the US. Inebriated and encircled by Chhouk Rin's bodyguards, I felt that I was in a pack of wolves.

That night Davide warned that Chhouk Rin wanting to go to Pailin with us was a trap. Chhouk Rin had to meet regularly with Hun Sen's secret police. Any information he gave them about my trip would raise his standing with the police. Chhouk Rin had already sold most of his land to pay $20,000 to the chief magistrate in the Kampot Province Tribunal. Chhouk Rin's commander, Sam Bith, and his gang had relocated to Pailin. They still hated Chhouk Rin for surrendering to the Cambodian Army. Under normal circumstances if Sam Bith's Gang saw us with Chhouk Rin, we would be held hostage. If Sam Bith was feeling magnanimous, we would get to choose how he killed us.

I had seen Sam Bith's file on Judge Mong Mony Chariya's desk.

Like Chhouk Rin, Sam Bith was convicted of murdering the backpackers and sentenced to life in prison. There would be many ifs traveling to Pailin to meet the architects of the Khmer Rouge Revolution with Chhouk Rin, even if he did not find out that I had met with the Supreme Court judge who sentenced him to life in prison. Sam Bith was also a candidate for a tribunal against the Khmer Rouge commanders for genocide. I remembered Judge Mong Mony Chariya saying the case against Sam Bith is still active. We just don't know his whereabouts.

After another bowl, Davide agreed to drive me to the mountains along the Thai border. There was no guarantee. Sometimes the road was impassable. Sometimes the rains turned roads into rivers and the riverbanks became roads. And there were bandits. It would be good to have Dr. Noun with us. Everyone loved Dr. Noun. Khat Mann would be our bodyguard. Penya would help with the car. I would pay $50 a day for the Defender, and $50 a day for Davide. In no way was I to pay Khat Mann more than $5 a day. And under no circumstances should Chhouk Rin come with us.

Chhouk Rin arrived unannounced at the Marco Polo with Dr. Noun, Khat Mann, and four armed men who kept eyes on the street, river, and all of us. Khat Mann said that I was taking Chhouk to the "disco" across the river. Noticing me noticing the pistols, Khat Mann said that Chhouk Rin was afraid of assassination. Once again, I was struck by the irony that Chhouk Rin needed bodyguards to protect himself from the Kampot townspeople twenty-seven years after the Khmer Rouge had "liberated" Cambodia.

The disco had one reflecting ball that did not work on the ceiling. Our bodyguards chose an empty table in the back with views of the large room's entrance and exit. Davide lifting a chair over the table for Chhouk Rin to sit accidentally slashed my forehead. I could feel the warm blood dripping down my nose and cheek, but there was no pain and I pretended not to notice, which amused Chhouk Rin. Davide handed me a wad of paper napkins that stopped the bleeding with direct pressure.

"Khat Mann gives everyone a nickname," Davide said. "Penya is Mr. Penguin, which is very funny because Penya looks like a penguin."

I was afraid to ask what my nickname was and Davide told me anyway, "Black Face." At first, I thought Black Face was a compliment. Cambodians considered themselves Black people in part due to their skin color, and their belief in ghosts and black magic. Black Face people were *barangs*. Listening to Davide, Khat Mann, Chhouk Rin, and Dr. Noun all talking in Khmer, punctuated by Mann-inspired fits of laughter while the sun sank into the Elephant Mountains across the Komchi River, I sensed Khat Mann lobbying for Chhouk Rin to accompany us to Pailin.

"You are the only foreigner Chhouk Rin has talked to," Davide said. "Drink. It is not polite for Chhouk Rin to leave empty beers on the table."

Chhouk Rin sat between Leakhena, a pretty, nineteen-year-old woman and Lena, a shy, sixteen-year-old with one eye that looked to the side. When a band with three women singers took the stage, everyone got up to dance the *romvong*, then sat down the second the music stopped. I counted getting up sixteen times to dance with hostesses then sitting down after each song. To my delight my sprained knee tolerated the *romvong's* small steps and fluid hand movements.

Drenched in sweat, I stepped onto the porch with one of Davide's joints to listen to the river's gentle gurgling and watch the lights reflecting across the smooth black surface from shanties on the opposite shore. Just as I was cooling down in a sea of endorphins, I heard a loud *tap, tap* on the window seconds before a fat man strolled onto the porch with his bodyguards. The Big Man's protuberant abdomen, fake Rolex watch, and fat fingers adorned with diamond rings suited his arrogant demeanor. I returned to our table where everyone was agitated except Chhouk Rin, who was incapable of showing any sign of weakness.

Davide whispered that the "Big Man" was the chief magistrate in Kampot Province who had accepted $20,000 from Chhouk Rin selling his land to avoid going to prison for killing the backpackers. Chhouk Rin knew that the magistrate would not do anything in a disco at night, especially with his armed bodyguards.

"This is a good time to ask Chhouk Rin to come with us to Pailin," Davide said with a straight face. "In 1979, when the Vietnamese Army invaded Cambodia, the Phnom Vor Gang went to Pailin to fight the Vietcong for eight years. That is where Dr. Noun operated on Chhouk Rin's leg in 1986. Many of the local people who gave him food would still be grateful for his service."

Raising a Tiger Beer, I officially asked if Chhouk Rin, Dr. Noun, Khat Mann, and Davide would travel to Pailin to try and meet Khieu Samphan and Nuon Chea. Because they were soldiers, I would pay everyone a daily ration of $10 a day plus expenses, on one condition. I paused to see how long it would take for Khat Mann to ask, "What mean condition?" to explain that their ration also included one magic pill a day "if" they promised to use a condom if they had sex. Chhouk Rin and Khat Man agreed. Dr. Noun beamed. I placed one Viagra into each outstretched palm like a demented priest.

As Chhouk Rin ordered more beer and hostesses, I knew that my desire to meet the Khmer Rouge "intelligentsia" might come at the price of selling my Calvinist soul. I also worried that fostering the Phnom Vor Gang's desire for the raging erections of their indiscriminate youth could lead to cheating on their wives, sexually transmitted diseases, infertility, and AIDS.

Davide said that it was better if Chhouk Rin traveled with us. Everyone knew that Chhouk Rin had trouble with foreigners. If Chhouk Rin were with us, there would be no problems. Once again, I failed to comprehend Davide's logic because there was none.

"I did not tell you before," Davide continued, "Sam Bith may still want to kill Khat Mann." In 1992, when the UN replaced the Vietnamese occupation, Khat Mann left the Khmer Rouge and worked with the French Foreign Legion. While Khat Mann was learning to speak French, Sam Bith heard that Khat Mann had deserted and gave the order to kill him. Two years later, when Khat Mann returned with a jeep that he had stolen from the French, Sam Bith did not say a word.

We worked as a team. Khat Mann examined the *kut loi* (check) to make sure they were not cheating me while Penya counted thirty-three empty Ankor bottles. The check came to $43. I had $42 and Penya chipped in $1. I was wondering where my small cash had gone as everyone but Davide got up and headed for the door.

Davide looked exhausted. I did not have to ask if he was all right before he said that he had been up for two weeks smoking opium. Being addicted to opium explained his appearance and volatile moods. I stifled anger. I was dependent on Davide to take me to Pailin. When we met two years ago, Davide admitted smoking on the weekends. With the stress of two children, renovating an old colonial house into the new Marco Polo, and trying to set up a sawmill in China to harvest teakwood he had illegally logged in Burma, Davide started to smoke opium regularly. For the past two months he was smoking ten bowls a day.

Davide tried but could not bullshit me. Besides having hepatitis C for twenty years, which was why he did not drink alcohol, Davide admitted that he had not had a medical checkup with blood tests and a chest X-ray in ten years. I made Davide laugh saying that being addicted to opium was better than having liver cancer. Davide waxed about an opium den in Phnom Penh. In an elegant room while lying on silk pillows, *apsaras* served him tea, gave massages, and prepared pipes of opium. At the end of his muse, I reminded Davide about his wife trying to kill him last year and suggested that he go to a Thai hospital and deal with his addiction before it killed him.

Instead of resisting, Davide agreed. He knew that he was not strong enough to drive to Pailin. His driver Po would take me. Po was trustworthy. His wife helped take care of his two children, Tito and Temujen. Davide sanctioned my traveling without him and warned that Chhouk Rin was a real killer. If he gave the order to kill me, Khat Mann would do it without thinking. An enormous weight avalanched from Davide's shoulders onto mine as I paid $350 for one week with the Defender. I did not have enough cash so Davide took my traveler's checks, for an additional $35, assuring me that he did not charge more than the bank.

TRAVELS TO PAILIN

Pailin was a Khmer Rouge stronghold on Cambodia's western border with Thailand throughout their communist revolution from 1975 to 1979, a decade of Vietnamese occupation in the eighties, and UN control in the nineties. In addition to military and financial support from China, the Khmer Rouge financed their war selling precious gems and timber across the porous border with Thailand.[82]

Ieng Sary, the Khmer Rouge foreign minister, profited from this illicit trade until 1996 when he surrendered to the Cambodian government. In exchange for defecting from the Khmer Rouge with 3,000 soldiers, he got to keep control of the gems and timber. Ieng Sary's surrender allowed the Cambodian government to move thousands of troops to Pailin, forcing a split in the Khmer Rouge hardliners and Pol Pot who moved to Anlong Veng.

Chhouk Rin, Dr. Noun, and Khat Mann arrived as planned at the Marco Polo at 6 a.m. When Khat Mann said that it was customary to bring dried shrimp, which were hard to get and considered a delicacy, when visiting "Big Men" in the mountains, we stopped at the Kampot market. Davide ridiculed my buying two kilos of dried shrimp, then drove without talking from Kampot to Phnom Penh's

Ponchetong International Airport in two hours. I wished him luck on his "urgent business" in China and hoped that he would get professional help withdrawing from opium instead of splurging on the money I had given him.

Stepping out of the Defender, Davide admonished me to be careful. If I had to piss, do it in the middle of the road. Otherwise, I could step on a land mine. With that, Davide walked into the airport with no luggage, and I was at the mercy of the Phnom Vor Gang.

Po navigated the Defender with the skill of an Olympic skier. At six feet tall Po towered over most Cambodians. He was pleasant, spoke no English, and passed everyone on the road, including ox-drawn carts dwarfed by mounds of hay and bicycles overloaded with poles of ducks hanging upside down. Slamming into potholes and eroded sections of the dirt track sent daggers of pain through my right knee. But unlike Sokha's Toyota, the Defender absorbed most disruptions in the road with ease. The Defender seemed invincible, until we had to circumnavigate eroded stretches of the road on terrain bristling with land mines.

Leaving the Tonlé Sap River Valley, Khat Mann pointed to a distant rice paddy where he and Chhouk Rin were lying down in the water as five Vietcong soldiers walked toward them. Three times Khat Mann wanted to shoot. Three times Chhouk Rin held his AK-47 down. Khat Mann surprised me by saying that he was scared and did not want to die. Chhouk Rin grinned as Khat Mann described the Vietcong soldiers almost stepping on them before Chhouk Rin stood up.

"And kill all," Khat Mann exclaimed. "Before when I fighting with Chhouk Rin, we walk two months from Phnom Vor to Pailin. Now I like to go by car." Khat Mann was the happiest I had seen him, sitting in the back seat next to Chhouk Rin, and asked if the US Army could give him a jeep. He was disappointed when I said I had no connection to the US Army, but his mood remained elevated all afternoon pointing out copses of trees and hillocks where he and

Chhouk Rin had battled the Vietcong. Po did not stop for gas or roadblocks or drunken policemen in hammocks under makeshift grass huts or washed out sections of the road where I handed 500 riels to children's eager, outstretched hands.

A flat tire at dusk made me worry that we might not make it to a town by dark. Khat Mann worried about bandits and hurried to change a flat tire. Seeing Khat Mann nervous made me feel insecure sitting by the side of the road writing in my journal. I questioned thinking that I was safer not carrying a weapon that could accidentally shoot me or be confiscated and used against me. Khat Mann and Chhouk Rin had pistols, AK-47s, and hand grenades. A large bowie knife bounced on the dash in front of the passenger seat. I did not need Chhouk Rin staring at me to remind me that writing was a crime during Angkor's rule, punishable by death, and that the pen could be mightier than an AK-47.

Wiping grease from his hands, Khat Mann surprised me. Chhouk Rin wanted me to write his story. Chhouk Rin was forty-eight years old. He looked ten years older. Chhouk Rin grew up in Phnom Vor and liked to go fishing before he joined the Khmer Rouge in 1971 to help Pol Pot free Cambodia from "foreign devils." When I asked how many times he had been wounded, Chhouk Rin smiled and pondered the question before boasting that he had been wounded more than a hundred times. I smiled recalling his first assessment that he had been wounded thirty times.

Chhouk Rin enjoyed talking about his halcyon days fighting the Vietnamese. When the Vietnamese evicted the Khmer Rouge from Cambodia in 1979 and established a puppet government, the Khmer Rouge were heroes to their people fighting Vietnamese occupation. After killing all the Vietcong in one village, Chhouk Rin went to the commander's hut to gather intelligence. When he stepped near the bed, a click was the last sound he heard on two feet. Khat Mann laughed describing how the front of Chhouk Rin's left foot was gone. It was hard to stop the bleeding and Chhouk Rin lost a lot of blood.

Khat Mann radioed to Pailin from the copse of bamboo where their gang of sixty Khmer Rouge soldiers were surrounded by 200 Vietcong. When Dr. Noun arrived two days later, Chhouk Rin's leg had swollen so much he could not walk. Dr. Noun made a cross of bamboo and tied Chhouk Rin down with his arms out to the sides in mock crucifixion. Khat Mann rode a bicycle all night to generate electricity for a small bulb to illuminate the makeshift operating theater. When Khat Mann's legs gave out, Dr. Noun made him pedal with his hands.

Dr. Noun had no problem amputating what remained of Chhouk Rin's left foot. Chhouk Rin's left leg was badly damaged. To replace torn segments of Chhouk Rin's left femoral artery, Dr. Noun harvested segments of the saphenous vein on his right leg. One nurse helped with sewing. In a modern hospital this would not be easy. In the Cambodian jungle it was monumental.

When the light went out, Khat Mann substituted a small bulb from his radio. The moment the light went on, two men standing guard were shot: one in the heart, another in the chest. Both died. Dr. Noun operated until sunrise when Chhouk Rin announced that he was going to die and demanded a pistol to fight the Vietcong while his gang escaped.

Learning that the entire operation had been done under local anesthesia, I was astounded by Chhouk Rin's tenacity. Dr. Noun gave injections of lidocaine only when Chhouk Rin screamed loud enough to give away their position. When Chhouk Rin's pulse became high from losing too much blood, Dr. Noun gave intravenous fluids. The grotesque scars on the inside of Chhouk Rin's legs bore witness to his will to live. He was a tough motherfucker.

When the gang came back the next day, they were surprised to find Chhouk Rin still alive and carried him away on the bamboo cross. For six months Chhouk Rin could not walk. Dr. Noun treated wound infections with *kramas* soaked in honey. I had heard of field surgeons in World War II using honey on bandages. Because honey is hygroscopic, pulling water away from anything, even glass, it deprives bacteria of the moisture needed to survive.

Khat Mann joked that the jungle had a lot of honey before delivering another punch line. The first day Chhouk Rin could walk, a Vietcong shot him in the ankle. Khat Mann and Chhouk Rin laughed like inebriated adolescents. Even Dr. Noun smiled. Penya sat in the back well of the car. He never laughed with the Khmer Rouge, lest it be mistaken for laughing at them.

Po drove without stopping for nine hours until we arrived in Kampong Chhnang well after dark. I got single rooms for everyone for $4 each at a small hotel guarded by petite Vietnamese women armed with high heels, short skirts, and cell phones. A painful right knee made me limp like an old man to a riverside restaurant where teenage waitresses shared our food and refilled our glasses after each sip of Tiger Beer. When Chhouk Rin ordered appetizers of giant prawns, the most expensive items on the menu, I reminded myself not to be "Cheap Charlie," especially as everyone's food, gas, lodging, and expenses was less than $100 a day.

Kampong Chhnang was a frontier town. After dinner Khat Mann insisted that we hunt for *chirans*. The Phnom Vor Gang smiled in broad agreement. They were on full scholarship with single rooms, united in their desire to check out the nightlife. Drinking to excess and chasing teenage prostitutes with the Phnom Vor Gang was enough to make my hair turn whiter. After giving everyone their daily ration, it was easy to escape.

At six in the morning, Po and I were the first to arrive at the restaurant for bowls of clear beef noodle soup with chilies, French bread, and strong Khmer coffee in a glass with half an inch of sweetened condensed milk on the bottom. I loved this fusion of traditional Khmer and French breakfasts and hoped there were no microbial repercussions. Khat Mann appeared clean-shaven demanding $20 for beers that Chhouk Rin had already paid for.

I did not have to ask about Khat Mann's escapades. He was incapable of not telling me about the two *chirans* that came back to their rooms. Once again Chhouk Rin could not get an erection, and Khat Mann had sex with both women. This time I laughed because Khat Mann and Chhouk Rin were laughing. Reiterating that drinking too much alcohol could negate the magic pill's effect, Khat Mann reiterated that the magic pill might not be possible for Chhouk Rin.

Po raised the hood when the Defender did not start. The battery had broken its restraints many kilometers ago spilling acid that left the alternator and fan belt in a tangled meltdown. After pushing the Defender to slip the clutch, Po and the gang went in search of a garage. Violent diarrhea restricted me to painful squats over a porcelain hole ruing the breakfast soup that gave me the Kampong Chhnang Two-Step.

Khat Mann returned two hours later asking who would pay $15 to fix the alternator. I gave Khat Mann $20 and asked him to get a receipt, imagining a steady stream of forged receipts in his handwriting. Not failing to disappoint, Khat Mann returned without a receipt or any change, but he had a new haircut. I was content to be tolerating tea and plain toast, told Khat Mann that he looked handsome, and was glad that he was easily flattered.

"If we talk to Khieu Samphan, you must pay extra money. If I caught, I maybe kill or go to prison."

"If we talk to Khieu Samphan, I will give you a $50 bonus when we get back to Phnom Penh."

"And $50 for Nuon Chea!"

"Only if we talk with him," I said. The prospect of an additional $50 for Khat Mann was a morale booster. The alternator had not been fixed. We still had to push-start the Defender, but my bowels were improving.

We made it to Battambang in three long hours while Khat Mann relived the nights' events. All conversation stopped when we passed the Battambang Tribunal, a traditional Cambodian building with carved wooden cobras poised to strike from the four corners of the roof. Khat Mann explained that the Kampot Tribunal was small compared to the one in Battambang, but they took a lot of money. This was an inside joke that Chhouk Rin had to sell a lot of his land to the Kampot Tribunal chief to stay out of prison.

Clouds of red dust and oppressive heat accompanied views of distant lone coconut palms standing sentinel over fallow paddies. It was too hot to keep the windows up and too dusty to keep the windows down. As we took turns opening and closing the windows, all our clothes and teeth turned the same shade of Khmer Rouge.

Climbing into the Cardamom Mountains, thick smoke from blistering infernos and crackling hillsides on both sides of the road choked our pace to a crawl. The once dense forests and stands of virgin timber were succumbing to settlers clearing land and burning the jungle to plant bananas and corn at the beginning of the wet season. Men, women, and children missing arms and legs appeared through the smoke in this surreal hell realm, a fitting refuge for the living architects of the Khmer Rouge Revolution who were responsible for two million deaths.

Pailin was a small mining town on the Thai border, a haven for smuggling and one of the last areas in Cambodia still controlled by Khmer Rouge soldiers. Unlike Rome that was also surrounded by seven hills, Pailin's were burning. Some of the blazes climbed a hundred feet up giant stands of bamboo and the trunks of enormous hardwoods. With the deforestation of large tracts of land, the winds would blow hotter and carry less rain. And when the rains came, they would erode the steep hillsides, clog the streams with silt, and kill the fish, making Pailin even more uninhabitable.

THE GHOST PARTY

"Maybe problem," Khat Mann said as we passed a man who lifted his head from a hammock. "That Sam Bith, our commander. After backpacker problem, Sam Bith order me to clear land on his coconut plantation. After one month I run away. Sam Bith may still want to kill me."

Khat Mann looked sheepish. There was something else. He could not conceal emotion if his life depended on it. "Is that all?" I asked and waited for him to confess. After Sam Bith defected to the government in 1996, Ta Mok gave his nephew, Dr. Noun, $10,000 for the Phnom Vor Gang to kill Sam Bith. Dr. Noun took the money and used it to build his house.

The Rambo knife on the dash suddenly seemed diminutive as I imagined Sam Bith's men having incentive to kill Chhouk Rin, Khat Mann, the good Dr. Noun and me. My mind was trapped in paranoid reruns unable to get Chhouk Rin's gun before he shot me. Po stopped at a thatched hut where a Khmer woman with ebony skin and short black hair sold cold drinks from a cooler. When Khat Mann asked if she knew where Khieu Samphan lived, the woman recognized Chhouk Rin, raised folded palms in respect, and offered him a Red Bull.

Khat Mann explained that this woman was a Khmer Rouge soldier. She was "black" from three decades of guerrilla warfare, including eight years fighting alongside Chhouk Rin against the Vietnamese around Pailin. When Chhouk Rin asked what the local politics were like now, she said the Khmer Rouge had a new party, the *Kana Paat Kmmoi*, the "Party of Dead Body."

"We say the Ghost Party," Khat Mann said, "because everyone is dead." Chhouk Rin, Khat Mann, and the woman laughed like ghosts. We left with no plans to meet again but we had directions to Khieu Sampan's house.

KHIEU SAMPHAN

Khieu Samphan was born around July 27, 1931, in Svay Rieng Province. The privileged son of a judge with Khmer and Chinese ancestry, he attended the Lycée Sisowath in Phnom Penh. After winning a government scholarship to study in France, Khieu Samphan was radicalized in Paris in the 1950s along with a handful of other Cambodian students who would later dominate the Khmer Rouge, including Pol Pot and his first wife, Khieu Ponnary, and her younger sister, Khieu Thirith, who married Ieng Sary.[83]

Khieu Samphan joined the Communist Party in France to confront their colonial rulers when Stalin was at the height of his power and personality. Chinese Communism was making great strides in 1949, consolidating power in mainland China and invading Tibet, then stopping the US in Korea in 1953. For the young Cambodian students and millions of French people, communism was the wave of the future.

Khieu Samphan was a natural organizer. He helped found the Khmer Student's Association, which the French authorities banned in 1956, followed by the Khmer Student's Union. Both organizations laid the foundation for Khmer Rouge Communism. Unlike Pol Pot who failed his exams, Khieu Samphan successfully defended his doctoral thesis, "Cambodia's Economy and Industrial Development," in 1959, the same year Chairman Mao's Communists wrested control of Tibet and the Dalai Lama fled into exile in India.

Returning to Cambodia to teach at the University, Khieu Samphan founded *L'Observateur*, a French language magazine critical of the Cambodian government headed by Prince Norodom Sihanouk. A year later *L'Observateur* was closed, and Khieu Samphan was arrested and forced to undress in public. Sihanouk nevertheless invited Khieu Samphan to be a deputy in the Sangkum, the Cambodian government's single party. As the undersecretary of state for economics, Khieu Samphan tried to implement his leftist policies to nationalize agricultural production.[84]

His brother summarized Khieu Samphan's communist ideology while serving in Sihanouk's government. "One day a Sino-Khmer merchant came to our house with a package for him. It was full of money. Later at dinner, he said that 'if you take money from the capitalists, you have to work for them. Then you're a traitor to the people because the capitalists are the enemies of the people.' After that businessmen would complain, 'No matter how we approach your brother, we get nowhere. He's hopeless. He'll never get along in this government.'"[85]

In 1963 with Sihanouk blaming Khieu Samphan for the rising prices of consumer goods, he gained the reputation of a hero fighting against the corrupt Cambodian government. In 1967 the right wing of the Cambodian government led by Lon Nol used the Samlaut Uprising of rural peasants in Battambang Province to violently suppress the leftists. When Khieu Samphan and two other men were accused of being communist agents and fomenting unrest, they fled into the countryside to join Pol Pot.

"There are those who want me to kill these three men," the Prince said. "But I won't do it. I'll let them kill themselves."[86]

Although Khieu Samphan had no military experience, he was commander in chief of Pol Pot's Khmer Liberation Armed Forces while they rose to power and overthrew the American-backed Lon Nol government on April 17, 1975. During the Khmer Rouge reign from 1975 to 1979, Khieu Samphan was the prime minister of Democratic Kampuchea. After the Vietnamese invasion, Khieu Samphan was the head of the Cambodian government in exile that maintained a seat at the UN. Khieu Samphan remained at the helm of Khmer Rouge politics throughout a coalition government with Sihanouk in 1982, succeeded Pol Pot as the leader of the Khmer Rouge in 1985, and represented the Khmer Rouge at the 1991 Paris Peace Accords.

In 1997, during an internal power struggle, Khieu Samphan fled with Pol Pot into the jungle when Ta Mok tried to kill them. At Khieu Samphan's last public appearance in December 1998, when he and Nuon Chea defected from the Khmer Rouge and were brought to Phnom to formally surrender, Khieu Samphan said that Cambodians should "let bygones be bygones."

The historian Ben Kiernan attributed Khieu Samphan's inability to take responsibility for the atrocities during the Khmer Rouge genocide to the fundamental "moral cowardice" of a man mesmerized by power but lacking any nerve.[87] But Khieu Samphan had a recent letter in the Cambodia Daily where he admitted that some mistakes had been made during the Khmer Rouge time. Khieu Samphan had not been specific, but it was the first time a Khmer Rouge leader had admitted any wrongdoing. I wanted to see for myself.

Single rooms at the Haeng Maes were $11 each and did not require ID or money up front. Everyone raced to clean up before meeting the Big Man. The thin wafer of soap proved ample when I could get no more than a trickle of water out of the handheld showerhead. I did my best to wash and was surprised by how much red dirt rinsed into the tub with so little water. Drying my hair and using a different part of the towel for each arm, each leg, and my torso turned the once-white towel into tangerine shades of a nuclear sunset.

I found Khat Mann in his bathroom staring at the hose with a nozzle connected to the toilet. When I showed him how water came out when he squeezed the handle and what it was for, he yelled, "I must show Per Noun." As if on cue hearing Khat Mann's outburst, Dr. Noun appeared in the doorway dressed in clean pants and a button-down shirt. His room did not have any plumbing problems. When he stepped within range, Khat Mann squirted him with water amid a tsunami of Mann-isms.

Dr. Noun's clothes dried in the heat as we drove to a small two-story house in the late afternoon bearing kilos of dried shrimp and fruits. When we knocked on the front door, Khieu Samphan's young wife said that he was not home. Khieu Samphan was still a good Communist and worked every morning in the fields. Accepting our gifts from the sea, she said we could return after dark, which we did. Po and Penya stayed in the Defender. Dr. Noun, Chhouk Rin, Khat Mann, and I took our shoes off at the entrance. Khieu Samphan's wife seated Dr. Noun and me in comfortable leather chairs around a glass table and poured tall glasses of ice water. Khat Mann and Chhouk Rin stood at attention with their backs to the wall.

We waited in near darkness as Khieu Samphan slowly descended the bamboo ladder from his loft. He appeared to be in excellent health for a seventy-year-old man, happily married to a woman half his age. A white crew cut framed his pudgy face. Khieu Samphan gave a warm welcome to Dr. Noun. He did not acknowledge Khat Mann or Chhouk Rin who looked awkward with their heads bowed and palms folded. Khieu Samphan was an amicable host and we exchanged pleasantries in French. When Khieu Samphan asked where I had learned *la belle langue*, I told him that my mother was born and married in Paris. I had studied for a semester in college at the L'Universite de Technologie in Bourges and worked at a small bookstore on the Left Bank, Shakespeare and Company.

"*Je le connais,*" Khieu Samphan said.

Khieu Samphan loved his time in Paris. The French people treated him well. He enjoyed French cuisine and walking the streets of the

Latin Quarter at night. Khieu Samphan's eyes sparkled recalling an affair with an Italian dancer. Then his eyelids narrowed when he asked how I met "these men." I said that I ran into Khat Mann by chance and Khieu Samphan said it was no accident. He did not trust Hun Sen. I mentioned being a physician and wanting to work with Dr. Noun, and Khieu Samphan replied that everyone in Pailin was grateful to Dr. Noun for his service to the Khmer people.

Chhouk Rin and Khat Mann remained pinned to the wall while Dr. Noun, Khieu Samphan, and I raised glasses of water to toast the cooperation between the US and Cambodia. When Khieu Samphan noticed my pretending to sip the water, he assured me that it was "boiled" and was delighted when I drank.

"Merci. Normalment, c'est necessaire je guardais mon stomach."

Khieu Samphan approved of my working with Dr. Noun and asked how Cambodians had treated me. When I replied that the Khmer people were gracious and hospitable, Khieu Samphan leaned closer to whisper in English, "You are not afraid of these men?"

"Not at all," I lied.

"I am sorry about what happened with the backpackers," Khieu Samphan said loud enough for Chhouk Rin and Khat Mann to hear. "You must understand we are at war. The American CIA and Lon Nol government attacked the Khmer people. After the Khmer Rouge liberated Cambodia, we are still fighting."

Inquiring about the US bombing of Cambodia, Khieu Samphan replied that the American bombing of Cambodia was wrong. He blamed President Nixon for directing American planes to start bombing Cambodia in the beginning of 1969. Many times the pilots did not see the Khmer Rouge because the soldiers were hiding in the jungle, and the pilots dropped their bombs on villages. Many innocent people and animals died.

"For this," Khieu Samphan said, "the Khmer people began to hate America. American bombing made people want to help the Khmer Rouge free Cambodia from foreign domination."

"People in the US only know about the Khmer Rouge killing fields. They don't—."

Khieu Samphan's tone was harsh and unforgiving. "On April 17, 1975, the Khmer Rouge army liberated Cambodia people from foreign devils! Under the Democratic Republic of Kampuchea only a few corrupt government officials who supported Lon Nol died."

The tension was palpable. I had broached a forbidden subject, mentioning the Khmer Rouge time. Khieu Samphan rose diplomatically and thanked me for coming. He said that he got up early and had to work on his memoir.[88] When I asked if he had a publisher, Khieu Samphan escorted me to the door and asked for my card.

Smoke obliterated the crescent moon as we walked to the Defender. Khieu Samphan looked like a nice old man and waved as we drove off without lights to avoid detection. Dr. Noun was elated. Chhouk Rin and Khat Mann did not speak. When we were out of earshot, Khat Mann said Khieu Samphan wanted my card to see if I worked for the CIA. Po and I pressed our heads to the windshield looking for potholes.

Although Khieu Samphan apologized for the backpackers' murders and confirmed that the hatred of US bombing had helped the Khmer Rouge recruit soldiers to overthrow foreign devils, he refused to assess the Khmer Rouge Revolution. Khieu Samphan was shrewd. He also associated Chhouk Rin and Khat Mann with Hun Sen, which made them traitors.

Chhouk Rin had not spoken with Khieu Samphan, but the meeting buoyed his spirits. Perhaps traveling with an American that he had not held hostage or killed bolstered his image. Even if he couldn't get an erection, Chhouk Rin had a pair of steel cojones.

SECOND WIFE

The Mountain Top restaurant outside Pailin had views of three fires burning in the distance, but the smoke cleared the mosquitoes. Chhouk Rin pushed a sixteen-year-old girl wearing a USA T-shirt and jeans toward me. Pancake makeup did not make Srey look any older or more attractive. Chhouk Rin said that she was a virgin and that I could take her. The idea of anyone having sex with this underage prostitute was more than depressing; it was a crime. Chhouk Rin was a ruthless, sexual predator.

Khat Mann said that Srey was Chhouk Rin's niece, and that Chhouk Rin had given her to me. When Chhouk Rin ordered Srey to sit down next to me, she leaned toward me for an instant then hit my arm. As the pain faded, compassion replaced anger for Srey having sex forced on her. Khat Mann grabbed another waitress's arm hard enough to elicit a wince. Slapping his face only encouraged Khat Mann to grab again. The plight of these women scared me. So did wanting to hit Srey.

"You know the first time I see pussy I fifteen years old," Khat Mann said. "I soldier fighting near border Vietnam. One day in summer, when not much rain and water low, I see three girls running across a stream. One girl lose her *krama* and I see her pussy. Small, small pussy! Very good!"

"When is the first time you *hope muon chiran*?"

"The first time I fuck I twenty-nine years old," Khat Mann said with a straight face. "Angkor not allow Khmer Rouge soldier to fuck."

Khat Mann's statement was in direct contradiction to accounts of women brutally raped and killed by Khmer Rouge soldiers. Loung Ung's *First They Killed My Father: A Daughter in Cambodia Remembers* details how girls were abducted at night.[89] Some were never seen again. Others returned beaten, disheveled, unable to look their family in the eyes, forever changed and at high risk of suicide. Sometimes soldiers returned with the girl and said they were married. It was the daughter's duty to have a child for Angkor, otherwise she was worthless and dispensable.

I had been so engrossed wallowing in the lowest common social denominator that I had not noticed Chhouk Rin talking to a beautiful woman with a shy boy who drank soda through rotten teeth that had never seen a toothbrush. The woman appeared to be in her late twenties. She had strong arms and steel eyes. Although Chhouk Rin had consumed twenty beers, he was on his best behavior, holding her hand, saying sweet words.

"Do you have ten dollars to give me secretly?" Khat Mann whispered. "This is Chhouk Rin's wife and son from when he fighting Vietnam in Pailin. Eight years ago, Sam Bith order Chhouk Rin to fight Vietnam in Phnom Vor. Chhouk Rin has not seen his wife for seven years. This is the first time he saw his son."

On my way to the bathroom, I slipped $20 into Chhouk Rin's back pocket. For once I felt sorry for Chhouk Rin. He was obviously attracted to his Pailin wife. He was also a soldier who followed orders and left his young wife and child he would never know to continue fighting the Vietnamese occupation. I paid the bill and relocated the gang to the Haeng Maes Disco. Besides killing and carnal pleasure, what happiness could there be for Chhouk Rin who was in his own words already a ghost?

NUON CHEA

Unlike Khieu Samphan who lived without bodyguards in the middle of town, meeting Nuon Chea had to be planned. In December 1998, after Pol Pot's death in April, Nuon Chea and Khieu Samphan sent a letter to Cambodia's prime minister offering to stop fighting in exchange for living with their families in Pailin. According to Davide, Nuon Chea lived on his own mountain with 10,000 Khmer Rouge soldiers who were surrounded by the Cambodian Army.

Nuon Chea was born Lao Ben Kon in Battambang on July 7, 1926. In 1941 during World War II, Battambang was incorporated into Thailand and Nuon Chea automatically became a Thai citizen. He was sixteen years old when he moved to Bangkok in 1942 and lived under the care of three monks from Battambang at the Wat Benjamabopit.[90] Using the Thai name Runglert Laodi, Nuon Chea completed the government's middle school at the wat, followed by two years of preparatory school at Thammasat University. Nuon Chea did well in his studies. He earned an academic scholarship when he enrolled in law school at Thammasat in 1946 and worked for three years as a low-level official in the Thai Ministry of Finance.

In 1947 Nuon Chea joined the leftist Thai Youth Organization and worked as a clerk at the Ministry of Foreign Affairs.[91]

The well-respected scholar of modern Cambodian history David Chandler notes that Nuon Chea was influenced by his cousin, Sieu Heng, who had also spent part of the war in Bangkok and joined the Indochinese Communist Party in Battambang in 1945.[92] During an extensive interview by Eiji Murashima with Nuon Chea in Thai, Nuon Chea said that he saw no future in numbers and wanted to be a diplomat.[93] While working at the Ministry of Finance he took and passed an exam to work at the Thai Foreign Ministry where he was placed in the Indochina office in charge of affairs with Burma and French Indochina.

When the Vietnamese branch of the Indochina Communist Party became aware of the Khmer who had joined the Thai Communist Party in 1950, they asked if he wanted to join in the struggle against French colonialism. In consultations with senior Vietnamese and Thai Communist officials in 1950, Nuon Chea transferred his membership to the Communist Party of Indochina.

Nuon Chea left Thailand without finishing his law degree and moved to Samlaut and Pailin in western Cambodia where he oversaw anti-French propaganda and newspaper publication. After Stalin's death on March 5, 1953, Nuon Chea traveled overland with the help of Thai and Lao Communist guides and spent two years being trained in Vietnam. He was in Vietnam with ten other Khmer Communists from March to May 1954 during the Battle of Diem Bien Phu. While the Vietnamese defeated the French, Nuon Chea was meeting the heads of the Lao Communist Party.

Nuon Chea returned to Cambodia in 1955 and met Pol Pot for the first time. Ben Kiernan, a Western scholar and authority on Cambodian Communism, describes Nuon Chea becoming the deputy secretary of the Communist Party of Kampuchea, better known as "Brother Number Two," in 1960.[94] As the leader of Democratic Kampuchea's People's Assembly, Nuon Chea traveled to China, Vietnam, and North Korea. Despite their differences, Nuon Chea felt that as a Communist, Pol Pot was a moral man who did not steal or drink.[95] Nuon Chea also respected Pol Pot for being educated in Paris, like Zhou Enlai.

When the Khmer Rouge Communists took over Phnom Penh on April 17, 1975, Pol Pot renamed Cambodia Democratic Kampuchea. As chairman of the People's Assembly, Nuon Chea was the architect of the regime's most radical policies and authorized the purges, detention, torture, and execution of Khmer Rouge enemies. After the Vietnamese invasion in 1979, Nuon Chea retreated with Pol Pot to the Khmer Rouge strongholds along the Thai border and continued to fight Vietnamese occupation.

Before going out in search of contacts to Nuon Chea, Khat Mann demanded $30 to cover the bill from the previous night. After peacefully liberating thirty beers, Chhouk Rin showed no sign of hangover when we had breakfast while Po and Penya found a mechanic to look at the clutch. Chhouk Rin was amused by my fishing with chopsticks in a bowl of Khmer noodle soup. Capturing a small ball of meat, I made noises to inquire if this came from a pig or a cow.

"In tree," Chhouk Rin said.

"Monkey?"

"Small-small."

Chhouk Rin drew an elongated rodent that I failed to recognize on his paper napkin until our young, bright-eyed waitress bringing French bread with butter and jam and Khmer coffee said, "Squirrel." The delicious balls of mystery meat were oval, tender, and spiced with chilies. I left it to another time to find out if these Pailin oysters were squirrel testicles. Within minutes of talking to our waitress, Chhouk Rin learned that Sri La was eighteen years old, worked eight hours every day at the Haeng Maes Restaurant and studied English for two hours at night. Sri La was a good girl, a "virgin." The only way to have sex with her was to get married.

When the brake could not be fixed, Po had a bottle of fluid to pour into a well when the clutch lost its resistance. Still afflicted with intestinal cramps and pain, I was happy to spend the day away from the Phnom Vor Gang and talk with Sri La at the restaurant. When the sun began to set, Sri La wrote, "*Ohn nuk Bong* (Little sister likes older uncle)" on my napkin. "When you go away, you can say, 'Bong nuk Ohn.' It means, 'You miss me.'"

Khat Mann burst into the dining room. We had to leave now if I wanted to see Nuon Chea. I had never seen Khat Mann so nervous, which made me nervous. With less than half an hour of daylight and twenty-five kilometers on an unpaved circuitous road to the top of Nuon Chea's mountain, it was impossible to arrive before dark. Driving after dark was too dangerous. I tried to get specifics: who he had talked to and exactly what was said. Khat Mann kept insisting that we leave immediately.

"I afraid I shit my pants," Khat Mann said. "Maybe they kill me or put me in prison. You are my commanding officer. If you want to go, I will go with you. But we must go now!"

Acid burning in my stomach made me acutely aware that I was a foreign devil in a Khmer Rouge lair. I pulled out a photograph of Zachary with his beautiful eyes and a disarming smile, and Kaley with her arm around her brother, part love, part chokehold. Kaley was four years old, three years Zachary's junior, but already as tall and well on her way to becoming the older-younger sister. Khat Mann looked relieved when I said it was too late to meet the Big Man. We would try again tomorrow.

The next morning a very excited Khat Mann screeched up on a moto before I finished my second coffee. He had found an alternate road to Nuon Chea's compound on the opposite side of the mountain, within view of the governor's house. For small money Khat Mann made it to the last checkpoint in sight of Nuon Chea's house and talked to Nuon Chea's wife. He said he was a Khmer Rouge soldier who met Nuon Chea in 1983 and 1985. He said he wanted to see Nuon Chea and she said no. I tried to not show any disappointment that might frustrate Khat Mann's efforts.

"Then I say I am soldier with the Phnom Vor Gang who fight in Pailin against the Vietnamese for nine years. I say that I am with American doctor who is friend Khmer Rouge. I say you have some dried shrimp and rice to give Nuon Chea."

Chhouk Rin became more agitated with each kilometer as the Defender forded two streams and crossed a rickety suspension bridge. Passing an unmanned checkpoint, I thought Chhouk Rin would jump out of the car. I had never seen Chhouk Rin anxious and attributed this to a healthy respect for Hun Sen's soldiers.

"Hun Sen soldiers are like old men," Khat Mann said. "They sleep in the middle of the day to get away from the heat." This was one of the funniest things I had heard Khat Mann say, but no one laughed. When Chhouk Rin got out at Nuon Paet's house, his commander in Phnom Vor who was serving the fourth year of a life sentence for killing the three Western backpackers,[96] I realized that Chhouk Rin was not afraid of Hun Sen. He was afraid Nuon Chea would kill him for being the first Khmer Rouge officer to surrender to the Cambodian army.

The scorched hills yielded to camps of people clearing land mines, planting corn, and making charcoal from large, smoldering tree trunks. I could feel eyes watching us from the jungle as we followed a dirt track past an antiaircraft gun and under the same raised metal pole outside the Special Forces training camp.

Khat Mann whispered to lock the doors when we parked in front of a simple wooden house on stilts flanked by bananas and bamboo. He did not want our car searched. He also told me to walk exactly where he walked, and not ask about Pol Pot time. When Mrs. Chea came out of the house to greet us, Dr. Noun and Khat Mann bowed their heads with folded palms. I did the same even though I was much older. After accepting my offering of rice, fruit, and dried fish, we followed her single file like ducks into her house.

Nuon Chea was a smiling seventy-six-year-old man who, like Khieu Samphan, had a round face framed by a white crew cut. Both men seemed pleasant on the surface. Before taking their shoes off at the base of the stairs, Khat Mann and Dr. Noun gave exaggerated bows. Nuon Chea greeted me with a handshake and seated me at a table across from a monk in saffron robes. Both the monk and a Buddhist altar for the Chinese New Year appeared to have been prepared for my arrival.

Nuon Chea welcomed me into his home where he lived with his wife, four children, and their families. They raised corn and sesame seeds on land rented from Ieng Sary's son, who was a Big Man in Pailin. Ieng Sary was also the deputy prime minister and foreign minister during Democratic Kampuchea.

When Nuon Chea saw me looking at the Buddhist alter, he said that he prayed to the Buddha, like his parents. His mother's grandmother and wife were both of Chinese descent. They had four children and ten grandchildren. Nuon Chea did not speak Chinese but he was fluent in Khmer, French, Thai, and Vietnamese. Khat Mann explained that I was an American doctor who had been working with Dr. Noun in Phnom Vor. Nuon Chea beamed at the beneficent Dr. Noun.

"*Combien de temps vous avez visiter Cambodge* (How many times have you been to Cambodia)?"

"*C'est mon troisieme fois* (This is my third time)."

Nuon Chea smiled lambs' eyes when he talked about the biggest problems facing Cambodia today. With Khat Mann translating, Nuon Chea said that Cambodia needed to solve the problems of poverty, the education crisis, and major diseases. If Cambodia could solve these problems, they could start building democracy in Cambodia. But the development process would be "little by little."

Nuon Chea said that Angkor Wat was not built in one year, which made everyone except me laugh. Nuon Chea wanted me to know that Americans are good people. Cambodians are good people. No one wanted to fight anymore. No one was looking for revenge.

"*Glo-bal-iz-a-tion*," Nuon Chea said, accentuating each syllable.

Nuon Chea said that now was the time for Cambodia to embrace all people and all countries. If Cambodians continued the old way of thinking, they could not overcome the difference between people and races. They could not make "friendships" with new people. Nuon Chea made the point that he was not talking about governments. He was talking about people: Americans, French, Vietnamese, and Chinese. All people must not look down on Cambodia. If you looked straight, you would see that all people were the same on the inside. The key to globalization was equality, freedom, and brotherhood.

"*Glo-bal-iz-a-tion*," Nuon Chea repeated. "*E-qual-i-te, li-ber-te, fra-ter-ni-te*."

Asking about his health sent Nuon Chea's wife to retrieve two medicines: diltiazem for hypertension and Ismo, a nitrate compound to increase blood flow to the heart. As nervous as I was, I realized that if Nuon Chea took one Viagra the sudden drop in blood pressure would kill him.

Nuon Chea was happy to talk about his health. His wife took good care of him. He ate three meals a day, had a nap in the afternoon, and slept four hours at night. After a heart problem and stroke three years ago, he went twice a year to a clinic in Chanthaburi, Thailand. For the first year he had difficulty moving his right arm and leg. Now he demonstrated his full recovery by moving both arms and legs.

When I asked if he took a baby aspirin a day to prevent future stroke or heart attack, Khat Mann said that Nuon Chea had a problem with bleeding from the stomach. Noting a second way to kill Nuon Chea underscored the importance of taking a thorough history. I proclaimed Nuon Chea to be in good health, which pleased him.

"Nuon Chea says he is in good physical condition because of running from American bombs," Khat Mann said. Asked what the American bombing was like, Nuon Chea said that America was a superpower, and that Cambodian people loved Americans. He welcomed foreign people from all over the world to help Cambodia develop.

"What effects did US bombing have on Cambodia?"

"He does not want to talk about the past," Khat Mann said without asking. "He wants to talk about the future. His interest now is having all people of the world live in peace and cooperate."

"*Glo-bal-iz-a-tion*," Nuon Chea repeated, lingering over each syllable like a demented old man. I asked if I could take one photo and Nuon Chea agreed if I sent him a copy. Photos were taken of Nuon Chea and me sitting next to each other, shaking hands for "globalization," with Dr. Noun and Khat Mann standing behind us. More handshakes escorted us to the door where Nuon Chea noticed that my sprained knee made getting my shoes on difficult. Nuon Chea looked sympathetic waving goodbye.

I felt grateful to Khieu Samphan for confirming that Cambodians began to hate Americans because of US bombing. Nuon Chea's espousing *glo-bal-iz-a-tion* without acknowledging the Khmer Rouge's responsibility for destroying Cambodia made me want to vomit. Surrounded by their families, something that would have been forbidden to them during the Khmer Rouge Revolution, neither Khieu Samphan nor Nuon Chea offered any assessment of the Khmer Rouge Revolution.

THE LIVER EATERS

Po parked pointing downhill in front of Nuon Paet's house so we could jump the clutch when we left. I had been so nervous when we dropped Chhouk Rin off on the way to see Nuon Chea that I did not have time to think about Chhouk Rin's commanding officer, Nuon Paet. In 1995, one year after the Western backpackers were murdered, arrest warrants were issued for Nuon Paet and his commander, Sam Bith, for killing the backpackers.[97]

Nuon Paet, who was renowned to eat his captives' livers, was arrested on August 1, 1998, and taken to the military prison in Phnom Penh.[98] After extraordinary pressure from the families of the backpackers, Nuon Paet was convicted on June 7, 1999, of killing David Wilson from Australia, Jean-Michel Braquet from France, and Mark Slater from England.[99] He was also ordered to pay $30,000 to the families of three Cambodians killed in the attack, $5,500 to the railroad, and an unspecified amount to the Wilson family who demanded $50,000 of their son's share of the ransom be donated to charity.[100]

At his trial Nuon Paet denied giving orders to kill the foreigners, which was true. He was following orders from Sam Bith. On the same day when Sam Bith and Chhouk Rin showed up at the trial to testify, they were informed that their immunity from prosecution regarding the backers' murder had been revoked. Sam Bith had received immunity for any involvement in killing the backpackers when he surrendered in 1997. So did Chhouk Rin when he surrendered and became a two-star general in the Cambodian Army.[101] Ten days after Nuon Paet's conviction, Sam Bith and Chhouk Rin were also charged with the backpackers' murders.

Nuon Paet's mother smiled her few remaining teeth as she served us young coconuts with straws. Sitting on benches in the shade under the teak house, Chhouk Rin reminisced with Nuon Paet's son, a scrappy twenty-year-old man who was born after the Khmer Rouge Revolution. Unlike Sam Bith, who was still "angry" at Chhouk Rin for being the first Khmer Rouge officer to surrender to Hun Sen soldiers, Nuon Paet and Chhouk Rin were friends.

Between sips of sweet, clear coconut water, Nuon Paet's son made a long and impassioned plea for Chhouk Rin and 1,000 of his men to help break his father out of prison. Prime Minister Hun Sen was smart. To capture Nuon Paet he enticed him with a business deal and sent a helicopter to pick him up in Pailin. Nuon Paet's wife lamented that her husband had a "bad spirit" so he wore a protection cord, a dried fetus that he cut out of a woman who was three months pregnant. Nuon Paet believed that no harm could come to him if he wore this fetal amulet around his neck. When Nuon Paet stepped off the helicopter in Phnom Penh, Hun Sen arrested him.

Nuon Paet's wife gave everyone an aluminum spoon to scrape slivers of translucent meat from the inside of our coconuts. Khat Mann noticed the apprehension on my face after he translated and reassured me that "No one speaks English," as if this would diminish the horror of a pregnant woman bleeding to death after her fetus was cut out.

Before leaving, Chhouk Rin agreed to help Nuon Paet's son free his father. Once again, I found it ironic that another Khmer Rouge officer had been charged with killing three foreigners while no architect of the Khmer Rouge Revolution had been tried for genocide. I only hoped that prosecuting the backpackers' murderers would help Cambodia's court system, which was loosely based on French civil law, arrest and try the Khmer Rouge leaders for crimes against humanity.

Dr. Noun reminded me that his uncle, Ta Mok, the chief of the Khmer Rouge military who killed Pol Pot, was arrested in March 1999 and taken to the military prison in Phnom Penh.[102] In the 1940s, Ta Mok fought French colonial rule and Japanese occupation. He earned the nickname the "Butcher" as commander in chief of the Khmer Rouge in 1977 when he supervised a series of purges, including 30,000 people in the Angkor Chey district.[103] After the Vietnamese invaded in 1979, Ta Mok moved his forces to northeastern Cambodia and continued to fight the Vietnamese occupation.

In a battle for power, Ta Mok killed Pol Pot in 1998 after trying him in a jungle court. I asked Dr. Noun about the circumstances of Pol Pot's death, but this was not the time for Khat Mann to indulge my queries.

Although Nuon Chea, the Khmer Rouge second in command; Khieu Samphan, the Khmer Rouge political leader; and Ieng Sary, the Khmer Rouge foreign minister, were all living freely, the Hun Sen government had formally applied to the UN to have an international tribunal with foreign and Cambodian judges to try the leaders of the Khmer Rouge.[104] Kang Kek Ieu, better known by his nom de guerre "Duch," who ran the Tuol Sleng torture center, gave himself up after two reporters for the *Far Eastern Economic Review*, Nick Dunlop and Nate Thayer, interviewed Duch at his home in Samlaut in 1999.[105]

Po let the Defender roll downhill before slipping the clutch. The engine did not start until we accelerated into a curve, scattering chickens and dogs. As luck would have it, there were no people, animals, or vehicles in the oncoming lane. When the road flattened, Po stopped on the corrugated dirt road and raised the hood. We were unable to push-start the Defender, but Po started the engine by touching one end of a thick wire to the battery and jamming the other end deep into the engine.

Depression accompanied the drive back to Phnom Penh as Po sped past the fires ravaging the jungle, a tank engulfed in smoke, and other mangled, rusted remnants of war. Po drove even faster when we got out of the mountains to the paved road on the delta. The Defender passed pickup trucks, ox carts, motorcycles with families of four, students in uniforms bicycling home from school, and trucks teetering under bales of cloth from Thailand.

I needed to be liberated from my frivolous quest and the Phnom Vor Gang and the cakes of red dust from passing every vehicle. Then Po drove off the road in Battambang to avoid driving over a small bridge that was missing a plank. No one was hurt, but Po spinning the wheels sank the Defender's chassis into loose dirt. Fittingly, we were stuck next to thousands of ducks with clipped wings that prevented their escape from an enormous outdoor pen.

I thought I would explode in the hours we were on display from curious pedestrians while Po tried to remove the clutch plate with a hammer and screwdriver, and a crane moved a large metal plate to complete the bridge. Even when a child offered bags of green mango slices sprinkled with red chili salt, I could not stop feeling sorry for pigs bundled in twine stacked on bicycles on their way to the slaughterhouse.

Resuming our frenetic pace, Dr. Noun used toilet paper to wipe the ever-accumulating layers of red dirt from his window and let the wind dispose of the paper. I did not have the energy to ask Dr. Noun not to litter. Suddenly a family on a motorcycle appeared next to my window. The man wore a surgical mask turned brown from the dust. His wife riding behind, and their young daughter standing on the seat between them, had *kramas* wrapped around their heads to protect them. For a moment, the girl looked terrified by her glimpse of a foreign devil before being swallowed by our wake.

We left Pailin at 6:30 a.m. and arrived at the Goldiana Hotel in Phnom Penh at 7:30 p.m. I got enough money from my safety deposit box to pay Chhouk Rin, Dr. Noun, and Khat Mann $100 bonuses, and $50 for Penya and Po. I could never have met Khieu Samphan and Nuon Chea without the Phnom Vor Gang and felt grateful for their efforts. Everyone seemed pleased except Chhouk Rin who had a harried look on his face when his cell phone rang. Without saying goodbye, Po drove Chhouk Rin and Penya off in the Defender. Khat Mann said that Chhouk Rin had a problem with his wife in Phnom Vor.

I got rooms for Dr. Noun and Khat Mann and told them to put their money in the hotel safe and get cleaned up for dinner.

BARBARIANS AT THE FCC

Dr. Noun perused the FCC menu while Khat Mann scanned the patrons for women he was attracted to, preferring well-dressed, full-figured Caucasian women in their twenties. He did not like Asians or any women of color. Backpackers were out of the question. Khat Mann wanted money. I couldn't resist teasing that he would have to be a "cunning linguist" if he wanted to have a foreign wife.

"Journalists!" Khat Mann hissed at four men with cameras coming up the stairs.

"Tourists," I corrected.

"Watching us!" Khat Mann said, focused on his prey. "I think many journalists here. In Khmer Rouge time, Pol Pot order us to kill all FCC people."

"What about me? You might need a doctor."

"You Bad Biography. Must kill."

A waiter pushing a dessert cart with assorted French pastries, tarts, cheeses, and fresh fruits distracted Khat Mann. After checking the menu, Khat Mann said, "In Pol Pot time when I soldier Khmer Rouge, I had a problem with civilization. Now I want to order seafood pizza."

After dinner Khat Mann insisted that I take him to the Martini Bar in honor of my forty-sixth birthday. I called Sokha and asked him to drive but did not tell him that Khat Mann was with us because he would not have come. By nine o'clock dozens of Vietnamese and Cambodian prostitutes packed the disco, open-air theater, food stalls, bar, and pool tables. Some of the prostitutes pinched. Others lunged at a suggestive glance. I ordered drinks for everyone, tipped the bartender $2, and watched Khat Mann walk up to a teenager with bodacious breasts and a stunning red silk dress who stood apart from her peers wearing T-shirts, jeans, and six-inch flip-flops.

The bartender said that she was sixteen years old. She was too young to work, but she paid the off-duty policemen at the door. She got pregnant last year from her father who stayed home with the baby while she worked. He threatened to cut her if she told anyone. Khat Mann was incensed with discrimination when he returned and yelled above the din, "She taxi girl! She not fuck Cambodia boy for five dollars. She want fuck *barang* for ten dollars."

REPERCUSSIONS

Khat Mann and a solemn Dr. Noun were waiting for me outside the Goldiana Hotel the next morning before I could have breakfast alone at the FCC. Dr. Noun's face was ashen. His head hung in shame. Khat Mann said that they went to another bar last night and brought *chirans* back to their hotel. Dr. Noun hid his money inside his prosthesis. When he woke up his *chiran* and his money were gone. Having warned Dr. Noun to be more careful, I did not want to pay him out of principle.

"For Dr. Noun no problem," Khat Mann said. "If he go home with no money, his wife big problem."

I thanked Dr. Noun and Khat Mann again for helping me meet the Big Men and started emptying my pockets. Dr. Noun and Khat Mann looked worried when I only came up with $50, but best friend smiles returned when I pulled a $50 bill from my sock for a total of $100. Dr. Noun had not lost face and we planned to meet in Kampot in a few days.

When I arrived at the Marco Polo, Chhouk Rin was in his third day of interrogation by Hun Sen's police. While Chhouk Rin was away, his wife told everyone that he was traveling to Pailin with an American doctor to meet Nuon Chea. Chhouk Rin had already been in prison once for eight months and faced life imprisonment. It could not have been worse timing for his wife to publicize our travels. So much for quiet time reading the last 349 pages of William Duiker's *Ho Chi Minh*.[106]

Po's wife came in from the kitchen in tears. Davide had called from China and fired Po. Davide said that it was Po's fault that he had to pay $250 to fix the car. Tears streamed down Set's cheeks. Davide paid Po $20 a month to drive. If Po did not work for Davide, they would have to leave Kampot. Set pleaded with me to talk to Davide. I said that I would and wondered how he was faring with opiate withdrawal.

The next morning Khat Mann asked if I was happy. I replied that I wanted to know how many soldiers the Khmer Rouge had in 1968 before American bombing, and how many soldiers they had every year after that, from 1969 until Pol Pot time in 1975. Then I would be happy.

Khat Mann said that I should talk to Mr. Muhn, Pol Pot's telegraph operator who translated Pol Pot's directives into telegraph and sent this information to his thirteen regional sub-commanders. As the Phnom Vor Gang's telegraph operator from 1979 to 1993, Khat Mann had spoken to Mr. Muhn many times. According to Khat Mann, Mr. Muhn had a "picture mind." He could remember everything. He was also married to Dr. Noun's sister and lived in Samlaut, near Pailin.

"Why didn't you tell me when we were in Pailin?"

"You not ask!"

A blue Toyota sedan with black tinted windows stopped in front of the Marco Polo. Plainclothes policemen with pistols got out on either side of Chhouk Rin, who looked calm and dangerous. I recognized the fat man with dark glasses from the Kampot disco. The oversized Rolex watch that hung from his right wrist and three-inch pinkie fingernails advertised that the chief of the Kampot Tribunal did not have to do manual work.

Hun Sen's henchmen scanned the road and riverbank while Chhouk Rin and the chief sat down with me at an outdoor table. Chhouk Rin was neither afraid nor impressed by his captors. Mimicking Davide, I yelled into the kitchen for Penya to bring cold beer for our guests.

When the fat man leaned back in his chair and began to talk, I did not need translation to see that he was an arrogant, corrupt, loathsome human being infused with the powers of the state. Khat Mann said that the tribunal chief was a "Big Man" and wanted to know what I was doing in Cambodia. I replied that I was a doctor interested in the health of the Khmer people and wanted to work with Dr. Noun.

"I told him already," Khat Mann said. "He want to know why you go to Pailin?"

I said Cambodia was a beautiful country. We had also traveled to Kampong Chhnang and Battambang, and I wanted to see more. The fat man's anger with my answer reminded me of Chhouk Rin threatening to kill me the first time we met "if anything bad happened because of our meeting." There was no doubt being interrogated with Chhouk Rin after meeting Khmer Rouge leaders qualified as something bad happening.

Chhouk Rin did not look nervous when the fat man asked what I had talked about with Khieu Samphan and Nuon Chea. I stuck with the truth. Khieu Samphan reminisced about his time in Paris. Nuon Chea was concerned with globalization. They both approved of Dr. Noun and me working together.

"Who is this man?" The fat man demanded in English, pointing his index finger at Chhouk Rin.

"He is my friend," I said.

The tribunal chief leaned back in his chair and did not cover his mouth while picking his teeth with a toothpick. His condescension paled compared to his corpulence. After several beers he tired of my giving the same answers and said that Chhouk Rin should go to Vietnam to "make friends." This was an obvious setup for the Vietnamese to kill Chhouk Rin if Hun Sen's secret police didn't beat him to it. Chhouk Rin did not flinch when Hun Sen's goons took him away.

"I think you not come back to Phnom Vor," Khat Mann said the next morning when I left.

"Mann, you say that every year."

GENOCIDE TRIBUNAL

I felt compelled to go to the US embassy in Phnom Penh where a female security guard at the front desk accepted my stating that I was a doctor from the US who wanted to talk to someone in the political section about a tribunal for the Khmer Rouge. A few minutes later I was chatting with the secretary for the US embassy's lawyer.

Sharon's enthusiasm for living in Phnom Penh just led her to sign up for another year. In Washington, DC, she would be living hand to mouth. In Phnom Penh her paycheck was deposited directly into her account at home. Any money she had here went under the mattress. I told Sharon about the excellent venison steak that I just had in Kampot. Sharon replied that the "natives ate crickets down there," and made me promise to have a rare roast beef sandwich and Häagen-Dazs ice cream in her honor when I returned to the US.

Wearing crisp khaki pants, white shirt, and tie, the embassy lawyer looked like a cleaner clone of myself. I explained that I was a physician who had taken an interest in the backpackers' murders in 1994 and asked about current US policy toward Cambodia.

The lawyer said that the US was the only government in the world that did not give direct aid to Cambodia. From 1979 to 1991, the US had refused to recognize the Hun Sen government, as one might expect after the Vietnam War. The US legislature enacted the Cambodian Genocide Justice Act in 1994, reaffirming the US commitment to bringing those responsible for mass crimes to justice. Some people in Washington still hated the fact that Hun Sen won the election in 1998.

"What affect did the American bombing have on Cambodia?"

"The US bombing displaced many people who were also disaffected."

"Do you think the bombing helped the Khmer Rouge recruit?"

"You said you were a doctor. You sound more like a journalist."

"I am interested in human rights and medicine. Do you think the economic and human carnage from American bombing helped the Khmer Rouge recruit enough soldiers to overthrow the Lon Nol government?"

"Probably. From 1969 to 1973, the Khmer Rouge developed into an orangutan that attracted people."

When asked about the chances of Cambodia having a tribunal, the lawyer made it clear that the intent of a tribunal had to have a limited scope to get the architects of the Khmer Rouge, not every functionary, or they risked destabilizing the country. The Cambodian courts were corrupt and would do anything Hun Sen wanted. The lawyer agreed that it was ironic that a few Khmer Rouge officers had been brought to trial for killing three Western backpackers, while no Khmer Rouge officer had ever been tried for genocide. The lawyer would not address the issue of US crimes against Cambodia, but he seemed interested in the fate of the Cambodian courts and people.

"In order for Cambodia to get past the genocide under Pol Pot, there must be an international tribunal. Hun Sen was the one who broke off talks with the United Nations when he couldn't control the outcome."

"What about Khmer Rouge leaders who have been given amnesty?"

"The amnesty issue is a red herring. The Cambodian government can bring Ieng Sary to court. His defense lawyer will raise the amnesty issue. It is up to the Cambodian courts, not the UN. The tribunal could say yes, we will honor amnesty, but there are still other crimes to prosecute him for. I'm not usually in the business of giving the UN much credit. The UN wants to say preexisting amnesty does not bar prosecution. Amnesty is a constitutional prerogative. You can't fuck with that!

"Genocide is not an easy case for the international lawyers to prove. Look at Rwanda and Bosnia. I wouldn't be surprised if prosecutors failed to meet the burden of proof. Witnesses are old and afraid. I'm afraid the Cambodian judges will do what Cambodian judges do every day. They will have someone like Nuon Chea in front of them and say that he is guilty. Then some fancy, international defense lawyer will go on and on that the evidence does not meet the burden of proof. Imagine having Khieu Samphan and Nuon Chea before the tribunal and being acquitted. At least the Cambodian court system can guarantee the verdict."

With talks between the Cambodian government and the UN on an international tribunal stalled, and none of the Khmer Rouge leaders charged or imprisoned, the prospects to try the perpetrators of the Khmer Rouge genocide seemed bleak.

It took the international community a long time to name the ultimate crime against humanity. A Polish lawyer named Raphael Lemkin was outraged when the Ottoman Turks sent hundreds of thousands of Armenians on death marches into the desert in 1915. Lemkin's initial efforts to get the European states to criminalize what the US ambassador to Turkey called "race murder" were dismissed.[107] When Hitler invaded Poland in 1939, Lemkin lost twenty-seven family members during the Holocaust. After emigrating to the US, Lemkin continued his struggle to get the international community to recognize and try to prevent any group of people from annihilating another. Lemkin coined the word *genocide* while working for the US War Department in 1944.

According to Lemkin, "Genocide has two phases: one, destruction of the national pattern of the oppressed group; the other, the imposition of the national pattern of the oppressor. This imposition, in turn, may be made upon the oppressed population which is allowed to remain, or upon the territory alone, after removal of the population and colonization of the area by the oppressor's own nationals."[108]

Lemkin's efforts culminated in the UN adopting its first human rights treaty on December 9, 1948, the Convention on the Prevention and Punishment of the Crime of Genocide. The treaty was adopted by the UN General Assembly unanimously but lacked any provisions for enforcement. It took the US four decades to ratify the treaty, and another decade for anyone to be convicted of genocide by the international community.[109]

Samantha Power's *A Problem From Hell: America and the Age of Genocide* dissects the history of US inaction during genocides of the twentieth century.[110] To name a few, the US stood by while the Ottoman Turks massacred over 1 million Armenians between 1915 and 1916. During World War II, the Nazis killed 6 million Jews and 5 million Poles, gays, Romas, and other "undesirables." Over 2 million Tibetans perished under China's military occupation of Tibet that started in 1959 and continues to this day. In Iraq the US supported Saddam Hussein while he used poison gas to kill 100,000 Kurdish villagers from 1987 to 1988 at the end of the Iran-Iraq War. The US was silent while nationalist Bosnian Serbs killed 200,000 Muslims and Croats between 1992 and 1995 before Bill Clinton pushed NATO bombing. In 1994, the Hutu-dominated government in Rwanda killed 800,000 Tutsi in a hundred days.

Tom Fawthrop called me on my last night at my hotel to "swap information." He was a journalist for the *Sunday Times* of London who was writing a book on Cambodia during the 1980s. Dressed in cargo pants outfitted for a safari, Tom was waiting at a table at the Pon Luk Restaurant on Sisowath Quay. Tom said that he had spent much of the last ten years in Phnom Penh writing articles for the

Sunday Times and local papers. He did not say how he got my number. His interest piqued when I said that I had met Chhouk Rin.

Tom said that Chhouk Rin had been a constant thorn in the Hun Sen government. The Phnom Vor Gang did not have money like Pol Pot's Gang in Pailin. The Khmer Rouge stopped receiving money and supplies from China after the Paris agreement in October 1991. Chhouk Rin's Gang had to rely on extortion, robbery, and kidnapping. After constant pressure from the British, French, and Australian embassies, Hun Sen was pleased with the arrest of Chhouk Rin's commanding officer, Nuon Paet.

"Do you know what Nuon Paet was wearing around his neck when he stepped off the helicopter in Phnom Penh?"

"No."

"A fetal amulet."

"How did you—?"

"I met Nuon Paet's family. His son wants Chhouk Rin to bring 1,000 armed men to break his father out of prison."

"How did—?"

Horse-trading continued with my asking what made Hun Sen defect to Vietnam as a Khmer Rouge officer before returning as prime minister. Tom said that Hun Sen was the head of a Khmer Rouge unit that lost a battle with the Vietnamese in 1973. Hun Sen feared Pol Pot wanted to kill him for failing Angkor and fled to Vietnam. It took several years for Hun Sen to convince the Vietnamese that he was not a Khmer Rouge double agent. When the Vietnamese invaded Cambodia in 1979, and the Khmer Rouge retreated to the Thai border, Hun Sen was installed as the world's youngest prime minister. He was twenty-six years old.

Regarding Hun Sen's ruthless reputation, Tom credited Hun Sen as the only Cambodian leader who had gone on record, as far back as 1989, that the Khmer Rouge would never be allowed back into power. At the same time there were Khmer Rouge embedded in all levels of the Cambodian government, army, and civilian population. Tom admired Hun Sen in the same way he admired Tito, the Yugoslavian strongman who presided over a country where Serbians, Croatians, and Albanians lived in relative peace before the country broke up.

"There is a fear that the peace is fragile," Tom said. "There are large numbers of unemployed. You don't want rank-and-file Khmer Rouge to de-integrate. They have many hidden arms caches. If there is a tribunal, the first job will be to not disrupt the peace."

US President George W. Bush appeared as an apparition on CNN's evening news as I packed. "Our war against terror is only beginning," Bush said, declaring that Iraq, Iran, North Korea, and their terrorist allies constituted an "axis of evil." The term *axis of evil* was a reference to the alliance between Germany, Italy, and Japan during World War II. Apart from a few thousand troops from Britain and Poland, international support for George W. Bush's Gulf War II paled compared to that orchestrated by his father, George Herbert Walker Bush, during Gulf War I when the US military repelled Iraq's invasion of Kuwait. In stark contrast to his father, George W. Bush wanted to promulgate an unholy war in the Middle East.

Meeting Khieu Samphan and Nuon Chea confirmed my suspicion that the American bombing of Cambodia had fueled a countrywide hatred of American foreign devils. Although it was difficult to gauge the animosity of people on the ground, it was clear that the destruction of lives and the economy from US bombing helped the Khmer Rouge recruit enough soldiers to fight and defeat the US-backed Lon Nol government. But this was not enough. I was trapped by my Western, didactic education. I wanted numbers.

PART IV

THE ANGRY SKIES

THAI RIOT

Buddha only knew how Chhouk Rin's interrogation with Hun Sen's secret police had gone. Davide fell off the internet for all of 2002. Although I was preoccupied by working at the clinic and official separation, I was also obsessed with meeting Pol Pot's telegraph operator who lived in Samlaut, the most heavily mined area in Cambodia. Even if he did not have a "picture mind," Mr. Muhn was in a unique position to estimate the Khmer Rouge troop strength before the onset of US bombing in 1969, until they overthrew the US-backed Cambodian army and government in 1975, two weeks before the Vietnamese Communists defeated the US in Vietnam.

I returned to the Land of Smiles in January 2003. On my last night in the States, Kate poached salmon while I read *Winnie-the-Pooh* on the couch next to Zachary. Kate and I got along better now than when we were married, but I did not want to get divorced. Kaley took center stage in the living room, perching on alternate legs with both arms to the side in a swan, pivoting clockwise. Each time Kaley's peripheral vision rotated out of view, Zachary tried to push her off balance. I tried to distract Kaley's desire for retaliation by saying that the children in Cambodia did not have many toys.

Perhaps she could pick out one of her own toys for me to bring to a child in Cambodia?

"My two tigers are really special," Kaley said.

"How about something you don't play with anymore. It would be a great gift to a child without any toys."

"I know!" Kaley exclaimed, sprinting across the living room to a box that had become a mass grave for unwanted toys. "You can take Piglet."

Piglet was a great choice. He was adorable and compact. After reading more bedtime chapters, I hoped that Zachary and Kaley would not lose their father at a young age as I had lost mine. I knew that my father dying of lung cancer a few days after my fifteenth birthday was caused by his smoking two packs of Camel unfiltered cigarettes a day. Returning to Cambodia for the fourth time, I knew that Chhouk Rin could order Khat Mann to kill me. I wanted to see my children grow up to pursue their own passions, but I could not conceive of not going back to the Land of Smiles.

I did not realize that I had forgotten to pack Piglet until registering at the Goldiana Hotel in Phnom Penh on January 28, 2003. It was hard to ignore the sign posted on US embassy stationary at the front desk.

WARNING FROM THE US EMBASSY
ALL AMERICAN CITIZENS SHOULD EXIT CAMBODIA IMMEDIATELY IN ADVANCE OF THE DISRUPTIONS ANTICIPTATED WITH THE UNITED STATES' IMPENDING WAR WITH IRAQ. ANYONE WHO REMAINS SHOULD HAVE PASSPORTS AND POSSESSIONS IN ORDER FOR IMMINENT DEPARTURE.

The *Cambodia Daily* reported that the US expected to unleash 3,000 smart missiles in the first twenty-four hours of Gulf War II, ten times the number used in Gulf War I. Meanwhile North Korea was flaunting its refinement of weapons grade plutonium. I failed to understand what the US military meant by "smart missile." How many innocent civilians would be killed or maimed by our smart and dumb bombs? During Gulf War I from January 16 to February 28, 1991, the US Army estimated that over 100,000 Iraqi soldiers died and 300,000 were wounded, while 148 US soldiers died and 458 were wounded.[111]

The next morning the Cambodian press and radio reported that Thai actress Suwanan Kongying, after being invited to visit the Angkor Wats Temples, replied, "How can I be invited to my own country? The Angkor Wats belong to Thailand." Until this moment, Suwanan Kongying's films were popular in Cambodia. As she denied the quote attributed to her, Hun Sen went on the radio saying, "The Thai actress is lower than a blade of grass."

Having breakfast at the FCC I heard the first hundred Cambodian University students on motorcycles carrying banners with lewd caricatures of Suwanan, and "Angkor Wat belonged to Cambodia." When the mob stopped across the street, one student climbed an aluminum flagpole and removed the Thai flag from the line of nations' flags represented along the riverbank. Dozens of other students ripped a large poster of Suwanan from a billboard.

Kaeng, my waitress at the FCC, said the Thai embassy in Bangkok had been stormed. Eight Cambodians had been killed and one man was beheaded. The students were very angry. Kaeng looked worried. Her mother took care of her one-year-old son while she was working. If things got worse, it would be too dangerous to ride her moto home.

By the afternoon the Thai phone company and Thai Airlines offices at Ponchetong International Airport were burning, mobs were attacking Thai hotels and restaurants throughout the city, and the Thai embassy was under siege. The Independence Monument cast a long shadow over groups of armed men and teenage boys lighting tires and rubbish at intersections. We took a circuitous route back to our hotel until a crowd torching a Thai cement factory blocked our return to the Goldiana. Sokha stopped the car and tried to call his wife on his cell phone.

I implored Sokha not to look anyone in the eyes as we drove past armed men on both sides of the road. At the next intersection dozens of men malingered around burning tires churning thick black smoke straight up into the still, sticky air. Two shots rang out behind us. We were trapped. Without time to think, Sokha zoomed in reverse and two men jumped out of the way as Sokha crossed a sidewalk and headed into an alley.

"Bad men," Sokha said, his voice trembling as he drove too fast through a narrow alley disrupting piles of trash and ripping laundry from clotheslines. I did not compliment Sokha on his driving until he got us back to the Goldiana where the hotel courtyard had no fence to protect Sokha's car or separate the lobby from the street.

"I go home," Sokha said as we walked to the hotel's glass front doors. "I worry my wife and children."

The moto men whispering among themselves across the street did not accost us as usual. By day the moto men were not safe. At night the same driver could rob or kill you. Gunshots from the nearest intersection made Sokha get back in his car, but he offered no resistance to my insistence and was not reassured by my pointing out that all of the violence was being directed against Thai businesses. Sokha was Chinese and Cambodian. His family would be safe at his home. We would be safe inside the Goldiana, which was Chinese owned.

A gang of men on motorcycles fired AK-47s into the air as they passed a group of Italian election monitors in the Goldiana lobby. The receptionist at the main desk did not flinch when I withdrew my valuables from the safety deposit box. She had seen this before. For me, an angry, drunken mob robbing the hotel guests and shooting the safety deposit boxes, or worse, was easy to imagine.

Sokha ran with me up two flights of stairs to my room where I left the lights out while stashing credit cards, cash, and my passport into money and ankle belts. Sokha could not stop worrying about his family so I asked him to put the beers and bottled waters from the fridge into a bag. If the gangs went room to room, we would be safer hiding on the rooftop laundry. Sokha was glad to have something to do and ran with me up four more flights of stairs to the rooftop that offered sweeping views of Phnom Penh under siege. Sokha glued himself to a wicker chair in the middle of the flat rooftop, mesmerized by enormous orange flames leaping into the night sky from a warehouse four blocks away.

Bursts of automatic gunfire erupted on the streets below as I crawled under rows of sheets hanging out to dry, looking for exits, scaring three women and five children huddled under a mosquito net. The Goldiana was taller than any nearby building. There were no rooftops to jump to. No gutters or pipes to climb down. If the hotel was attacked, Sokha and I would have to hide in the potted ferns and tropical plants on the balcony facing the street.

I did not burden Sokha with my assessment. Hotel guests getting out of the elevator were asking if the gunfire was fireworks as an explosion and great ball of flames erupting from the Mobitel Semam Thai gas station near the Thai embassy unsettled an angry young Cambodian man wearing jeans and a hip-hop T-shirt. The sides of his head were shaved. The top had uneven gel spikes.

"Once again Phnom Penh is under fire," Tony said. "This is all because of that fucking Richard Nixon. None of this would have happened if the US hadn't bombed Cambodia."

Tony was born in a Thai refugee camp after his mother fled Cambodia when the Khmer Rouge took over. He grew up in Massachusetts and was on his first trip to Cambodia with six friends who had also grown up in exile. Their van was attacked this morning by a mob that started breaking windows until he spoke Khmer.

"They thought we were Thai," Tony continued. "That fucking Thai bitch said Angkor Wat is part of Thailand! You can't take away our national monument! That's ours!" The sound of glass breaking from hundreds of windows at the Lucky Market two blocks away punctuated Tony's rant. "This is bullshit, man. We saw dozens of people ransacking Thai hotels. Hundreds of people attacking the Thai embassy. This has nothing to do with students. Hun Sen goons hired glue-sniffers and thugs to attack the Thai embassy."

The gunfire did not scare me. Isolated shots from the same places in the nearby streets were probably from individuals protecting their property or firing warning shots. The motorcycle gangs were terrifying. Sokha begged to go home, but I convinced him to drink warm beers that tasted horrible but helped us relax. We would not learn until later that Thailand had just sent commandos to evacuate 400 Thai nationals at the airport, and Thai Prime Minister Thaksin halted all business with Cambodia. Thaksin also demanded that Cambodia pay to rebuild the Thai embassy and apologize for inciting violence against Thai interests.

The sounds of gunfire and breaking glass continued all night. From our rooftop vigil we monitored playboys cruising the streets, new fires erupting, and red phosphorous tracer bullets zipping into the black sky. As the gunfire escalated into a symphony with hundreds of simultaneous rounds, marauding crowds vandalized Thai hotels, Thai restaurants, and Thai market stalls in an orgy of anti-Thai violence.

The chaos reminded me of something John Ackerly had mentioned after we witnessed the Chinese military suppress Tibetan nationalist demonstrations in Lhasa in the fall of 1987. According to John, the riot we saw in Tibet was not technically a riot. By definition, a riot was random violence done by an angry mob. The violence in Phnom Penh tonight was being directed at Thai businesses, just as the angry Tibetan mob had attacked a Chinese police station where Buddhist monks were being killed. Underneath it all, racism reared its ugly head.

The Cambodian psyche had been traumatized by centuries of foreign domination, French colonization, an auto-genocide, and Vietnamese occupation. Cambodians had few businesses of their own.

Everything they consumed was manufactured abroad. Yesterday Thai cell phones, Thai food, and Thai movies were popular and envied. Today all Cambodians were united in their hatred of Thai people and anything Thai. Regardless of what the Thai actress said, it sparked the Cambodians' deep-seated sense of inferiority, of being second-class citizens in their own country where the most visible signs of prosperity and wealth were owned by Thai, Chinese, or foreign corporations.

The *Cambodia Daily* blamed Hun Sen for letting the riot get out of control without any security for the Thai embassy, except for a few police that showed up to watch the crowd. In another clear sign of mischief, Mam Sonando, the head of the independent Beehive Radio, had been arrested for spreading false rumors that eight Cambodians had been killed in Bangkok. These rumors fueled enough violence to close the Thai border indefinitely, which would cause food and gasoline shortages. Until the riot, the Thais had fixed the price of gasoline at 16.9 baht/liter in advance of Gulf War II that was expected any day.

With an election coming up, it seemed that Hun Sen had manufactured the Thai actress wanting to steal Cambodia's national symbol and allowed the mob to ransack the Thai embassy and Thai businesses. In response to the Thai ambassador's frantic calls to Hun Sen requesting police protection, Hun Sen was reported to say, "Look out your window. The police are already there." No police or firefighters came. Calculating that he would benefit from championing nationalism, Hun Sen set back international assistance to Cambodia for another decade.

In the morning we drove to check on Sokha's family and survey the damage. Thousands of people of all ages wrapped *kramas* around their faces to shield them from smoke rising from smoldering buildings and piles of trash. Soldiers with a tank had erected a temporary barbed wire fence to protect the Thai embassy from further looting. The embassy's facade had many broken windows but appeared intact. For the next mile, acrid smoke spewed from fires still burning at the

Thai gas station, cement, textile, and beer factories. At the Lucky Market, where we had heard glass breaking for hours the previous night, windowpanes that covered one whole side of the building lay in shards.

Hun Sen was a survivor. After the UN sponsored elections that resulted in a coalition government in 1993, Hun Sen staged a coup d'état in 1997 using grenade attacks and assassination to silence his political opponents. In the upcoming election in July 2003, Hun Sen would retain power with less than 30 percent of the vote thanks to widespread voter fraud, paying 5,000 riels ($1) to each voter, in addition to political violence and intimidation by Hun Sen goons.

BREAKING DOWN

When Sokha found his wife and two children glued to the Cartoon Network, the same channel that Zachary and Kaley watched, we both cried. Sokha's wife would not let him drive me to Kampot and return without stopping until we had a bowl of Khmer chicken soup. As predicted, the marijuana in the soup made me fall asleep on the drive down to Kampot.

Davide looked healthier than last year. He said he was treated like royalty at Sulchum Hospital in Bangkok while his body went through the rigors of opiate withdrawal. I didn't believe him until he showed me hospital and pharmacy receipts for seven days including prescriptions of Pangesic sublingual .2 mg, Catapres, Quomem, and Tranxene for $750. Lighting a large joint, Davide said that he would never smoke opium again. He could not drink alcohol because of his hepatitis C. Marijuana was the only thing left that helped him relax.

"Did you ever see Po look under the fucking hood?" Davide exclaimed. The dark circles under his eyes and sallow complexion had improved. His temper had not. "I told the fucking guy to look under the fucking hood and to call me if there is any fucking problem. Instead, he ruins my car and I have to pay $400. That's a lot of money in Cambodia. So yes, I fire the fucking guy."

Davide was right. Po had driven nonstop from Phnom Penh to Kampong Chhnang and did not look under the hood until there was trouble. But this was one year ago and Davide was inflating the price. I felt sorry for Po. When Davide found out that I had paid Po $50 after going to Pailin, the equivalent of two and a half month's salary, he fired Po and rehired Po ten weeks later. My bonus had subsidized Po's unemployment.

When I mentioned that I wanted to meet Pol Pot's telegraph operator, Davide surprised me by not knowing that Mr. Muhn was married to Dr. Noun's sister, but he agreed to drive me to Samlaut in his Toyota truck, which was more comfortable than the Defender and easier to repair.

"You have to be careful how you make your questions," Davide said. "The Khmer Rouge will say anything they think you want to hear, especially if money is involved. No matter what happens don't ever make the Khmer Rouge lose face. And don't give Mann more than $10 a day. If you give him more he will just want more." Davide had no objection to my paying him $50 a day for the Toyota pickup truck, and another $50 a day for his services.

My right cheek swelled grotesquely chewing my first bite of spaghetti carbonara. Before I could finish my third bite the swelling and pain reached my ear. There was no treatment for a blocked parotid gland, except sucking on something bitter and taking an antibiotic to prevent infection. If I was lucky a tiny stone would eventually dislodge itself from the salivary duct. Until then, eating any solid food or carbohydrate was off the menu. I tried massaging along the jaw toward my chin and asked for a sliced lemon.

Parting the ferns that shielded us from the street, Khat Mann was amused by my predicament and finished my spaghetti. I told Khat Mann that I wanted to go to Samlaut to meet Mr. Muhn and asked if there would be any problem for him or Dr. Noun coming with me. Khat Mann did not answer and raced off to get Dr. Noun, or so I thought.

Po's corpulent wife appeared from the kitchen and laughed when she saw the golf ball swelling on my right cheek. Set said that I looked like a chipmunk, asked if it hurt, and laughed before I could answer. I knew that Set blamed me for Davide firing her husband the previous year. She also laughed because I was a doctor and no medicine could help me. But Set said she had a cure and drew the outline of a tiger on my right cheek with assurances that I would be better tomorrow.

The next morning Davide drove Khat Mann, Penya, and me toward Kep. I thought we were going to Phnom Vor to get Dr. Noun, but we passed the statue at the bend in the road to Kep and followed the dirt track to the Kep Killing Fields Memorial. The older monk, who spoke English, remembered me and retrieved a hatchet from his room. Khat Mann lingered behind the acolytes in orange robes who accompanied us to the wooden shed and watched them take turns chopping at the termite mound that blocked the door painted ochre a long time ago.

When the door was finally pried open, Khat Mann stared at the pile of long bones from arms and legs on the left, and skulls stacked on the right as they came into view. The older monk looked uncomfortable. He knew that Khat Mann killed everyone in this mass grave when he was a child soldier for the Khmer Rouge. "I know these bones," Khat Mann said, mesmerized by his midden. Asked if he ever had nightmares, Khat Mann nodded. His face was solemn, transfixed by the physical remains of the New People he had murdered.

It was over a hundred degrees when we followed Khat Mann's cousin who wanted to show me 200 mass graves at the base of Kep Mountain. Hon was barefoot and wore only a *krama* around his waist. As we traversed parched rice paddies, everyone followed single file, careful to step in Hon's footsteps. We walked a long kilometer to dozens of subtle mounds the size of swimming pools where little vegetation grew because of the "spirits." Closer inspection revealed pieces of clothing sticking up from the dirt. Even if each of these mass graves did not hold up to 500 people, thousands of people died unnatural deaths in the Kep Killing Fields.

A teenage boy saw us returning to Hon's house and scampered up a coconut tree to drop a dozen large green coconuts. Infants and toddlers ran like chickens under Hon's stilted house where the extended family lounged in the shade. Older men and women sat on a wooden platform. I was surprised that I had more gray hair than all the elders combined, including the oldest woman with a wrinkled face.

"Dr. Brake," Khat Mann said, "He, my cousin."

"*She* is your cousin."

"He look like me?"

"*She* looks like you."

Khat Mann recounted that during the Khmer Rouge time his father had a new house because he had a Good Biography. When the Vietnamese invaded in 1979, Khat Mann hid in the jungle. His father did not know that he was fighting the Vietnamese. Hon's wife, her face wizened from decades of hard work outdoors, said that two times everyone thought Khat Mann was dead. Twice they made a ceremony for him, donating 3,500 baht ($90) to the temple for the gods.

As Khat Mann opened each coconut with four strong, swift chops of a machete, it was not difficult to imagine that the coconuts were heads. Knowing that Khat Mann had killed some members of Hon's extended family, I wondered if his wife wished that Khat Mann had died or accepted it as karma. When everyone was sipping the cool coconut water, Khat Mann needed no prompting to sing a Khmer Rouge liberation song, seated on a stool with his back to the elders who looked frightened while he sang

"Did you see the expression on the old woman's face?" Davide said. "She was terrified!"

"I scared, too," Khat Mann said without turning around to see the elders' furrowed brows. "All the hair on my arms stand up." Khat Mann performed another Khmer Rouge song for going off to Phnom

Penh to fight. Once again, the elders' faces cringed as Khat Mann sang.

> The fighters swim across the river
> And go up the hill many months
> Go by the rock and the base of the tree
> Sleep on the ground
> On the seventeenth of April
> There was liberation of Cambodia
> And the Cambodia people
> Shine all over on the sky
> Like a rifle to the blue sky
> Pol Pot make the black face clouds
> Disappear from the Cambodia sky
> The sunshine, the reputation clear.

A call on Khat Mann's cell phone interrupted his soliloquy. He had to go home and watch the baby while his wife bought rice to feed the family while he was gone. I smiled at the child soldier turned babysitter. Dr. Noun appeared as we left Hon's house and said the tiger on my cheek was strong medicine. He also gave me two pre-folded paper packets from his pocket containing erythromycin and Tylenol. I thanked the good Dr. Noun and asked if he would go back to Pailin so I could meet his brother-in-law, Mr. Muhn.

Dr. Noun's face lit up with the prospect of another road trip. He agreed to go even if we had to take a bus. I offered to pay all expenses plus $10 for each day that we traveled, and I paused to watch Khat Mann's and Dr. Noun's expressions evolve before setting the hook, "Plus one magic pill a day."

"Chhouk Rin come with us!" Khat Mann insisted the first of many times.

I drank too much whiskey watching the moonlight cast silver darts across the Komchi River. Nothing about this trip made sense. Khat

Mann would sell his own mother to the highest bidder. Davide's recovery from opioid addiction was questionable. Chhouk Rin lost his appeal and faced a life sentence for killing the backpackers. Going to Pailin with Chhouk Rin might help him curry favor with Hun Sen's police but could be disastrous for me. Not doing Chhouk Rin's bidding could also jeopardize my life.

An obese American couple pushed a Cambodian infant in a stroller into the Marco Polo as I contemplated the last ice I could trust for a week. I asked Davide if Cambodia still permitted adoptions after the State Department discovered the agencies were fronts for criminal gangs who charged $20,000 for each baby stolen from unsuspecting mothers.

"What did he say?" the mother-in-waiting asked.

"We're leaving," the husband muttered.

"You talk too loud when you're drunk," Davide nodded in agreement.

Dr. Noun and Khat Mann arrived at the Marco Polo the next morning in time for breakfast. Khat Mann reiterated that Chhouk Rin was going to Pailin with me and was waiting at a restaurant in Phnom Penh in the company of Hun Sen police. I could well imagine the spread that Chhouk Rin had prepared for himself and explained that Chhouk Rin already had "police problems" and would have more "police problems" if we traveled anywhere together. Khat Mann did not need to understand. He was following orders.

Davide tried to entice Khat Mann with a scheme to capture and kill eight Nigerians who controlled the heroin coming into Phnom Penh with the help of corrupt Cambodian policemen. Khat Mann readily agreed to take the Nigerians hostage and torture them. Davide said he wanted to torture the "Bad Man" who got him addicted. Khat Mann could kill the other seven. If the Bad Man talked, Davide would take this information to the CIA station chief at the US embassy. Davide's vehemence was alarming.

Rays of sunlight streaking through burgundy clouds brought color to the dawn. Rolling the windows up protected us from the dust trails kicked up by every vehicle on the road, but the absence of air moving compounded the oppressive heat and Khat Mann repeating that Chhouk Rin was waiting in a restaurant and would be very angry with me if I did not come. I tried distracting Khat Mann with his favorite subject, sex: oldest, youngest, bad smell, good smell, first time, and last year in Pailin when Chhouk Rin had not been able to get an erection but liked watching Khat Mann with two *chirans*.

Khat Mann did not need provocation. In one village during Pol Pot time Khat Mann noticed that every day another chicken disappeared. After seven days Khat Mann went into a house and saw a Khmer Rouge soldier "fucking one chiran."

"He fucked a girl?"

"No. He fuck chicken. The chicken dead. Khmer Rouge soldier not allow to fuck."

"What did you do?"

"I shoot him," Khat Mann said. "If boy soldier lay down with girl soldier and fuck, Angkor say, 'Must kill.'"

"Enough pussy talk!" Davide screamed as the Toyota hit a pothole hard enough to buck Penya and Dr. Noun to hit their heads on the roof. Khat Mann was too dense to buck.

Davide extolled Pol Pot's Khmer Rouge Revolution as the first true Khmer movement since the Angkor kings ruled Southeast Asia from the ninth to the thirteenth centuries. Like the ancient kings whose mastery of irrigation and slave labor allowed them to grow two or three crops of rice a year, instead of one, Pol Pot tried to re-create the glory of the Khmer Empire, using "New People" evacuated from the cities as slaves.

According to Davide, Sihanouk was the biggest traitor of Cambodia, not the Khmer Rouge. Sihanouk sold out to the Communists by exhorting people to join the Khmer Rouge in 1970 when he went into exile. If Sihanouk had allied with the Americans like the king of Thailand, Cambodia would be a developed country today. Although the king of Thailand and Sihanouk were the same age, the king of Thailand is reported to have told Sihanouk, "Look what you have done. You have destroyed your own country."

After each call from Chhouk Rin, Khat Mann repeated that Chhouk Rin was waiting for me at the restaurant, that he had ordered food, and that the police would be angry if I did not meet them. I could not think of anything dumber than meeting with Chhouk Rin and his police handlers or having him lose face. He must have been desperate to use me as a bargaining chip.

"Chhouk Rin already order $30 of food and beer," Khat Mann yelled. "Who is going to pay?"

"How many times do I have to say no fucking way."

For hours I thought Khat Mann would hit me. I tried to think of what it was like for Khat Mann being a child soldier for the Khmer Rouge: to kill or be killed until killing became routine. Whatever Khat Mann had seen or done, he was smart enough to become a telegraph operator to escape the front lines, malleable enough to work for the French Foreign Legion when the Khmer Rouge wanted to kill him, and wily enough to return to his gang years later with a stolen jeep and have all sins forgiven.

"The engine is fucked," Davide shouted above clanking. Davide drove to a large garage in Phnom Penh where two men began to disarticulate the transmission into pans of solvents. This could take days. I bought my freedom by getting the gang rooms at a Chinese hotel, paying their daily ration plus an extra $10. We had only been on the road for three hours and already I needed to escape.

MALCOLM CALDWELL'S MURDER

Drinking American coffee in the Renaksé Hotel garden, Davide revealed his obsession with learning who gave the orders to kill the Scottish journalist Malcolm Caldwell in his room on the second floor moments after he interviewed Pol Pot in 1979, three weeks before Vietnamese troops invaded Cambodia and the Khmer Rouge fled to the Thai border. To showcase the Khmer Rouge Revolution, Pol Pot invited Malcolm Caldwell, who was sympathetic to the Communists, along with Elizabeth Becker from the *Washington Post*, and Richard Dudman of the *St. Louis Post Dispatch* to stay at the Renaksé Hotel in December 1978. After two weeks of touring a scripted, sanitized version of the Khmer Rouge Revolution, the journalists had seen nothing that would confirm refugee accounts of starvation and massacres.

Davide referenced Becker's account, *When the War Was Over: Cambodia and the Khmer Rouge Revolution*.[112] In her own words, Becker admitted, "We were the original three blind men trying to figure out the elephant. At that time no one understood the inner working of the regime; how the zones operated; how the party controlled the country; how the secret police worked; that torture and extermination centers . . . even existed; the depth of the misery and death... We had the tail, the ears, the feet of the monster but no idea of its overall shape."

Unlike most of the Western journalists in Cambodia, Elizabeth Becker had lived among the Cambodians for three years. During Becker's and Dudman's one-hour interview with Pol Pot, the Khmer Rouge leader was paranoid about Vietnam and warned, "A Kampuchea that is a satellite of Vietnam is a threat and a danger for Southeast Asia and the world... for Vietnam is already a satellite of the Soviet Union and is carrying out Soviet strategy in Southeast Asia."[113]

Davide said that Caldwell's interview with Pol Pot at the Renaksé Hotel lasted three hours. Afterward Caldwell was in great spirits and went to his room to write. When soldiers barged into Becker's room and one man screamed, "It's not him," she hid under her bed. After she heard gunshots, soldiers came to escort her to Caldwell's room to witness his corpse lying in a pool of blood, and the body of the "assassin" on the lobby floor downstairs.

On Christmas Eve the Khmer Rouge put Caldwell's body and the American journalists on a flight to Beijing. The next day Vietnam launched Operation Blooming Lotus, invading Cambodia with 150,000 troops. Davide said that to this day it was a mystery who gave the orders to kill Malcolm Caldwell, and that he would do anything to find out. I was preoccupied with Chhouk Rin ordering Khat Mann to kill me before meeting Nuon Chea again.

"This is important!" Davide said. "Caldwell was a journalist who was sympathetic to the Cambodian and Vietnamese Communists. It was a shock when he was killed."

Seeing the Toyota's reassembled transmission the next morning instilled tremendous admiration for Cambodia's mechanics who had survived the Khmer Rouge Revolution and performed miracles in small villages to keep makeshift vehicles running. Khat Mann demanded $5 for a room where he had taken his *chiran* or he would go back to Kampot. Five dollars was a pittance to get him back on the road, and once we left Phnom Penh he stopped mentioning Chhouk Rin.

Davide cursed our first flat tire on the smooth stretch of elevated dirt road next to the Tonlé Sap River. He had paid $120 for new tires before our trip. After Khat Mann and Penya changed the tire, we stopped by the side of the road in the next town where two men found a leak by submerging the inner tube in a tub of water and looking for bubbles. A growing crowd gawked at the *barang* while the mechanic melted glue to patch the leak.

Time slowed when my peripheral vision glimpsed a man handing a pistol to a child. The boy fumbled twice loading a clip into the butt then aimed at everyone around him before settling on me. I tried not to show any emotion or fear and did not look directly at the boy. As a *barang* I stood out and was an obvious target. No one else seemed alarmed, and I was relieved when the inner tube was patched. Khat Mann changed the tire in record time and we resumed our trek to Khmer Rouge strongholds in the Cardamom Mountains along the Thai border.

"Gangsters," Davide said as a black Toyota sedan with no plates passed us in a blinding plume of red dust that forced us to a crawl. Khat Mann lunged from the back seat for the bowie knife on the dash. As the dust settled and Davide resumed his frenzied pace, we were all glad to see a government checkpoint where the black Toyota had been stopped to search for guns. For once I was glad to see Hun Sen soldiers who waved us on.

Despite two flat tires we made it to Pailin by 9:30 in the evening, twelve hours after leaving Phnom Penh. Checking into his room next to mine at the Haeng Maes Hotel, Khat Mann handed me a bottle of shampoo that he had bought for me.

"Very good for hair," Khat Mann said.

I was thrilled the hotel had enough water for a shower to wash the road dirt from every orifice. When I squirted the shampoo onto my hand, I did not expect a black color that would not rinse off my hand. Although the shampoo had only been on for a few seconds it left a mark. Khat Mann tried to trick me into painting my hair black, but mischievousness was better than madness.

Khat Mann said that he wanted to see a woman downtown who had raised him and put on a clean shirt. We followed him through the two-story town to a dry good's store in the central market. I did not understand what the elderly woman said. The devastation on Khat Mann's face and hunched shoulders spoke volumes. Davide explained later that when Khat Mann went up to the old woman and queried, "Mother?" She replied, "That was a long time ago. I do not recognize you now." I felt sorry for Khat Mann losing his mother to an American bomb and his stepmother not recognizing him. I also understood that being an orphan made it easier for the Khmer Rouge to turn Khat Mann into a child soldier, which was why militias around the world conscripted children to kill civilians in uncivil wars.

Dr. Noun, Khat Mann, and Penya were itching for a night on the town. Grabbing my hand to inspect the black spot on my palm, Khat Mann insisted that I "paint my hair black." Tonight we would hunt for chickens. Chickens liked black hair. Not gray hair. Khat Mann was as irascible as he was persistent. I gave everyone their daily ration and said that I was staying with Sri La.

"Ohhhh!" Khat Mann approved. "Very good!"

It worked. Khat Mann put Viagra in his mouth, money in his sock, and led the Phnom Vor Gang into this smuggler's town like cowboys during a roundup. I was happy to see that Sri La was still working at the outdoor restaurant. Her youthful exuberance was a good sign for any virgin in a frontier town.

"Strong medicine," Sri La said inspecting the tiger on my cheek that swelled when I sipped one noodle from the clear beef broth. Sri La's concern was an oasis in a tumultuous ocean. We had a quiet dinner exchanging Khmer and English words. With none of the gang in sight, I slipped into my room for a much-needed night's sleep.

The next morning driving to the outskirts of town, I assumed we were going to Nuon Chea's house, but Davide said it was impossible for me to meet the Big Man this year. Nuon Chea had talked to the CIA attaché from the American embassy six months ago. In the year since I had met Nuon Chea, two American women journalists tried to meet him and were turned away. Many Cambodian and Western journalists had also tried to interview him. For sure Nuon Chea had no desire to talk to any foreigner. If there was ever a tribunal, Nuon Chea could get the death sentence or life imprisonment.

Davide stopped to ask the first of many people for directions to Phnom Malai, the last stronghold of the Khmer Rouge without any Hun Sen soldiers, or roads. When the pavement ended, we were pointed to small streams that fed into a flood plain. I tried arguing, but Davide was right. Nuon Chea lived like a prisoner in Pailin surrounded by the Cambodian Army. Once I talked to him for the second time, we would be followed by the Hun Sen Secret Police and the Khmer Rouge. If Khat Mann and Dr. Noun could get us through the checkpoints, we would try and meet General Mau, the last Khmer Rouge general to surrender to the Hun Sen government, in 1988. Pol Pot's wife and daughter also lived there.

As a minister in Democratic Kampuchea's Department of Economics, General Mau was one of the few people who lived in Phnom Penh after the Khmer Rouge evacuated everyone to the countryside. This meant that General Mau would know who gave the order to kill Malcolm Caldwell. We also had to get back to Pailin before dark. I knew Davide *was* right. I just wanted to be included in the decision-making process. I suppressed anger into the well of nightmares to avoid saying anything that would jeopardize the trip.

We drove all morning along a lattice of interconnecting dirt tracks and shallow riverbeds where giant reeds prevented any vistas. When the tracks ended in a swamp, we drove along a dry riverbed that would have been impossible during the rainy season. Penya used a typical Khmer Rouge greeting, "Hope bai? (Have you eaten rice today?)"

before asking settlers in pajama pants burning the hillsides for directions to Phnom Malai. Most people smiled and shook their heads.

"You add too much fucking oil," Davide screamed at Penya during a routine inspection of the engine. Penya said that he had checked the oil level before we started this morning. It was low so he added some more. Davide yelled again for Penya to do what he was told, not what he thought.

Davide's bellicosity reminded me of my father throwing a roast beef across the room because it was overcooked, hitting me with a canoe paddle from the stern if I did not paddle hard enough, yelling after dinner that he was never coming back and slamming the door. After smoking a cigarette outside under the stars, he always came back inside. Unlike my father's explosive temper, Davide held on to his rage.

When we reached the 1,000-foot stone slabs protruding from the earth like prehistoric dinosaur spines along Cambodia's northwest border with Thailand, Khat Mann got directions to General Mau's house from children in the market. I bought twenty kilos of rice and fruit before two children led us on bicycles into an idyllic neighborhood with red, white, orange, and vermillion sprays of bougainvillea along clean dirt paths and teak houses on stilts shaded by coconut, jackfruit, papaya, and mango trees.

General Mau was sitting under his house, chain-smoking cigarettes with the most callused fingers I had ever seen and white roots beneath his crew cut painted black. General Mau did not seem to mind Davide introducing himself and engaging him in conversation. He started as a commando with the Khmer Rouge in 1970. During Pol Pot's Democratic Kampuchea from 1975 to 1979, General Mau was one of the few people who lived in Phnom Penh with Pol Pot after everyone was evacuated to the countryside.

Davide talked with General Mau for over one hour. Because General Mau worked at the Ministry of Economics during Democratic Kampuchea from 1975-1979, he knew that Ny Kan worked under

Ieng Sary at the Ministry of Foreign Affairs, which meant that the decision to kill Caldwell came from Pol Pot to Ieng Sary.

Davide's logic went like this: Caldwell's meeting with Pol Pot lasted several hours. It was general knowledge that no one interviewed Pol Pot, they listened to him without interrupting. Pol Pot spoke French and some English. Caldwell only spoke English. After the interview Ieng Sary came in to listen to the tape. Unlike Pol Pot, Ieng Sary was fluent in French and English and realized that Pol Pot had told Caldwell about his plans to attack Vietnam. The Khmer Rouge had been infiltrating southern Vietnam since 1977.[114,115] Caldwell was a Communist and would warn the Vietnamese.

"Until now," Davide said, "the Khmer Rouge have blamed Son Sen, the minister of culture, for giving the direct order to kill Malcolm Caldwell. Everyone thought the order to kill Caldwell went from Pol Pot to Son Sen to Ny Kan—who sent the man. Today we have proven that the direct order to kill Caldwell came first from Pol Pot to Ieng Sary to Ny Kan, the other way around. This is important because Son Sen is dead. It is very easy to say it is his fault because he is no longer here. But Ieng Sary is living in a nice house in Phnom Penh.

"The Khmer Rouge put all of the fault on the dead," Davide continued, "because they are dead! So when you ask, 'Who did this?' they say, 'Is this man.' That is always the answer you get when you ask any Khmer Rouge a question. But General Mau did not know what I was talking about, and I take a round turn to get to the point. Ieng Sary is responsible for Malcolm Caldwell's murder. If one day there is a trial for the Khmer Rouge leaders, I think it would be nice to ask him in a clean way. And maybe justice will be done. I doubt it, but we can try."

POL POT'S UN SECRETARY

When Davide learned that Democratic Kampuchea's secretary to UNTAC that ran the country in the 1990s lived down the street, we returned to the market for more fruit and rice. Unlike the architects of the Khmer Rouge Revolution, Teph Kunnal was much younger. He spoke English and was used to talking with foreign dignitaries. He was also married to Mae Son, Pol Pot's widow.

While Teph Kunnal welcomed us to sit at a large mahogany table under his house, Dr. Noun talked with Pol Pot's wife and her eleven-year-old daughter under a mango tree. The acid in my stomach reminded me that we would not have time to leave Phnom Malai before dark. Teph Kunnal looked much younger than his fifty-six years. He had an athletic build, no gray hair, and stood over six feet tall.

With the unhurried grace of a diplomat, Teph Kunnal answered Davide's questions about the origins of the Khmer Rouge as a political entity. On June 26, 1951, Ho Chi Minh dissolved the Indochina People's Party and formed three parties: the Pathet Lao, the Cambodia Revolutionary Party, and the Vietnamese People Worker Party. Pol Pot returned to Cambodia from Paris in December 1952. Son

Sen returned in 1955. On September 13, 1960, Pol Pot was at the "Railroad Meeting," that started the split between the Cambodian and Vietnamese Communist Parties.

Pol Pot assumed the leadership of the Cambodian Communists in 1962, when Lon Nol soldiers killed his predecessor—Tou Samouth. It was not only Nuon Chea's decision, but the decision of the entire party. Pol Pot led the Khmer Rouge until 1989 when Pol Pot, Khieu Samphan, Nuon Chea, and Son Sen all decided that Son Sen was the new leader. Two years later, in December 1991, there was a large meeting in Pailin to downgrade Son Sen when he wanted to make an agreement with the Hun Sen government.

Teph Kunnal's quick, inquisitive eyes gave me the impression that I could ask any question. I was also competing with Davide, who hated being interrupted when I asked about Pol Pot's relationship with China.

"Pol Pot first went to China in 1964," Teph Kunnal said. "He was impressed by Mao and Chou Enlai, who also spoke French. Pol Pot had extensive contact with Chou Enlai and Deng Xiao Ping. Pol Pot went to Beijing in 1980 and met with Deng Xiao Ping. Deng Xiao Ping only asked one question, 'How is leadership and order?' Pol Pot said, 'Leadership is intact. Eighty percent of the cadres support us.' Deng Xiao Ping told him, 'OK, I support you.'"

I was not surprised to hear that China supported Pol Pot at the same time the CIA was supplying arms to the Khmer Rouge when Vietnamese soldiers routed them to camps along the Thai border to fight their common enemy, Vietnam.

Teph Kunnal outlined three stages of the Khmer Rouge Revolution. Under Pol Pot's leadership, the first stage of Democratic Kampuchea was to build roads and dams and grow enough rice to become self-sufficient. Pol Pot used the same methods for irrigation as the ancient Khmer kings, enlisting the general population to dig irrigation canals. Like the Khmer kings, the Khmer Rouge hoped to triple the yearly production of rice. The second stage of the revolution was intended to develop industry, build rubber plantations, and begin to export. Now Teph Kunnal wondered if Cambodia could become a nation after all its roots had been destroyed.

"Who decided to evacuate the cities?"

"It was Pol Pot's decision to evacuate the cities."

"What about the 1.2 million people in Phnom Penh who had taken refuge from the American bombing? They would have been sympathetic to the Khmer Rouge, yet they were labeled as April 17 people."

"That is not a question!" Davide sputtered and asked about the relationship between Pol Pot and Son Sen in October 1979.

"The Thai government pushed for an alliance to fight the Vietnamese," Teph Kunnal said without altering his tone. "When Son Sen went to shake Pol Pot's hand, Pol Pot said, 'You have blood on your hands.' But beside this, Pol Pot viewed Son Sen as a true patriot."

"What effect did American bombing have on Cambodia?"

"The American bombing gave the Khmer Rouge an enemy to fight," Teph Kunnal said. "The bombs did not kill many people. But they destroyed Cambodia's economy. This is what made people hate America. There were two other reasons Cambodians hated America. First, the US had sided with South Vietnam. Second, the US bombed Cambodia directly."

When I asked if the Khmer Rouge would have done anything different, the jugular veins on Davide's neck distended.

"There were three main reasons why the Khmer Rouge Revolution failed," Teph Kunnal said. "First, there was poor communication between Pol Pot and his commanders. Second, some of the regional commanders acted like little kings. And third, pride. It was the decision in 1992 by Khieu Samphan and Pol Pot to not join phase two with the United Nations that marked the end of the Khmer Rouge as a political force."

Teph Kunnal apologized that he had work to do. Like Khieu Samphan and Nuon Chea, Teph Kunnal was gracious and hospitable despite our imposition into his home. And Teph Kunnal had critiqued the Khmer Rouge Revolution, something I had hoped for but not thought possible. As we backed out of the driveway, Teph Kunnal waved goodbye, Pol Pot's wife and daughter standing by his side like the proverbial happy family. I wanted more time to talk with Teph Kunnal, but time had run out.

POL POT'S DEATH

Darkness struck like a hammer as Davide drove too fast on unfamiliar terrain, too fast for bandits lurking in the shadows. For nine hours Davide did not stop driving. No one said a word except Khat Mann who talked incessantly with Chhouk Rin on his cell phone. The threat of being attacked peppered everyone's fears until we reached a small mining town that would never be on a map. It was after midnight but dozens of people were at the only outdoor restaurant celebrating the Chinese New Year with fireworks and inebriated cheers. After the first sip of curried coconut soup, my cheek drained a foul effluent with the immediate relief of pain.

Dr. Noun said that he talked with Pol Pot's wife, Mae Son, while we were talking with Teph Kunnal. When Pol Pot got sick, Mae Son said that Ta Mok would not give him medicine or food and took her away so she could not feed him. She thought Ta Mok was going to kill her and their daughter. Ta Mok wanted to kill everyone close to Pol Pot. Teph Kunnal, Khieu Samphan, and Nuon Chea had survived by escaping into the mountains.

I knew of the journalist Nate Thayer who gained worldwide notoriety in July 1997 when he was permitted to visit the jungle camp in Anlong Veng where Pol Pot was being tried for treason. Thayer documented his interview in his book, *Sympathy for the Devil: Living Dangerously in Cambodia: A Foreign Correspondent's Story*.[116] In October 1987, Nate Thayer became the second Western journalist besides Elizabeth Becker of the *New York Times* to interview Pol Pot.[117]

"First," Pol Pot said, "I want to let you know that I came to join the revolution, not to kill Cambodian people. Look at me now. Do you think . . . am I a violent person? No. So, as far as my conscience and my mission were concerned, there was no problem. This needs to be clarified. My experience was the same as that of my movement. We were new and inexperienced and events kept occurring one after the other that we had to deal with. In doing that, we made mistakes as I told you. I admit it now and I admitted it in the notes I have written. Whoever wishes to blame or attack me is entitled to do so. I regret I didn't have enough experience to totally control the movement. On the other hand, with our constant struggle, this had to be done together with others in the communist world to stop Kampuchea from becoming Vietnamese. For the love of the nation and the people it was the right thing to do but in the course of our actions we made some mistakes."[118]

Thayer was allowed to visit Anlong Veng and see Pol Pot on April 16, 1998, one day after he died, but the details of his death remained elusive.[119] I asked Dr. Noun how Pol Pot had died, and Davide, still basking in the aura of solving the mystery surrounding Caldwell's murder, admitted this was a good question.

Dr. Noun spoke at length before Khat Mann translated. In the late nineties before he died, Pol Pot became *ch kuot* (crazy), and jealous of the other Khmer Rouge leaders. In 1997, Pol Pot killed Son Sen, his number one general. When Ta Mok heard about this, and that Pol Pot planned to kill all the remaining Khmer Rouge leaders, Ta Mok put Pol Pot in a bamboo cage and tried him in a jungle court. Knowing Ta Mok was going to kill him, Pol Pot asked Teph Kunnal to marry his wife and raise his daughter, which he did.

When the US embassy found out that Ta Mok was going to kill

Pol Pot, they sent someone with a suitcase of cash. Ta Mok was smart. He also talked with the Chinese who had supplied the Khmer Rouge with weapons, ammunition, and advisors since the 1970s. Not wanting Pol Pot to talk to the US, the Chinese government gave Ta Mok $1 million for his family, outbidding the Americans, in return for Pol Pot's death.

Dr. Noun said the Khmer believe that old spirits can depart and new spirits can come into this life on the New Year. Ta Mok killed Pol Pot with a "poison" at midnight on the last day of the Khmer New Year so his spirit could never come back to this world. I tried to elicit the kind of poison that could kill Pol Pot that quickly to no avail. In the end, cremating the body erased all evidence. The Khmer Rouge, forever lacking in ammunition, had improvised to prevent Pol Pot's reincarnation.

Pol Pot's death was an apt metaphor for the demise of the Khmer Rouge Revolution. In essence the Khmer Rouge cannibalized themselves. Not allowing new recruits after 1975, when the Khmer Rouge ousted the US-backed Lon Nol government, and the constant purges of child soldiers and cadre leaders suspected of having ties to the US, Vietnamese, and Russian intelligence services assured the eventual demise of the Khmer Rouge as an effective military and political force.

BROTHER NUMBER TWO AGAIN

Khat Mann arrived before sunrise to report that Nuon Chea was still protected by 10,000 Khmer Rouge soldiers and their families, and that his wife said we could come up the road on the back of the mountain. Hun Sen's troops guarded the main entrance on the other side of the mountain.

"If Nuon Chea has a little bit of intelligence," Davide said, "offer to help him publish his story outside of Cambodia. At a tribunal they will only ask him questions to put him in prison. He is the only one alive who can clarify history. After Pol Pot died in 1988, Hun Sen made Khieu Samphan and Nuon Chea come into Phnom Penh to sign an agreement signaling the end of the war. Both men are wanted for a tribunal. They have no amnesty like Ieng Sary and Chhouk Rin. Khieu Samphan has less to worry about. No one will testify against him. Nuon Chea has the most to lose. He was always in the inner circle. When you met him last year, did he have the laser eyes of a killer?"

Another gush of fetid fluid from my cheek flavored the sober edge of fear as we bought twenty kilos of mangos, green grapes, dried fish, and the best rice. Driving twenty-five kilometers through scorched jungle on the back road to Nuon Chea's house, I was blinded by my desire to meet the highest living architect of the Khmer Rouge Revolution who was responsible for 2 million Cambodians' deaths. An acrid haze clinging to the nearby hills heightened the adrenaline pacing my heart and acid burning my stomach as we drove past the antiaircraft gun and under the raised metal bar guarding Nuon Chea's compound.

Wearing a white windbreaker with a "Bad Boy" monogram over his heart, Nuon Chea was waiting for us at the top of the stairs. His wife accepted our gifts and sat us at the table. The small altar remained on the wall but the monk was noticeably absent. Nuon Chea had aged. He said that he was glad to see me and asked if I had the photo I had promised to give him. I was embarrassed that I had forgotten and said that I didn't have his mailing address, which was true, and offered to send him another. Davide introduced himself in Khmer and invited Nuon Chea and his family to stay at his Marco Polo Restaurant and Guest House in Kampot.

When I asked about his health, Nuon Chea replied that he had a second stroke six months ago but did not want to talk about the past. Cambodia needed to look to the future. Nuon Chea was still intoxicated with the words *glo-bal-iz-a-tion*, *e-gal-it-e*, *li-ber-te*, and *fra-ter-ni-te*, but he took more time to enunciate each syllable. Nuon Chea continued that in every country of the world a man is born (*cut*), grows old (*chi*), becomes ill (*chu*), and dies (*slop*).

"*Slop!*" Nuon Chea exclaimed, the word rolling off his lips like a guillotine. Everyone went through this. This was life. According to Nuon Chea, today Cambodia needed help from all countries. Nuon Chea said that he had no bad feelings for any people. He loved the Americans, Chinese, Vietnamese, even Thai. He said Cambodia must be friends and work together with all countries to rebuild. When people forgot this, they made war. There was no reason to fight. Peace was very important.

"*Glo-bal-iz-a-tion*," Nuon Chea repeated through his few remaining teeth that did not match. If I heard him say *Glo-bal-iz-a-tion* one more time I thought I would vomit. I said that I had met Khieu Samphan the previous year and asked how he was doing. Nuon Chea said that Khieu Samphan's son had arrived yesterday with a car from Anlong Veng. They left this morning on vacation.

Davide refused to ask Nuon Chea about a tribunal, the effects of American bombing, and what it was like fighting against and with the US. Nuon Chea chatted with Dr. Noun and Khat Mann, who had been sitting upright and mute, like old friends. Out of enormous frustration, I reached out and touched the "Bad Boy" monogram on Nuon Chea's windbreaker.

"Don't touch him!" Davide yelled too late and jumped up. Khat Mann froze. The room fell silent. Nuon Chea did not register any emotion. I asked Nuon Chea in French what it was like when he was in the army, and I was surprised when tears welled in his eyes.

"So many deaths," Nuon Chea replied in English. "I know what it feels like to go to war and leave my family."

I had found a nerve. Nuon Chea's second stroke had left him vulnerable emotionally. When a loud screech accompanied my reaching into my daypack and pulling out my pocket-sized Olympic camera, Nuon Chea's wife relocated her chair behind me.

"What are you doing?" Davide screamed.

"One photo?"

"I told you no photographs," Davide said, but Nuon Chea was a ham for having several pictures taken sitting next to me, and with Dr. Noun, Khat Mann, and Davide. Once we were safely in the car, Davide said he liked this motherfucker better than he thought.

As predicted, a white Toyota sedan followed us to the outskirts of Pailin. Fording a stream, Davide said that I had a spirit watching over me. Touching an ordinary Khmer was considered impolite. Touching a Khmer Rouge general was punishable by death. Anyone else who touched Nuon Chea would have been killed. Davide drove fast enough to stay ahead of Hun Sen's police.

As if on cue, Chhouk Rin called Khat Mann on his cell phone and demanded that we meet for a "farewell dinner." Khat Mann reiterated that I did not want Chhouk Rin to be mad at me. Between each kilometer and each call on his cell phone, Khat Mann became quieter, except when he turned to me and asked if he would get in trouble for telling me that Vietcong soldiers had fucked a water buffalo.

I was frustrated by Nuon Chea's pablum, my naïve attempt to get him to acknowledge atrocities committed in his name, and Davide's refusal to translate my questions. Compared to Teph Kunnal's summation and critique of the Khmer Rouge Revolution, Nuon Chea was a smiling motherfucker. I was also acutely aware of Khat Mann's growing distance and fear that harm would come to him because of our association, and Chhouk Rin's anger that I made him lose face by not meeting him with Hun Sen's secret police.

MR. MUHN

Pol Pot's telegraph operator lived in Samlaut, the most heavily mined part of Cambodia, and the world. The Cambodian Mine Action Center (CMAC) estimates there are between 4 and 6 million unexploded mines in Cambodia, with the majority scattered along the Thai border. According to the UN, if the world applied its present technology, it would take 100 years to clear all the land mines from Cambodia, 1,100 years to clear all the land mines in the world.[120] Unlike the journalist Nic Dunlop who spent years tracking Duch to this remote Khmer Rouge enclave in 1999, I had two distinct advantages. Khat Mann was Pol Pot's telegraph operator in Phnom Vor and had talked with Mr. Muhn hundreds of times, and Dr. Noun was Mr. Muhn's brother-in-law.

Khmer Rouge soldiers defending their jungle sanctuaries for two decades against the Cambodian Army, and Vietnamese occupation from 1978 to 1989, deserve much of the blame for the casualties inflicted by land mines. But the lion's share goes to the American and Chinese sponsors of the war. CMAC has also found mines in Cambodia made in South Africa, Bulgaria, Chile, the former Czechoslovakia, East Germany, Hungary, India, Iran, Iraq, North and South

Korea, Poland, the former USSR, Thailand, Vietnam, and the former Yugoslavia.

Davide sped for two hours on dirt roads to stay ahead of Hun's secret police. As the sun reached high in the sky, burning jungle gave way to rolling hills where men in blue uniforms with metal detectors combed the ground and thatched huts. Red flags and metal signs with a skull and crossed bones: *DANGER MINES*, marked mines that a separate crew in black flak jackets and helmets detonated. Hundreds of red flags and an inordinate number of children and adults missing limbs reminded me of Nuon Chea temporarily recalling the horrors of war.

Davide was so relieved to find a woman sitting by the road who poured forty-one liters of gas from old soda bottles into the tank that he apologized for not filling up in Pailin, and joked that he was in a hurry to leave. To his credit, Davide had gotten us safely in and out of Khmer Rouge strongholds. My biggest worry was meeting Pol Pot's telegraph operator and Davide or Khat Mann refusing to translate.

When Mr. Muhn was not at his thatched home, the oldest of four children went in search of his father. We retraced our route to the Samlaut market where a juvenile monkey on a ladder attacked anyone within range of its leash. The market provided kilos of fresh beef, chicken, fish, fruits, and vegetables. When a man squatting under a thatched roof revealed a block of ice under mounds of rice husks, I found a plastic washtub and filled it with beer and ice.

Proud of my creation, I showed Khat Mann my washtub of "*Angkor glace.*" Khat Mann took me aside and said that I should give some money to Dr. Noun if we met Mr. Muhn. Dr. Noun had not gotten money for meeting Nuon Chea. Khat Mann did not fail to repeat that Dr. Noun was Ta Mok's nephew, that Dr. Noun's sister was married to Mr. Muhn, and that Dr. Noun had a Pure Biography. I complimented Khat Mann for being a great translator and bodyguard and promised that I would give Dr. Noun and Khat Mann each $100 bonuses when we got back to Phnom Penh if we met Mr. Muhn. Khat Mann and Dr. Noun beamed. We were on the same team again for the moment.

"I hope beer does not make Muhn crazy," Khat Mann said. "Muhn is a very ugly man. When children see him, they cry and run away."

Mr. Muhn's wife, Ouch Nim, accepted our offering of food and started cooking. She had the same gentle demeanor and round cheeks as Dr. Noun. To everyone's amusement, Khat Mann found the collapsible chair and generator that he used to run his telegraph and provide light while Dr. Noun operated on Chhouk Rin. Setting up the pedals, Khat Mann cycled from a sitting position, then on his back. Touching an exposed wire and getting shocked ignited raucous laughter.

"Number one!" Khat Mann exclaimed. "Made in China!"

Mr. Muhn's arrival interrupted Khat Mann demonstrating how to lay anti-tank mines. Mr. Muhn had the same leathery complexion as Chhouk Rin from decades under the sun. He was fifty-seven years old, bald but not ugly, and welcomed me with a handshake. We posed for pictures at Khat Mann's direction before sitting cross-legged in a circle on the front porch. Mosquitoes feasted on my arms and legs while Ouch Nim and her children served beef sautéed with chilies and cabbage, chicken sautéed with scallions and basil, smoked fish on bamboo skewers, and sliced cucumbers, tomatoes, and onions. I heaped more food on my anti-mine casing than I had eaten in a week.

Mr. Muhn was pleasant, thoughtful, and played with his children. He joined the Khmer Rouge after hearing Sihanouk on the radio when he was twenty-five years old. Sihanouk had gone into exile in China where he made regular pleas for all Cambodians to help the Khmer Rouge overthrow the Lon Nol government. Everyone knew that the American CIA was behind the Lon Nol coup.

Khat Mann explained that Mr. Muhn translated everything Pol Pot said from Khmer into "telegraph" and sent this to regional commanders who forwarded the message to the radiomen in their districts. Mr. Muhn also received their replies. Khat Mann was proud that he was "Pol Pot's radio man in Kampot" and repeated that Mr. Muhn had a "picture mind."

Eyeing my journal, Mr. Muhn asked if I was a journalist. His question was a trap. The Khmer Rouge despised journalists as much as Lon Nol soldiers and the CIA. This was also ironic because my bribing the Phnom Vor Gang with a daily ration and Viagra violated journalists' unwritten code of ethics. Opening my notebook to a blank page, I said that I was a physician interested in how the Khmer Rouge came to power.

Mr. Muhn, Dr. Noun, and Khat Mann watched me draw a big oval Cambodia with the Tonlé Sap Lake in the north, and the Tonlé Sap and Mekong Rivers converging in the south. I labeled Vietnam to the east and Laos to the north. It did not take long for Khat Man to note the similarity between my map and a vagina and touch the Tonlé Sap, giggling like a schoolboy.

When asked if he had seen any Americans in Cambodia, Mr. Muhn said that he had not seen any US soldiers but he knew they had entered Cambodia many times. Mr. Muhn traced his finger from Laos to Vietnam and Cambodia where the Americans bombed the Ho Chi Minh Trail in the late sixties. Pointing to Cambodia's eastern border with Vietnam, Mr. Muhn said the US started bombing Vietcong soldiers who had crossed the Cambodian border in 1969 to hide from US bombing in Vietnam. When the Vietcong moved farther into Cambodia to avoid the bombing, more bombs followed.

Khat Mann said that Phnom Vor did not see many bombs until 1973 when the entire country was bombed. He demonstrated with upraised arms what it was like when a bomb exploded. "After bomb fall," Khat Mann said, "many people want to join Khmer Rouge." Mr. Muhn surprised me when Khat Mann said, "Mr. Muhn want to thank you for American bombs. He say America bombs give Cambodia people many ponds for frog. And frogs are easy to steal!"

Like Teph Kunnal, Democratic Kampuchea's UN representative, Mr. Muhn answered any question. In 1973, Mr. Muhn stayed close to the Vietnamese border where he saw many B-52s drop bombs. Another plane, with a hole in the middle of the tail, was for intelligence. The Khmer Rouge called this plane *chan srai*. There was also a C-130 cargo plane that dropped food and ammunition for Lon Nol soldiers.

Khat Mann boasted that Mr. Muhn was very smart. One day Mr. Muhn got an American walkie-talkie from a Lon Nol soldier who had been killed. For two weeks Mr. Muhn hid near the Lon Nol soldiers and listened to them talk on the radio to their planes. When he learned the codes, he pretended that he was a Lon Nol commander and called the American planes at the last minute to change the coordinates and drop food and ammunition to Khmer Rouge soldiers instead of Lon Nol soldiers. Mr. Muhn did this many times, which is how he got to try American food. He liked canned fish, chocolate, cigarettes, sugar, and coffee. At first no one knew what toilet paper was for.

Mr. Muhn said that before the Americans bombed Cambodia, the Khmer people did not know about America. But after 1973, when the US bombed the countryside every day for six months, many people became angry at America and joined the Khmer Rouge. I asked how many troops the Khmer Rouge had in 1968, before America started bombing. Davide yelled that it was impossible to get exact numbers and refused to inquire about the Khmer Rouge troop strength.

I stifled thoughts of punching Davide. Sensing that I was losing control, Khat Mann spoke to Mr. Muhn in Khmer. After a while Khat Mann said the Khmer Rouge had only a few hundred "propaganda officers," and they did not have guns, before America started bombing. Pointing to my map, I asked how many soldiers the Khmer Rouge had in different parts of Cambodia in 1969, after the first year of US bombing.

"This is not a question!" Davide barked.

In consultation with Dr. Noun, Mr. Muhn divided Cambodia into five slices of a pie according to their radio call signs. Ta Mok was 160. Sam Bith was 140. There were also 180, 190, and 170. Mr. Muhn wrote down 12 times 4 = 48, 48 times 4 = 192, 192 times 4 = 768, 768 times 4 = 3,072, and 3,072 times 4 = 12,288. After Dr. Noun and Khat Mann both agreed, Mr. Muhn wrote the number 12,288 next to each of the five sections with a call sign.

Khat Mann translated that the Khmer Rouge had 1,000 soldiers in 1970, when the Vietnamese Communists came to Cambodia to help fight the Lon Nol regime. In 1972, the Khmer Rouge had two battalions in the north and two battalions in the south, approximately 24,000 soldiers. After America bombed the whole countryside in 1973, the Khmer Rouge recruited three new battalions in the south, and three battalions in the north. They also had new battalions on the Vietnamese and Thai border for a total of twelve battalions.

I reclaimed my notebook and checked their addition. Before the Americans started bombing in Cambodia in 1969, the Khmer Rouge had approximately 200 propaganda officers. By 1972, the Khmer Rouge had recruited 24,576 soldiers. By 1973, after eight months of carpet-bombing the entire country, the Khmer Rouge had 73,728 soldiers, enough to overthrow the US-backed Lon Nol government.

I knew the numbers were not accurate but they were similar to Western intelligence estimates of 68,000.[121] When I asked Khat Mann again how many soldiers the Khmer Rouge had at the end of US bombing in 1973, he repeated that the Khmer Rouge had 60,000 soldiers. I took this as an auspicious number, not a statistic, but I was elated. The numbers were not as important as the fact that there was a method to their calculation. When I asked Mr. Muhn what he thought of America now, he said that he liked America. He believed in human rights and democracy and wanted to learn English.

I said that between 1975 and 1979, the UN estimated that between 1 to 2 million Cambodians died during the Khmer Rouge time out of a total population of 6 million. Mr. Muhn looked astonished and reclaimed my journal and started writing numbers on several pages. From 1970 to 1974, the Khmer Rouge fighters were outside Phnom Penh. During this time many people went to Phnom Penh to avoid the American bombing.

"Rich people," Khat Mann said referring to everyone in Phnom Penh before the Khmer Rouge overtook the city. "Rich people from city cannot adapt to everyone equal, and everyone grow rice. In countryside not much rice. Pol Pot say village people not have rice because rich people in city take all. When village people hear this, they want to kill all city people."

"Why do you think Pol Pot said this?"

"I think Pol Pot like village people because they easy to control," Khat Mann said.

"What happened to the people from Phnom Penh who were moved to the countryside?"

Dr. Noun and Mr. Muhn conferred before Khat Mann said that 20 to 25 percent of the New People died from malaria, diarrhea, and starvation. Pol Pot protected people with skill, people who could grow rice, because Pol Pot had no skill. People who were lazy, people who earned money from poor people, people who supported Lon Nol, people with Bad Biographies were killed. After detailed consideration and addition, Mr. Muhn and Dr. Noun agreed. During "Pol Pot time" from 1975 to 1979, 18 percent of the Cambodian population died, approximately 1 million people, but most of these deaths were not from the Khmer Rouge.

I was familiar with the Khmer Rouge's perspective that they had liberated Cambodia from foreign domination that started with six centuries of Siamese and Vietnamese invasions after King Suryavarman VII was dethroned in 1218, and a hundred years of French colonial rule. I also knew that Pol Pot used slave labor to remake the Khmer empire, like the God Kings that dominated Southeast Asia from the ninth to thirteenth centuries. I was impressed by Mr. Muhn's calculation of Khmer Rouge troop strength in relation to US bombing, and by his frank acknowledgment of the magnitude of deaths during the Khmer Rouge Revolution.

Mr. Muhn said that he was worried for the future of the mid-level Khmer Rouge leaders. Hun Sen government soldiers watched all the Khmer Rouge in Samlaut and Pailin. If it were any consolation, I told Mr. Muhn that the UN had just withdrawn from trying to have an international tribunal. As I got up to stretch, Mr. Muhn asked if he could ask me a question. I was flattered. I had asked him enough questions about taboo subjects.

"Mr. Muhn want you to drop one more bomb here," Khat Mann said, pointing to tall grass behind the house. "Mr. Muhn want one more pond for frogs."

THE ANGRY SKIES

As the children cleared our plates of anti-tank mine casings, Davide insisted that I talk with Mr. Muhn's wife. Davide was incensed by my quest for numbers and said that Ouch Nim had more interesting things to say. Straight jet-black hair framed Ouch Nim's cherubic face. She looked younger than her forty-one years and showed us a picture of her as a young soldier standing at attention with four rows of *Nari Yotea* (Virgin Combatants or Virgin Warriors). Ouch Nim was thirteen years old when she joined the *Nari Yotea*.

Ouch Nim used my map of Cambodia to point out the routes that she hiked from Koh Kong in Thailand over the Elephant Mountains, carrying supplies of food and ammunition to the Khmer Rouge troops on the front lines. What measured 200 kilometers on the map could be two or three times as long because the terrain and American bombing made it impossible to walk in a straight line. Davide laughed when Ouch Nim said that she was not very strong and could only carry fifty kilos. Some of the older girls carried sixty kilos.

Ouch Nim described what it was like when the Americans started bombing. In 1969 and 1970 she did not see many bombs. But as the Americans bombed more of the countryside, she saw many bombs that were dangerous for her gang and forced them to hike at night. During the day they were afraid to go out in the open and hid in the jungle.

"One day Ouch Nim saw a bomb kill five girls who were hiding in a bunker. Many times she saw American bombs kill thirteen-, fourteen-, and fifteen-year-old girls. When the skies became angry, everyone hated America."

JUSTICE IS FOR THE GODS

Driving back to Phnom Penh, Davide said that it was difficult for Westerners to understand how Cambodians viewed justice. If a woman planting rice stepped on a land mine and lost her leg, it was her fault. In the West people might take pity on the woman. In Cambodia she would be robbed. She lost her leg because she had done something bad in a previous life. It was her karma. Justice was for the gods, not humans. In this land of smiles where so many people had been killed, I thought of Chhouk Rin and how many times he had been wounded and how many people he had killed. What happened to a soldier's psyche who had been so close to death for so long that he saw himself as a ghost?

"Once you become wounded you feel you are worthless. You really don't give a fuck if you live or die. You are a piece of shit. If this happens more than once, it is difficult to come back to a family or get married or live in one place."

The Toyota developing an oil leak did not stop us from reaching Phnom Penh before sunset. When I got money from my safety deposit box at the Goldiana, Khat Mann seemed disappointed with his $200 bonus and asked again if anything bad would happen to him because he told me that Vietnamese soldiers had fucked a water buffalo. Khat

Mann's concern for his safety was understandable. My contact with him could get him killed by the Vietnamese-dominated Hun Sen government. I was more concerned for my safety and what Chhouk Rin was thinking.

Without saying goodbye or thank you, Davide told me to leave Cambodia immediately, then drove Dr. Noun, Khat Mann, and Penya to Kampot. But I did not want to leave without talking to Youk Chhang and someone in "defense intelligence" at the US embassy. Eating my first salad in weeks confined me to my hotel room the following day. As soon as I could tolerate tea and toast, I called Youk Chhang to ask what mechanisms Cambodians had to forgive their captors.

"In all of the world's great religions," Youk Chhang said, "Islam, Christianity, Judaism, if you commit a crime, you must pay. I have read the Bible and the Koran and Buddhist texts. If a man kills another man, he must be punished. For Cambodians to get beyond the Khmer Rouge genocide, they must have a tribunal for the leaders of the Khmer Rouge Revolution. Khieu Samphan and Nuon Chea are old men. It would be a shame if they died before they could be tried."

"Is there a chance the Khmer Rouge could return to power?"

"The Cambodian people will never allow the Khmer Rouge to take over again. Not after what they have done. If the Khmer Rouge came to my door right now, I would kill them."

DEFENSE INTELLIGENCE

It paid to show up early for a 10 a.m. meeting with the US embassy defense attaché, Chief Warrant Officer 2 John L. Kribbs. One year ago, I remembered visa applicants seated in long rows inside a metal cage. Today, days before George W. Bush launched Gulf War II, the cage was empty. I passed through the outer perimeter where guards patted me down, recorded my passport number, and issued a pass that let me through another metal detector and search before entering the political wing of the US embassy.

Captain Jones introduced himself as Colonel Kribbs's secretary. He apologized that the colonel was out on the range and seated me on a camouflage couch with camouflage cushions in front of a floor to ceiling map of Cambodia covered with a clear plastic sheet. Black symbols scribbled on every province attested to this being a busy time of year. Captain Jones had short, thinning hair and appeared at ease. He had been in Cambodia for two months of his two-year tour, and his wife was already much happier. He had been stationed in war zones in Macedonia and Algeria. He had also been in Inner Mongolia. Cambodia was isolated and backward, but his wife liked him coming home every night.

Captain Jones agreed that Cambodia was more developed in the sixties than it was today, twenty-four years after the Khmer Rouge regime. Pol Pot destroyed the country. In 1960, Cambodians lived in peace despite the US war in Indochina. People had enough to eat. Cambodia exported rice and rubber. The captain also agreed that the carpet-bombing in 1973 helped the Khmer Rouge cause. Captain Jones pointed to the northeastern provinces bordering Vietnam and Laos.

"The Vietnamese troops regrouped in Cambodia to launch strikes against US troops in South Vietnam. They built schools and hospitals in the Cambodian jungles that were legitimate targets."

Regarding the Cambodian people, Captain Jones said the Khmer villagers had no educational background. They didn't care about the future or tomorrow. All they cared about was how they were going to live today. Captain Jones admitted that he was to the right of Attila the Hun, right next to Dick Cheney. He had one son in the military and thought it was our duty to fight world tyranny after it came to our soil on 9/11. Captain Jones also believed there were already more than enough reasons to attack Iraq, Iran, and North Korea.

"Do you think the American bombing helped the Khmer Rouge rise to power?"

Captain Jones looked in my eyes. "We have God on our side, son. Don't forget that. Are you a Communist?"

"I'm a humanitarian."

"What do you do with monsters like Osama bin Laden and Saddam Hussein?"

"Not support them in the first place."

Captain Jones and I would not see eye to eye but he did not take offense at my questions and said that Cambodia was ruled by a very corrupt 1 percent of the population. There was no middle class. Most people were poor villagers who were easy to brainwash. The villagers did not know politics.

When I asked if American bombing helped the Khmer Rouge recruit an army, Captain Jones admitted that the Khmer Rouge were scattered, poorly trained, and not well organized before 1973. The carpet-bombing in 1973 helped the Khmer Rouge to recruit. "You have to understand that Pol Pot was not the sharpest tool in the shed. You take the wrong man, Pol Pot, at the right time and the right circumstances and you have a disaster. The Khmer Rouge had children twelve to fourteen years old doing most of the killing. When the child soldiers got older or started to question what they were doing, they were killed."

"What is the Defense Department's main job in Cambodia?"

"The Defense Department's main function as an organization is to try and assess what the people need and get the most bang for our buck. It's not rocket science. Right now, Cambodia needs basic development: infrastructure, roads, clinics, and schools."

For once I was in 100 percent agreement with the military attaché and asked what happens now that the UN pulled out of a tribunal to try the architects of the Khmer Rouge?

"After the Thai riot, Cambodia was pulled off the map. The embassy's chief concern right now is repatriating the Montagnards back to Vietnam. Personally, I think it's better if there's no tribunal. One of the Khmer Rouge generals died last week. What's his name?"

"General Maes."

"Something like that. The leaders of the Khmer Rouge are all old men with health problems. They're not going to live much longer. One worry with a tribunal is that it gets the Khmer Rouge to start fighting again. Look what happened in Liberia. Right now, the Cambodian Army can't even hold Pailin."

FAREWELL TO HARM

When Davide called to say that Chhouk Rin had ordered Khat Mann to kill me, I lost my ability to distinguish between fantasy and reality, paranoia and fear. Two gunshots punctuated my last dinner at the FCC. No tourists looked over the balcony to see three policemen wrestling a playboy to the ground. Looking past Sisowath Avenue bustling with pedestrians, monks, tourists, and beggars to the enormous new Sharp and Suzuki billboards on the opposite bank of the Mekong River, with florescent red and blue lights reflecting across the water, I hoped that development would be kind to Cambodia.

When I got back to the hotel, I called Khat Mann who answered on the first ring. He sounded distant. Gone were his adolescent jubilations. There were heavy traffic sounds in the background. "You are still at the Goldiana!" Khat Mann yelled above the din. Paranoia gripped every part of my being.

"Where are you?"

"I at my house. When you come to Kampot?"

Kampot did not have traffic. I was a snail traversing a razor's edge. Khat Mann was already in Phnom Penh on his way to the Goldiana.

"I'll see you next year," I said, calculating the time it would take Sokha to get me to the airport.

"Chhouk Rin very angry you not pay money," Khat Mann said.

It was a classic lose-lose situation. The Khmer Rouge could kill me and blame Hun Sen goons. Hun Sen goons could kill me and blame the Khmer Rouge. Killing in Cambodia was like giving out a speeding ticket at a NASCAR race. Three opposition politicians from Sam Rainsy and FUNCINPEC (National United Front for an Independent, Neutral, Peaceful and Cooperative Cambodia) parties had been murdered in the last month. Hun Sen attributed the executions at gunpoint in broad daylight to robbery. I called Sokha and said that I had a "Pol Pot problem" and needed to get to the airport.

As I packed, King Abdulla of Jordan was on CNN after a meeting with US President George W. Bush. The US invasion of Iraq for the second time in a decade was imminent. Wolf Blitzer quoted President Bush telling King Abdulla he was going to "smash Saddam Hussein because we are the mightiest nation in the world, and you are either with us or against us."

Sokha slalomed down both lanes of Monivong Boulevard while I searched for Khat Mann on the crowded streets where there would be no witnesses. Chhouk Rin had already been convicted of the backpackers' murders and faced life imprisonment. He was angry at me for being interrogated by Hun Sen's secret police and not inviting him on another trip to Pailin. Worse, my not meeting him in Phnom Penh for a second interrogation by his police escort made him lose face.

Sokha cried when the guard would not let un-ticketed passengers into the Ponchetong International Airport that was still scarred by fire damage from the Thai riot. A three-story glass wall separating the terminal from the parking lot made us an easy shot for anyone driving by.

"Same-same my brother," Sokha said. "Cambodia not safe. Pol Pot kill. Understand?"

"I understand," I said, giving Sokha a $200 handshake.

As the tension washed off in waves, it took months to not take it personally that Chhouk Rin ordered Khat Mann to kill me. Without Chhouk Rin, Khat Mann, and Dr. Noun, I would not have learned how the Khmer Rouge manipulated the villagers' hatred of US bombing and foreign devils into the hatred of everyone living in cities. I would not have seen how this animosity, combined with the human and economic devastation from American bombing, and King Sihanouk's pleas, enabled the Khmer Rouge to rise from a rag-tag group of Maoist-inspired Communist guerrillas and defeat the US-backed Cambodian government.

Cambodia's genocide is unique because the Khmer Rouge killed one quarter of their own people. For me the question remained if the Khmer Rouge were more brutal in Cambodia than the Chinese Communists still are in Tibet. There was no doubt that the US bombing of Cambodia was a crime against humanity, and that the destruction and hatred on the ground helped the Khmer Rouge rise to power and fueled their genocide.

SLOUCHING TOWARD A TRIBUNAL

Ironically, the Cambodian court system's pursuit of the Phnom Vor Gang kidnapping and killing three Western backpackers, not the violent deaths of 2 million Cambodians, helped pave the way for a tribunal to try the architects of the Khmer Rouge Revolution for crimes against humanity from April 17, 1975, to January 6, 1979. Sam Bith was arrested in March 2002 and charged with conspiring to kill David Wilson from Australia, Jean Michel Braquet from France, and Mark Slater from England.[122] On December 23 of the same year Sam Bith was sentenced to life in prison where he died on February 15, 2008.[123,124] Chhouk Rin was sentenced in absentia for the backpackers' murders in 1994, but he was not arrested until October 26, 2005.[125] After he lost his appeal in February 2005, it was rumored that Chhouk Rin was being held in Phnom Penh's military hospital where he was dying of AIDS.

It took thirty-one years for the Cambodian and international courts to come together and prosecute five senior leaders of the Khmer Rouge for crimes committed during Democratic Kampuchea, twelve years after the dissolution of their political and military operations.[126] The US Congress passed the Cambodian Genocide Justice Act to bring the leaders of the Khmer Rouge to trial for crimes against humanity, war crimes, and genocide on April 30, 1994.[127] Three years later Cambodia's two prime ministers petitioned the UN for help with the trial.

The Cambodian National Assembly founded the Extraordinary Chambers in the Courts of Cambodia (ECCC) in 2001. According to the ECCC the death toll during the Khmer Rouge regime was between 1.7 and 2.2 million people: 800,000 of the deaths were violent. Although an agreement between the UN and the Royal Government of Cambodia was signed on June 6, 2003, and ratified by the General Assembly, progress was still painstakingly slow before the ECCC was fully functional in 2007.

Condescension from the head of the UN Office of Legal Affairs, Hans Corell, insisting that all the judges and prosecutors be internationally trained, that the trial be conducted outside Cambodia, and withdrawing from negotiations in February 2002 when he could not get his way, delayed the ECCC from starting the tribunal for years. NGOs and human rights groups like Amnesty International and Human Rights Watch prolonged the debate with legitimate concerns that the seriously flawed Cambodian judiciary would bow to the corrupt Cambodian government. The US and China were also wary that any trial of the Khmer Rouge could bring out embarrassing details of their support for the genocidal regime.

In 2006, my documentary film, *The Angry Skies: A Cambodian Journey*, won Best Political Documentary in Los Angeles and Best Feature Documentary in New York at the New York International Independent Film & Video Festival. The film also played on television overseas to pressure Cambodian President Hun Sen to accept an international tribunal trying the architects of the Khmer Rouge regime for crimes against humanity in Cambodia.

Despite the odds, the needs of the Khmer Rouge victims to have an accounting of a regime that killed at least one person in every family outweighed any political grandstanding. In July 2006, there was an elaborate ceremony in Phnom Penh to swear in twenty-seven

Cambodian and foreign judges for a special tribunal to try five architects of the Khmer Rouge Revolution.[128] The alleged crimes committed by the Khmer Rouge included enslavement; extermination; murder; rape; torture; persecution on political, racial, and religious grounds; and other inhumane acts. It took another year until June 2007 for the judges to agree on the procedural rules. Thanks to extra funding from Canada, India, and Japan, the tribunal had $53 million for a trial expected to last three to four years.[129] Both the pretrial and trial chambers were composed of three Cambodian and two foreign judges. The Supreme Court chamber was composed of four Cambodian and three foreign judges.

On July 31, 2007, Kang Kek Ieu, alias Duch, the commander of Tuol Sleng torture chambers, became the first Khmer Rouge leader to be indicted and transferred to the custody of the ECCC.[130] At the landmark trial for the leaders of the Khmer Rouge Revolution, Duch testified that he was running one of 198 Khmer Rouge torture centers throughout Cambodia. He was following orders from Nuon Chea and would have been killed if he did not.

To back up Duch's claim, he testified that 200 Tuol Sleng guards had themselves been tortured at Tuol Sleng. In 1977, when the Khmer Rouge started purging their own troops in the eastern zone, up to a hundred prisoners were tortured every day, including Khmer Rouge cadre leaders, before Duch sent them to Choeung Ek for execution. Duch was convicted of crimes against humanity, murder, and torture on July 27, 2009, and sentenced to thirty-five years in prison. Although he appealed his conviction, Duch was expected to serve at least nineteen years due to a reduction for time already spent in prison.[131]

Nuon Chea, Khieu Samphan, Ieng Sary, and Ieng Thirith were indicted by the EEEC on September 15, 2000. Nuon Chea was eighty-two years old when he was arrested and brought to the tribunal on September 19, 2007. According to an interview with the Associated Press, Nuon Chea continued to deny any wrongdoing. "I was president of the National Assembly and had nothing to do with the operation of the government."

Ieng Sary, Pol Pot's seventy-seven-year-old brother-in-law and his wife, Ieng Thirith, seventy-five years old, were taken by the police from their home in Phnom Penh to the ECCC on November 12, 2007.[132] According to prosecutors, as former Khmer Rouge deputy prime minister, and foreign minister, Ieng Sary planned, directed, and coordinated the Khmer Rouge policies of "forcible transfer, forcible labor, and unlawful killings." Ieng Thirith, the former minister of social Affairs, was accused of "planning, direction, coordination, and ordering of widespread purges . . . and unlawful killing or murder of staff members from within the Ministry of Social Affairs."

Khieu Samphan, the commander of the Khmer Rouge Liberation Armed Forces, was seventy-six years old when he suffered a stroke the day after Ieng Sary and Ieng Thirith were arrested.[133] When Khieu Samphan was formally detained on November 17, 2007, he retained his eighty-three-year-old friend and lawyer from their left-wing student days in Paris in the 1950s. Mr. Verges had previously represented the former Yugoslav president Slobodan Milosevic, the Nazi Gestapo officer Klaus Barbie, and the Venezuelan terrorist Carlos the Jackal.[134] On April 24, 2008, Verges caused the adjournment of a pretrial hearing because thousands of documents had not been translated into French, one of the official languages of the tribunal. Mr. Verges understood if his client died before he could be convicted, he won.

In January 2008 the tribunal revised its budget from $56.3 million to $169.7 million and extended the projected end date to 2011.[135] This compares to $6 million spent for the hybrid UN tribunal in East Timor, and $10 million a year for the court trying 400 defendants in Bosnia and Herzegovina. So far, the Cambodian tribunal had cost $34 million for each of the five defendants, money that some argue would be better given to the victims and their families.

I visited the ECCC in Phnom Penh in February 2011. Although Khieu Samphan's lawyer would not let me past the guards, I learned that Khieu Samphan's and Nuon Chea's wives visited their husbands once a week to bring food, medicines, and clothing, things that would never have been allowed under their own regime. If the ECCC did not hasten its pace, the Khmer Rouge leaders remaining in the docket would die from illness and old age. Ta Mok, who killed Pol Pot in 1998, died in prison in 2006. Both Nuon Chea and Khieu Samphan were frail before they had strokes. Ieng Sary was admitted to the hospital with a heart condition in February 2008.

On Friday November 15, 2018, Nuon Chea was convicted of committing genocide against Cambodia's minority Muslim Cham and Vietnamese; Khieu Samphan was convicted of committing genocide against the Vietnamese.[136] Nuon Chea was ninety-two years old. Khieu Samphan was eighty-seven. Both men were also convicted of crimes against humanity and sentenced to spend the rest of their lives in prison.

After being convicted, Khieu Samphan maintained that "he was not aware" of the heinous acts committed by other leaders. Nuon Chea, ever the political ideologue who wanted to turn Cambodia into an agrarian utopia, remained defiant to the end.

Although the tribunal had many critics for only trying five Khmer Rouge leaders, corruption, and spending $300 million to review hundreds of thousands of documents and interview hundreds of people, three of the five architects of the Khmer Rouge Revolution were convicted of committing crimes against humanity. Ieng Sary was eighty-seven years old when he died in prison on March 15, 2013, awaiting trial.[137] Ieng Sary's wife was released from the tribunal when the court found that she had dementia.

Even a flawed tribunal was better than no tribunal for the perpetrators and victims of the Khmer Rouge genocide. The historical record also needed straightening. Unfortunately, time has passed for Henry Kissinger, who died November 27, 2023, to answer the charge that the US bombing of Cambodia was an act of state-sponsored terrorism.

EPILOGUE

My travels in Cambodia with victims and perpetrators of the Khmer Rouge genocide helped me understand how difficult it is for the US to win an insurgency of its own making. President Nixon and Henry Kissinger used faulty intelligence and lies to secretly conduct war on Cambodia. Six hundred thousand Cambodians died before the US Congress halted the US bombing in 1973. On Aril 17, 1975, the Khmer Rouge defeated the US-backed Lon Nol government and army. Pol Pot was pleased that the Khmer Rouge Communists had defeated the US two weeks before the Vietnamese Communists defeated the US. For four years the world had scant information of the 2 million Cambodians who perished under the brutal communist regime.

President Johnson also misled the American people to go to war in Vietnam that killed over 2 million Vietnamese and 50,000 Americans, created 10 million refugees, and destroyed Vietnam's economy and environment. The US government still does not recognize that we secretly dropped more bombs on Laos than on any other country, killing more than 50,000 people. Unexploded cluster mines continue to maim and kill Laotian civilians today.

Four days after al-Qaeda's September 11, 2001, attack on the

World Trade Center towers and the Pentagon, the US Congress passed the Authorization for Use of Military Force Against Terrorists. "Our war on terror begins with al Qaeda, but does not end there," George W. Bush said. "It will not end until every terrorist group of global reach has been found, stopped and defeated."

When the US benefited from an international outpouring of sympathy, George W. Bush invaded Afghanistan. But instead of finding Osama bin Laden and dismantling the al-Qaeda network that had attacked the US and relocated to the remote mountains of Pakistan, Bush demonized and invaded Iraq on March 20, 2003. At the time Iraq had nothing to do with Al Qaeda. George W. Bush was misinforming the American people and the world that Iraq had attacked the US on 9/11 and that Iraq had weapons of mass destruction that could strike the US within minutes.

During America's longest war, 7,000 US soldiers died in Afghanistan and Iraq, along with 177,000 national and military police, 46,000 civilians, and 53,000 "opposition fighters."[138] These statistics are far from accurate and do not include civilian casualties, 30,177 American veterans taking their own lives after they came home, and more than 5 million refugees. And now, after the US abandoned two decades of war and trillions of dollars invested in the Afghan Army and civil society, the Taliban defeated the US and control a fundamentalist, Islamic state.

Preemptive wars are not only illegal and contrary to a wide body of international laws and agreements, they are crimes against humanity. Whether or not George W. Bush's and Dick Cheney's neoconservative cabal are ever held accountable for lying the US into war and occupation of Iraq, hundreds of thousands of Iraqi soldiers and civilians have been killed, over 1 million Iraqi children and civilians have died from diseases directly attributed to Gulf Wars I and II, millions of refugees further destabilize the Middle East and Europe, and American taxpayers inherit a multitrillion-dollar price tag.

Wars are even more expensive when they are fought with borrowed money. The Brown University Costs of War Project estimates that by the end of 2019 the US has borrowed $5.9 trillion to fight wars in Afghanistan and Iraq and take care of disabled veterans.[139] And this does not include interest payments.

Israel razing Gaza with US bombs is the latest example of the US sponsoring crimes against humanity. After Hamas soldiers raped and killed more than 1,200 Israelis and took 250 hostages on October 7, 2023, Israelis' anger and desire for revenge is understandable. So is the difficulty of fighting an enemy embedded in the community.But carpet-bombing Gazans' hospitals, homes, and infrastructure has displaced 90 percent of the population and killed over 50,000 Palestinians, mainly women and children. Blocking international aid to over 1 million Palestinians who are starving is also a crime against humanity. Once again, American bombs are in danger of creating more "terrorists" than they kill.

The US is currently conducting counterterrorism operations in eighty countries on six continents where extremists and militant Islam are forging more potent and lethal alliances. It is not too late to reduce our militaristic approach to worldwide domination. What if a fraction of the US Defense Department's $778 billion budget, which is larger than the combined military budgets of China, India, Russia, United Kingdom, Saudi Arabia, Germany, France, Japan, South Korea, Italy, and Australia, helped impoverished communities around the world build wells, roads, clinics, and schools?

Imagine.

ALPHABETICAL LISTING OF CAMBODIANS MENTIONED IN *THE ANGRY SKIES*

SAM BITH   Khmer Rouge general, Nuon Paet's superior officer.

NUON CHEA   "Brother Number Two," chairman of Democratic People's Assembly responsible for the most radical policies of purges, detention, torture, and execution of "enemies."

YOUK CHHANG   Cofounded the Documentation Center of Cambodia that collected 34,000 Khmer Rouge soldiers and hundreds of thousands of individual accounts of torture, rape, and murder by the Khmer Rouge.

NHEK BUN CHHAY   Deputy chief of Royal Cambodian Air Force.

KANG KEK IEU   "Duch," head of the Tuol Sleng interrogation center that tortured and killed 20,000 "enemies."

NY KAN   Worked at the Ministry of Foreign Affairs under Ieng Sary.

DR. KROH   Physician in Kho Sala.

TEPH KUNNAL   Secretary of Democratic Kampuchea during the United Nations Transitional Authority in Cambodia (UNTAC); married Pol Pot's wife after Pol Pot's execution by Ta Mok.

KHAT MANN   Child soldier and radio operator for Phnom Vor Gang.

GENERAL MAU   Worked at the Ministry of Economics during Democratic Kampuchea from 1975 to 1979.

TA MOK   "The Butcher." The most feared Khmer Rouge general, who killed Pol Pot in 1998.

OUCH NIM Nari Yotea, virgin warrior; Dr. Noun's sister; married to Mr. Muhn.

DR. NOUN Surgeon for Phnom Vor Gang; Ta Mok's nephew.

NUON PAET Khmer Rouge commander; Chhuok Rin's superior officer, known to eat his captives' livers.

POL POT Born Saloth Sar. Principal architect of Khmer Rouge Revolution; president of Democratic Kampuchea from April 17, 1975, to January 6, 1979.

CHHOUK RIN Warlord in Phnom Vor; first Khmer Rouge officer to surrender.

TOU SAMOUTH Pol Pot's predecessor; leader of Cambodia's Communists; killed by Lon Nol soldiers in 1962.

KHIEU SAMPHAN Commander of Khmer Liberation Armed Forces that overthrew US-backed Lon Nol government; prime minister of Democratic Kampuchea during Khmer Rouge genocide; head of Cambodian government in exile after the Vietnamese invasion in 1979.

SON SAN The highest ranking Khmer Rouge general.

IENG SARY Foreign minister and deputy prime minister of Democratic Kampuchea.

HUN SEN Former Khmer Rouge officer who defected to Vietnam in 1973. In 1979, when the Vietnamese invaded Cambodia, Hun Sen became the world's youngest prime minister at twenty-six years old who ruled Cambodia until 2023 when he passed control to his son, Hun Manet.

SON SEN Member of the Communist Party of Democratic Kampuchea; oversaw security apparatus and Tuol Sleng.

MAE SON Pol Pot's widow.

IENG THIRITH Democratic Kampuchea's minister of social affairs; Ieng Sary's wife.

BIBLIOGRAPHY

Becker, Elizabeth. *When the War Was Over: Cambodia and the Khmer Rouge Revolution*. Public Affairs, 1986.
Becker, Elizabeth. *When the War Was Over: Cambodia's Revolution and the Voices of Its People*. Touchstone Books, 1988.
Bizot, Francois. *The Gate*. Translated from French by Euan Cameron. Alfred A. Knopf, 2003.
Chandler, David. *Brother Number One: A Political Biography of Pol Pot*. Westview Press, 1999.
Chandler, David. *The Tragedy of Cambodian History: Politics, War, and Revolution since 1945*. Yale University, 1991.
Chandler, David. *Voices from S-21: Terror and History in Pol Pot's Secret Prison*. University of California Press, 2000.
Chandler, David. *A History of Cambodia*. Westview Press, 2008.
Duiker, William J. *Ho Chi Minh*. Allen and Unwin, 2000.
Dunlop, Nic. *The Last Executioner: A Journey into the Heart of the Killing Fields*. Walker & Company, 2005.
Hitchens, Christopher. *The Trial of Henry Kissinger*. Verso, 2001.
Kamm, Henry. *Cambodia: Report from a Stricken Land*. Arcade, 1998.
Kiernan, Ben. *The Pol Pot Regime: Race, Power, and Genocide in Cambodia under the Khmer Rouge, 1975-1979*. Yale University Press, 1996.
Kiernan, Ben. *How Pol Pot Came to Power: Colonialism, Nationalism, and Communism in Cambodia, 1930-1975*. Yale University Press, Second Edition, 2004.
Lindqvist, Sven. *A History of Bombing*. The New Press, New York, 2001. Albert Bonniers Forlag, 1999. Originally published in Sweden as *Nu dog du*.
Mouhot, Henri. *Voyages a Siam et dans le Cambodge*. Librairie Hachette Paris, 1868.

Ngor, Haing, and Roger Warner. *A Cambodian Odyssey*. Macmillan, 1988.

Picq, Laurence. *Beyond the Horizon, Five Years with the Khmer Rouge: A Western Woman's Firsthand Account of the Drama, Passion, and Horror of Pol Pot's Cambodia*. St. Martin's Press, 1989.

Ponchaud, Francois. *Cambodia, Year Zero*. Penguin, 1978.

Power, Samantha. *A Problem From Hell: America and the Age of Genocide*. Basic Books, 2002.

Sallay, Michael, and Mitch Weiss. *Tiger Force: A True Story of Men and War*. Little Brown, 2006.

Samphan, Khieu. *Reflections on Cambodian History from Ancient Times to the Era of Democratic Kampuchea*. Documentation Center of Cambodia, 2007.

Shawcross, William. *Sideshow: Kissinger, Nixon, and the Destruction of Cambodia*. Hogarth Press, 1979.

Swain, Jon. *River of Time: A Memoir of Vietnam and Cambodia*. Berkley Books, 1995.

Ung, Luong. *First They Killed My Father: A Daughter of Cambodia Remembers*. HarperCollins, 2000.

Vickery, Michael. *Cambodia 1975-1982*. Silkworm Books, 1984.

NOTES

INTRODUCTION

1. Marvine Howe, "2 American Mountaineers Tell of Witnessing Tibet Protests," *New York Times*, November 13, 1987.
2. John Ackerly and Blake Kerr, MD, *The Suppression of a People: Accounts of Torture and Imprisonment in Tibet* (Physicians for Human Rights, 1989).
3. Blake Kerr, MD, "Witness to China's Shame, How Human Rights and Families Suffer in Tibet," *Washington Post*, February 26, 1989.
4. John Ackerly and Blake Kerr, MD, "Torture and Imprisonment in Tibet," in *The Anguish of Tibet*, ed. Petra Kelly, Gert Bastian, and Pat Aiello (Parallax Press, 1991), pp. 110-128.
5. Blake Kerr, MD, "Tibetans under the Knife," in *The Anguish of Tibet*, 96-109.
6. Blake Kerr, MD, *Sky Burial: An Eyewitness Account of China's Brutal Occupation of Tibet* (Nobel Press, 1993).
7. Estimates of the number of Cambodians who perished while the Khmer Rouge ruled Cambodia vary from 1.3 to 2.8 million. Two million seems to be the most accurate.
8. Simon O'Dwyer-Russell, "SAS Training Jungle Fighters," *Sunday Telegraph*, September 24, 1989, 14.
9. Robert Karniol, "UK Trained Cambodian Guerrillas," *Jane's Defence Weekly*, September 30, 1989, 629.
10. The Phnom Vor Gang killed Jean-Michel Braquet from France, Mark Slater from Britain, and David Wilson from Australia after a three-month hostage-taking in 1996.
11. Haing Ngor, *A Cambodian Odyssey* (Macmillan, 1988).
12. Elizabeth Becker, *When the War Was Over: Cambodia's Revolution and the Voices of Its People* (Touchstone Books, 1998).

13 Ben Kiernan, *The Pol Pot Regime, Race, Power, and Genocide in Cambodia under the Khmer Rouge*, 1975-1979 (Yale University Press, 1996).
14 David Chandler, *The Tragedy of Cambodian History: Politics, War, and Revolution since 1945* (Silkworm Books, Yale University, 1991).
15 Laurence Picq, *Beyond the Horizon, Five Years with the Khmer Rouge: A Western Woman's Firsthand Account of the Drama, Passion, and Horror of Pol Pot's Cambodia* (St. Martin's Press, 1989).

SOFT TRAVEL TO HARD PLACES

16 H. Bruce Franklin, *Star Wars: The Superweapon and the American Imagination* (Oxford, 1988), ch. 7.
17 James William Gibson, *The Perfect War: Technowar in Vietnam* (Atlantic Monthly Press, 1986).
18 Sven Lindqvist, *A History of Bombing* (New Press, 2000), 163, originally published in Sweden as *Nu dog du* (Albert Bonniers Forlag, 1999).

KISSINGER, NIXON, AND THE AMERICAN BOMBING OF CAMBODIA

19 Don Oberdorfer, *Tet* (Doubleday, 1971), v.
20 Michael Bilton and Kevin Sim, *Four Hours in My Lai* (Viking, 1992), 21.
21 Larry Berman, *No Peace, No Honor: Nixon, Kissinger, and Betrayal in Vietnam* (Free Press, 2001).
22 Christopher Hitchens, *The Trial of Henry Kissinger* (Verso, 2001).
23 William Shawcross, "The Secret," in *Sideshow: Kissinger, Nixon, and the Destruction of Cambodia* (Hogarth Press, 1991), first published in Great Britain by Andre Deutsch Ltd., 1979.
24 Shawcross, "The Coup," in *Sideshow*.
25 Henry Kamm, *Cambodia: Report from a Stricken Land* (Arcade, 1998), 66-67.
26 "Transcript of President's Address to the Nation on Military Action in Cambodia," *New York Times*, May 1, 1970, 2.
27 Shawcross, "The Bombing," in *Sideshow*, 280-299.
28 National Foreign Assessment Center, *CIA, Kampuchea: A Demographic Catastrophe* (Library of Congress, 1980), 2.
29 Shawcross, *Sideshow*, 350.
30 Hitchens, *The Trial of Henry Kissinger*, 42-43.
31 Luong Ung, *First They Killed My Father: A Daughter of Cambodia Remembers* (Perennial/HarperCollins, 2000).
32 Kramas are red-and-white-checkered cloths wrapped around heads and waists, warn as belts or sarongs, by men and women.
33 Kiernan, *The Pol Pot Regime*, 48.

34 A French Jesuit Priest named Francois Ponchaud coined the term "Year Zero" in his book *Cambodia, Year Zero* (Penguin, 1978).

SIEM REAP

35 Cambodian Ministry of Information, *Angkor Guide*, 2000.
36 David Chandler, *A History of Cambodia* (Westview Press, 2008).

THE ANGKOR WATS

37 Henri Mouhot, *Voyage dan les rayaumes de Siam, de Cambodge, de Laos, et autre parties centrale de l'Indochine* (1863); English title: *Travels in the Central Parts of Indochina, Cambodia, and Laos during the Years 1858, 1868 and 1860.*
38 *Apsara* is Sanskrit for a beautiful female spirit or goddess. Apsaras are depicted as nymphs or celestial maidens proficient in dance throughout Hindu and Buddhist cultures.
39 George Coedes, *Angkor* (Oxford University Press, 1963); George Coedes, *The Indianized States of Southeast Asia* (University of Hawaii Press, 1968).

MR. LAND MINE

40 United Nations Department of Humanitarian Affairs, United Nations Mine Clearance and Policy Unit, Department of Humanitarian Affairs, September 1977.
41 "Landmine Monitor Report 2000," *Phnom Penh Post* 9, no 19 (September 15-28, 2000).

FAST BOAT

42 Michael Yamashita, *Mekong: A Journey on the Mother of Waters* (Takarajima Books, 2005), 53.
43 Nick Ray, *Vietnam, Cambodia, Laos & the Greater Mekong* (Lonely Planet, 2007).
44 Chandler, *The Tragedy of Cambodian History*.
45 Chandler, *A History of Cambodia*.

PHNOM PENH'S NIGHTLY DEATH

46 Mikel Flam and Kgo Kim Cuc, "Children of the Dust," *Bangkok Post*, February 23, 1997.
47 Chris Seper, "Police Sweeps Help Clean Up Child Prostitution," *Christian Science Monitor*, January 8, 1988.
48 Laura Bobak, "For Sale: The Innocence of Cambodia," *Ottawa Sun*, October 24, 1996.

49 Cameron W. Barr, "Asia Traffickers Keep Girls in Sexual Servitude, Criminal Groups Deceive and Lure Poor Villagers," *Christian Science Monitor*, August 22, 1997.
50 *Yum yum* is slang for "oral sex." *Boom boom* is slang for "sex."

TUOL SLENG
51 David Chandler, *Voices from S-21: Terror and History in Pol Pot's Secret Prison* (University of California Press, 2000).

DON'T BREAK
52 *Barang* is a Khmer word for "foreigner."

CHILD SOLDIER
53 Tom Fawthrop, "Radio Transcripts Point Finger at Paet," *Phnom Penh Post*, August 7-20, 1998.

MERCENARY
54 "Transcript of President's Address to the Nation on Military Action in Cambodia," *New York Times*, May 1, 1970, 2.

KEP KILLING FIELDS
55 John Avedon, "The Long Night: 1966-1977," in *In Exile from the Land of Snows* (Vintage Books, 1986), 291.

LARIAM DREAMS
56 US Population Bureau's 1998 world demographic report and census carried out with UN assistance.
57 J.J. Rummel, "Statistics of Vietnamese Democide," March 24, 2014, lines 777-785, http://www.hawaii.edu/powerkills/SOD.TAB6.1B.GIF.

JEAN-MICHEL BRAQUET, MARK SLATER, AND DAVID WILSON
58 "Phnom Penh," *AFP*, June 7, 1994.
59 Bruce Cheesman and Yvonne Ridley, "Murdered Briton's Mother to Face Khmer Rouge Guerrilla," *The Observer*, June 6, 1999.
60 "The Long Road from Genocide to Justice," *Sydney Morning Herald*, August 7-20, 1998.
61 Tom Fawthrop, "Radio Transcripts Point Finger at Paet," *Phnom Penh Post*, August 7-10, 1998.
62 "Two Ex-Khmer Rouge Charged for Tourist Murders, *Reuters*, June 21, 1999.

THE ELEPHANT BAR
63 "Khmer Rouge Chief Cleared of Backpackers' Murders," *Birmingham Post*, July 19, 2000.
64 Nick Ray, *Lonely Planet: Cambodia*, 3rd ed. (Lonely Planet Publications, April 2000).

AIDS IN THE JUNGLE
65 Heng Soy, "Hun Sen: UNTAC Brought AIDS to Cambodia," *KI-Media*, January 23, 2008.
66 Milton Osborne, *Sihanouk, Prince of Light, Prince of Darkness* (Silkworm, 1994).
67 Soizik Crochet, *Le Camboge* (Karthala, 1997).
68 Helen Vesperina, "Cambodia's Aids Struggle," *BBC News*, November 20, 2000.
69 Marie Charles, NIH National Library of Medicine, HIV epidemic in Cambodia, one of the poorest countries in Southeast Asia: a success story, 2024, https://pmc.ncbi.nim.nih

DOCTOR KROH AND AMERICAN BOMBING
70 Ben Kiernan, *The Pol Pot Regime, Race, Power and Genocide in Cambodia Under the Khmer Rouge, 1975-1979* (Yale University Press, 1996), 24.
71 Ben Kiernan, *The American Bombardment of Kampuchea*, quoting an interview with journalist Bruce Palling and Catholic missionary Francois Ponchaud in Paris, 21-22.

SEARCHING FOR THE TRUTH
72 Jane Ardley, *The Tibetan Independence Movement: Political, Religious, and Gandhian Perspectives* (Routledge, 2002).
73 Kenneth Conboy and James Morrison, *The CIA's Secret War in Tibet* (University Press of Kansas, 2002).
74 Richard Bennett, "Tibet, the 'Great Game' and the CIA," *Asia Times*, March 26, 2008.
75 Ramananda Senqupta, "The CIA Circus: Tibet's Forgotten Army. How the CIA Sponsored and Betrayed Tibetans in a War the World Never Knew About," *Outlook*, February 15, 1999.

POL POT
76 David Chandler, *Brother Number One: A Political Biography of Pol Pot* (Westview Press, 1999).
77 Ibid., 36.

YOUK CHHANG AND THE DOCUMENTATION CENTER OF CAMBODIA
78 *Searching for the Truth*, Magazine of the Documentation Center of Cambodia, edited by Youk Chhang, Wynne Cougill, Julio A. Jelders, Phnom Penh, Cambodia.

TUOL SLENG SURVIVORS
79 Van Nath, *A Cambodian Prison Portrait: One Year in the Khmer Rouge's S-21* (White Lotus, 1988).

VICTORY COCONUTS
80 William J. Duiker, *Ho Chi Minh* (Allen & Unwin, 2000).

THE PHNOM VOR GANG
81 Joseph R. Fraley Jr. is a pseudonym.

TRAVELS TO PAILIN
82 Andrew Netty, "Khmer Rouge Stronghold Gets Market Lesson," *Southeast Asia*, October 29, 2008.

KHIEU SAMPHAN
83 Chandler, *Brother Number One*, ch.3.
84 Indo-China, "Khieu Samphan: Out of the Jungle," *Time*, April 28, 1975.
85 Ibid.
86 Ibid.
87 Ben Kiernan, "Don't Blame Me, It Was My Prime Minister, *The Long Term View*, VI, no. 4 (Spring 2005), 36.
88 Khieu Samphan, *Reflections on Cambodian History from Ancient Times to the Era of Democratic Kampuchea* (Documentation Center of Cambodia, 2007).

SECOND WIFE
89 Ung, *First They Killed My Father*.

NUON CHEA
90 Eiji Murashima, *The Young Nuon Chea in Bangkok (1942-1950) and the Communist Party in Thailand: The Life in Bangkok of the Man Who Became "Brother Number Two" in the Khmer Rouge* (Documentation Center of Cambodia, 2009).
91 Ibid.
92 Chandler, *Brother Number One*, 53.

93 Murashima, interview with Nuon Chea, August 12, 2003, *The Young Nuon Chea in Bangkok (1942-1950)*.
94 Ben Kiernan, *How Pol Pot Came to Power: Colonialism, Nationalism, and Communism in Cambodia, 1930-1975*, 2nd ed. (Yale University Press, 2004), 59.
95 Murashima, interview with Nuon Chea, August 12, 2003.
96 "Phnom Penh," *AFP* June 7, 1994.

THE LIVER EATERS
97 Minister of Foreign Affairs Alex Downer, "Arrest of Nuon Paet," media release: AF105, August 1, 1998.
98 The Nuon Paet Case: A Resource File Prepared by *Cambodia Today* in Cooperation with the NGO Forum on Cambodia, http://www.ngoforum@ngoforum.org.kh.
99 Minister of Foreign Affairs Alex Downer, "Trial and Conviction of Nuon Paet," media release: FA 64, July 7, 1999.
100 Ker Munthit, "Khmer Rouge Commander Convicted," Associated Press, June 7, 1999.
101 "Two Ex-Khmer Rouge Charged for Tourist Murders," *Reuters*, June 21, 1999.
102 "Ta Mok, Khmer Rouge Leader Who Inflicted Untold Miseries on His People during and after the Regime of Pol Pot," *Sunday Times*, July 22, 2006.
103 "Obituary: Ta Mok," *BBC News*, July 21, 2006.
104 "Landmark Khmer Rouge Trial Starts," *BBC News*, February 17, 2009.
105 "Two Ex-Khmer Rouge Charged for Tourist Murders."

REPERCUSSIONS
106 Duiker, *Ho Chi Minh*.

GENOCIDE TRIBUNAL
107 Samantha Power, *A Problem From Hell: America and the Age of Genocide* (Basic Books, 2002), chs. 1—4.
108 Raphael Lemkin, *Axis Rule in Occupied Europe: Laws of Occupation, Analysis of Government, Proposals for Redress* (Carnegie Endowment for International Peace, Division of International Law, 1944), 79.
109 *A Problem From Hell*, 60.
110 Ibid.

THAI RIOT

111 1991 Gulf War Information: http://www.cryan.com/war/

MALCOM CALDWELL'S MURDER

112 Becker, *When the War Was Over,* 409.
113 Ibid, 426.
114 John Sharkey, "Vietnam, Cambodia Exchange Bitter Charges," *Washington Post,* January 1, 1978, A8.
115 David Binder, "Vietnam Holds Cambodian Region after Bitter Fight, U.S. Aides Say," *New York Times,* January 4, 1978, A1, A6.

POL POT'S DEATH

116 Nate Thayer, *Sympathy for the Devil: Living Dangerously in Cambodia: A Foreign Correspondent's Story* (Penguin Putnam, 1999).
117 Nate Thayer, "Dying Breath: The Inside Story of Pol Pot's Last Days and the Disintegration of the Movement He Created," *Far Eastern Economic Review,* April 30, 1988.
118 Nate Thayer, Day of Reckoning," *Far Eastern Economic Review,* October 30, 1997, 14-20.
119 Nate Thayer, "Finding Pol Pot," *Newsletter of the Center for Public Integrity* 7, no. 2 (March 1999).

MR. MUHN

120 Landmines in Cambodia: http://www.mekong.net.
121 "Cambodian Civil War: Military Developments under the Khmer Rouge, Khmer Rouge Ground Forces," http://en.wikipedia.org/wiki/Cambodian_Civil_War.

SLOUCHING TOWARD A TRIBUNAL

122 "Fed: Downer Welcomes Sam Bith Arrest," *AAP General News,* May 23, 2002.
123 "Cambodian Court Decision on Sam Bith Welcomed by Mike O'Brien, Australian Prime Minister," M2 Presswire, December 23, 2002.
124 "Convicted Khmer Rouge Commander Dies," AP Online, February 15, 2008.
125 "Convicted Killer of Western Tourists Arrested after Eight Months on the Run," AP Worldstream, October 25, 2005.
126 Parvathi Menon, "Khmer Rouge Tribunal Indictment after 31 years," *The Hindu,* September 18, 2010.

127 "Cambodian Genocide Program, Chronology 1994 to 2004," Yale University, 2024.
128 Simone Montlake, "Killing Fields Tribunal Judges Sworn In," *The Guardian*, July 3, 2006.
129 "Tribunal Finally Ready to Probe Killing Fields," *Globe and Mail*, June 14, 2007.
130 "Duch: Khmer Rouge Prison Chief Charged," KI Media, July 31, 2007.
131 "Convicted Khmer Rouge Jailer Duch Will Appeal," *BBC News*, July 27, 2009.
132 Sopheng Cheang, "Police Enter Home of Khmer Rouge Ex-Foreign Minister in Apparent Move to Arrest Him for Trial," Associated Press, November 12, 2007.
133 Sopan Cheang and Munthis Ker, "Khmer Rouge Ex Head of State Suffers Stroke," Associated Press, November 11, 2007.
134 "Lawyer Scolds Tribunal Judges," Associated Press, April 24, 2008.
135 Sebastian Stangio, "Cambodia: Whose Tribunal Is It Anyway?" *Spiked*, February 18, 2008.
136 Seth Mydans, "2 Aging Khmer Rouge Leaders Are Found Guilty of Genocide," *New York Times*, November 17, 2018.
137 Seth Mydans, "Ieng Sary, Former Official of Khmer Rouge, Dies at 87," *New York Times*, March 15, 2013.

EPILOGUE

138 Watson Institute International & Public Affairs, "Costs of War Project," Brown University, 2022, costsofwar@brown.edu
139 "End the War in Afghanistan: Editorial," *New York Times*, February 4, 2019.

www.ingramcontent.com/pod-product-compliance
Lightning Source LLC
LaVergne TN
LVHW091626070526
838199LV00044B/955